Professional Digital Photography

ISBN 0-13-099745-5

90000

9 780130 997456

Professional Digital Photography

Bill Erickson
Frank Romano

Prentice Hall PTR
Upper Saddle River, NJ 07458
http://www.phptr.com

Library of Congress Cataloging-in-Publication Data

```
Erickson, Bill.
    Professional digital photography / Bill Erickson, Frank J. Romano
      p.    cm.
   Includes index.
   ISBN 0-13-099745-5 (alk. paper)
   1. Photography--Digital techniques Handbooks, manuals, etc.
  2. Digital cameras Handbooks, manuals, etc.  3. Image processing-
  -Digital techniques Handbooks, manuals, etc.  I. Romano, Frank J.
  II. Title.
  TR267.E75  1999
  778.3--dc201                              99-18428
                                               CIP
```

Editorial/Production Supervision: Craig Little
Acquisitions Editor: Tim Moore
Manufacturing Manager: Alexis R. Heydt
Marketing Manager: Bryan Gambrel
Cover Design Director: Jerry Votta
Cover Design: Talar Agasyan

The publisher offers discounts on this book when ordered in bulk quantities.
For more information, contact the Corporate Sales Department at 800-382-3419,
fax: 201-236-7141, email: corpsales@prenhall.com or write Corporate Sales Department, Prentice Hall
PTR, One Lake Street, Upper Saddle River, NJ 07458

Printed in the United States of America
  10 9 8 7 6 5 4 3 2 1

ISBN 0-13-099745-5

Prentice-Hall International (UK) Limited, *London*
Prentice-Hall of Australia Pty. Limited, *Sydney*
Prentice-Hall Canada Inc., *Toronto*
Prentice-Hall Hispanoamericana, S.A., *Mexico*
Prentice-Hall of India Private Limited, *New Delhi*
Prentice-Hall of Japan, Inc., *Tokyo*
Prentice-Hall (Singapore) Pte. Ltd., *Singapore*
Editora Prentice-Hall do Brasil, Ltda., *Rio de Janeiro*

ACKNOWLEDGMENTS

Thank you to my family and friends for their support and patience, to my colleague Frank Romano for his help in bringing this book to life, and to John Szczesniak and Brian Jackson for their contributions. A great deal of thanks to my mother for typing her fingers to the bone, and a special thanks to Jennifer, without whom I wouldn't have gotten started in the first place.

Also thanks to Truly Donovan, copyeditor extraordinary, Richard Romano for the camera images from the Micro Publishing Press archives, and Craig Little who continues to make hard jobs easy.

AUTHORS

Bill Erickson is Director of Color Imaging Technologies for the RIT Research Corporation, a subsidiary of the Rochester Institute of Technology. He has held advanced technology positions at various corporations in the imaging and printing industries and, from time to time, still uses the first camera he ever owned.

Frank Romano is a professor in the School of Printing Management and Sciences at the Rochester Institute of Technology.

INTRODUCTION

We cannot overestimate the importance of pictures and the roles they play in society—how the evolution of picture taking has influenced, even shaped, life as we know it. Why is an image worth a thousand words? Think how the art and science of photography is being changed and enhanced by the ability to scan, store, and print pictures, and how networked computers allow us to put them any place, on anything, any time ... almost.

The camera you have now works fine; you can even get prints in an hour in four sizes if you want to. Why do you need or even care about digital anyway? Film works; it works well. "Photographic quality" has long been considered the ultimate standard. Where does digital fit and what advantages does it offer?

Digital revolution has become digital evolution. We're past the "gee whiz" phase; now what do we do with it? What can we do with it?

A lot happens when you push the button and someone else does the rest. Conventional photography deals with the basic science of how objects, light, cameras, film, chemistry, and photo paper all conspire together to stop time and put it on something we can pass around or put on the wall. This book deals with advances in photography in the light of the emergence of digital technology.

You can get a scanner that does 4800 dpi, and an inkjet printer that prints 1200 dpi, free with the PC you buy down the street. What does that mean and what is the connection to photography? Well, you have most of your own photo publishing system. How does the photo get from paper or film to digital output, and what is digital anyway? How do you get pictures from film to computer and how do you take a picture without using film at all? We'll tell you.

The ideas behind making a photo print in *Time* magazine, putting an image into a Powerpoint sales presentation, or printing a poster for the entrance of a gallery for next week's opening are pretty much the same. You can even get rid of a pimple, an ex-husband, and annoying power lines in the process, and make the grass look greener, too.

Why is the fisherman's sweater you bought from L.L. Bean more of a teal than the turquoise it is in the catalog, why is it that the TVs at Sears never match, and why is the print you got from that free inkjet printer a whole lot different than the one you saw on the monitor? We'll tell you.

Images take up a lot of space and once you've got them you'll want to send them places. What do you do when you need to find some you took the other week and send them out fast. Soon you'll be knee deep into storing, sorting, searching, transmitting, and receiving images. We'll even give you the photographic low-down on databases, networks, platforms, and the ubiquitous Internet.

The power of the press belongs to those who have one. Now just about everyone has one and they're all a little different. How do you get images out of the computer and onto paper, or film, or cloth, or snowboards. We'll tell you why WYSIWYG isn't and what you can and cannot do about it.

A little technology can be a dangerous thing—both boon and bane. Where do things appear to be headed and how much of it do you even want to deal with? We'll tell you.

TABLE OF CONTENTS

Chapter 1

THE DIGITAL WORLD

Some rules regarding this book:

1. The subject of digital photography is enormous and lies at the top of a pyramid of interacting technologies, techniques, and information. We could never cover everything. The important things are covered in depth, related issues for understanding, supporting issues for breadth, and obscure things only mentioned. Pay attention to the long sections. This book is designed to tell you what you need to know to get started and keep going, not bog you down with details you'll never need to know. We encourage you to refer to our peers and yours. You can always find more detail, but you will not always have a lot of time to wade through dissertations on the spectral values of cyan. We cover the important stuff.

2. Things change. By the time you read this book, the information in it will be three months old and that's if you buy it the moment it comes out! Which we know you will, as the information in it is far more interesting than the latest release of Windows Whatever that sells about a million copies the first week it comes out.

3. We are intentionally not too specific on makes and models or specific features as we know it will all change as soon as we type the words describing them. Instead, use this book as a reference and apply it to your own situations. As fast as things are changing, we imagine that a year from publication you will look back on this fondly as the "good old days."

4. It depends. Nothing is clear cut in digital imaging except that things will get better, faster, and cheaper. All things depend on other things. The best digital camera in the world is at the mercy of whatever is used to print out the final image and the path the image took to get there.

5. Don't wait to get started. Remember #2 above and realize that as soon as you buy a piece of equipment, it is obsolete. An overstatement, sure, but the sooner you resign yourself to that simple fact, the better you will feel when you see your month-old camera on sale for $100 less than you paid for it. Technology is like a flowing river, you might as well jump in and start swimming or you'll wait forever on the banks, never getting anywhere.

6. Understand and use the Internet. A connection to the World Wide Web is like having a library, computer store, photo gallery, instructor, mentor, and Girl or Guy Friday at your desk 24 hours a day, seven days a week. It's the fastest and easiest way to find anything out, communicate, and, perhaps more importantly, share images. Start at www.LatentPixel.com to get started as a jumping off point for everything and anything relating to digital photography.

7. When we say "PC" we mean any desktop computer regardless of its flavor. While the Macintosh has long been the front-runner in digital capture, manipulation, and output, the lines are clearly blurring (how's that for a non-statement?) and what once was no longer is. You can bet that the folks at Microsoft have big plans for digital photo imaging and output and, in fact, they already have a full head of steam. So, we use the term "PC" but really intend to be platform-neutral.

8. Make mistakes. Digital is cheap, all those 1s and 0s are disposable and the only way you'll progress is to shoot and play and print and do it again.

We start with the required short and superficial historical record of photography.

History of photography

Photography has been around, in one form or another, since the early 1800s or so and hasn't undergone any dramatic changes since then. Sure, we have gone from wet glass plates to thin flexible polyester films but, for all intents and purposes, we capture images the same basic way we always have. Two needs that photography has met since those early days are convenience and quality. These needs carry through to the digital world as well and, until met, promise little success for the manufacturers of digital cameras. They know this and are, slowly but surely, taking steps toward solving these problems.

In 1888 photography met one of the two challenges of convenience and quality through the efforts of George Eastman. Eastman introduced a handheld, easy-to-use camera with the philosophy of "You push the button, we do the rest." It worked, and photography took off like wildfire. Suddenly this almost-magical method of capturing time and printing it out to be shared was within the reach of just about everyone. The quality was quite a bit less than earlier photographs using large cameras fixed on tripods, but it was a picture, and not all that bad a picture at that. It was convenient and allowed everyone to get into the picture-taking act. Digital photography is not quite to this point yet.

Eastman's philosophy helped build a company that is synonymous with photography, in general, to this day, the Eastman Kodak Company, known simply as "Kodak" around the world. And it is known *around the world*. Kodak is one of the most recognizable names on the planet, primarily because photographs have become so important in our lives. Snapshots at home, magazine ads, catalogs, wall portraits, billboards, packaging—photographs permeate our lives completely. The picture is the single most cross-cultural communications device ever invented. It transcends all language, geographic, social, and economic barriers. Remember this, because it is this strength that is propelling the digital photography world as well.

The world's love of photography and the ability to stop time and share it with others spawned a huge industry. As this industry follows the same digital path nearly every industry is faced with, new challenges arise and new companies become leaders. Traditional photographic companies are trying to reinvent themselves to become leaders in the digital photographic world as well.

As photographers, we are familiar with a world of photography heralded by traditional names like Kodak, Fuji, Agfa, Ilford, Lucky, Nikon, Canon, Minolta, etc. As we discuss photography in a digital domain, these photographic companies are joined by names foreign to the photography world such as Hewlett-Packard, Microsoft, Epson, Adobe, and Quark. As we make the transition from a purely analog world to a digital world, these names are taking their place next to, and occasionally ahead of, the traditional bearers of photography's standards.

Which invites the question, what is photography anyway, aside from its technical definition? For professional photographers, it is the process of freezing in time an idea, a scene, or a moment. It is accomplished often under difficult conditions and only through the application of specialized equipment and techniques. It is also a way of life and livelihood.

Professional photography is all about image quality. As a result, the film, papers, and chemicals that have been developed to serve this market are highly specialized. Professional photographs are generally taken using positive or negative film 2-1/4 inches (6 cm.) in width on up to 8 x 10 or even larger. Exposure is tightly controlled by the photographer through the use of a light meter or flash meter that helps to determine the correct mix of film speed, shutter speed, and aperture to achieve a correct exposure.

After the exposure is made, the film is sometimes processed in the studio but more often than not sent out to a professional photographic laboratory to be processed and printed. The resulting prints or transparencies are sharp and saturated. This is photographic quality. Nobody ever sees it. Nobody ever sees it, you say? Well, almost nobody. The photographer does and the client does, but unless it is a family portrait or a bit of framed wall art, few people have the opportunity to appreciate the quality of an image taken professionally. Once they are captured, most photographs we see are digitized, halftoned, robbed of a great deal of saturation and color range, and printed on regular old paper through a lithographic printing press. Perhaps this means that it is the lithographic press and the variety of papers that can be printed on it that we ought better use as a measure of quality.

The imaging chain

The imaging chain shown here holds true for traditional photography as well as digital photography and all flavors in between (known as hybrid). In traditional photography, the capture stage is accomplished by pushing the shutter on your camera, allowing light to pass through the lens and hit the film. The film itself is the key aspect of the storage phase, as silver halide particles respond to the light that has just hit them, holding it as a latent, or invisible, image to be developed later. Once processed, this latent image changes to a visible image that serves as a storage vehicle throughout the imaging path, to be duplicated at any time in the future.

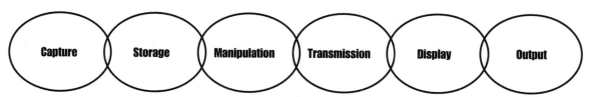

The imaging chain

The manipulation stage in the photographic process is a little bit fuzzier. Manipulation can be accomplished during film processing where longer or shorter development durations can be introduced (known as push or pull processing) but it is more prevalent in the printing phase. Photographs are usually manipulated during printing when variables such as contrast, lightness, and color balance can be controlled. However, aside from some highly specialized darkroom techniques, the ability to substantially manipulate traditional photographic images is minor.

Transmission of photographs, in the strictest sense of the word, is accomplished by hand, post, FedEx, and carrier pigeon. Aside from some specialized digital transfer processes such as those employed by the Associated Press for their member newspapers and prepress operations for print production, this is still very much true today. It is interesting to note that for quite some time now, photographs have been transmitted digitally using fax machines.

The ability to capture images and then store them on some sort of semi-permanent media (no media is permanent), interact with and manipulate them, catalog them, sort through them, and print them is really what is driving the digital photo industry. People will be able to see the advantages in being able to instantly access any image they take or have ever taken.

Once you have an image, whether it starts from a 35 mm camera on film or it starts from a digital camera, what do you do with it? The whole concept of photo albums changes a little bit. While we will still have photo albums, we will add to them the concept of on-line photo libraries, albums that can be shared and viewed by family members or clients all around the world, at the same time or at any time they choose.

What is digital anyway?

Now that we have discussed photos and images, what is the difference? Nothing really. For most of our discussions, images are what photos become once they are digitized—that is, reduced to spots or dots, or zeroes and ones. The word "image" takes photography from the traditional view of pictures on film- and paper-based emulsions and expands it to include pictures on monitors, T-shirts, disks, e-mail, paper, and just about anything else you can imagine. So how do we get from here to there?

Pictures or images?

The difference between a picture and an image is mostly semantics and, truthfully, one can be a synonym for the other. Purists may argue that an image is created while a picture is taken (as in taking a photograph) but we will argue that many a picture created with crayon found its way to the door of our refrigerator years ago, back when an image was something your agent worked on for you to get you a better role.

Pictures traditionally have been slices of life captured by a camera onto film. This definition held up for many years up until scanners and computers came into the picture (bad pun, unintended). Once a picture, be it photograph, drawing, or painting, was scanned and digitized, it no longer had the same physical properties as the original. A different term was needed and the word "image" fits nicely.

Webster's, in defining the word "image," uses words such as "form," "representation,""likeness," and "embodiment." In this sense, the digital form of a picture, photograph, or painting fits the word "image" and makes it easier to differentiate between traditional imagery and its digital form. While we are still taking pictures with a digital camera, "images" gives things a digital feel.

How we got from pictures to images

Digital imaging had its beginnings back into the 1960s. The 1970s saw it blossom into a mainstream, albeit high-end, business with giant specialized imaging systems and specially trained operators. The lion's share of these digital imaging companies were called color separators and their trade soon became the key to the entire printing process. Theirs was an exclusive fraternity, open only to those with the money and the wherewithal to invest it in equipment, technology, and personnel. It was a club of millionaires, because that was the entrance fee just to get started in the business. And once in, you could charge nearly any price, if you were good enough, and make millions more scanning photos and selling color-separated film for offset lithographic printing.

That all changed in 1984 when Apple invented the Macintosh, the computer for the rest of us. The Macintosh opened the door of computing to everyone. Its graphical persona was immediately embraced by the printing and publishing world.

Soon the ability to create images with text and graphics on the Macintosh bloomed into the ability to create full-color images, to import text and graphics including image files into the computer, lay them out on a page, and then spit them back out either as film separations or as a laser print. The business of color publishing became available to anyone with the ability to buy a modest system and learn a few computer tricks. Art collided with science on the desktop and the two have been wed ever since. For those of you buying this book hot off the press (in its first printing) not quite ten years have passed since this time.

Another important factor in this new world of digital color was the introduction of color copiers and their ability to bring color output to the masses. Xerox, for example, had a color copier 20 years ago, a great first attempt but just too expensive to produce and the world was not ready for it. Canon turned the world on its ear in the late 1980s with its introduction of the CLC line of color copiers. These devices first found their way into graphically inclined offices, then eventually locations like Kinko's. Color suddenly became accessible to anyone within driving distance of a quickie copy center. Soon these copiers were interfaced to computers, instantly combining desktop digital imaging systems with quality mini color printing presses. Today color laser printers are no longer an anomaly and color inkjet printers are as common as doorknobs.

On the input side, the single technology that really influenced desktop digital imaging was the introduction of desktop scanners. These devices work more or less like copiers in reverse, turning paper prints into electronic information and sending them to the computer. Handy, but you were still limited to a relatively low-resolution image that looked okay on screen but did not necessarily print out very well on paper.

Then along came Kodak with Photo CD, a 4-3/4 inch plastic disk holding 100 high-resolution photographic images of your choice. Photo CD made a huge impact on the graphic design and printing market. Interestingly, it did not do too much for the photographic world, which was still firmly entrenched in silver halide technology and for the most part devoid of an output device that could match the quality of that process. Suddenly high-quality digital scans were available to anyone, and you could get them at the local photo lab.

Photo CD was an excellent enabler for the creation of high-quality photographic output. With a little tweaking, Photo CD images were, and are, sufficient to produce a good quality 8 x 10 print for printing, but there were few reasonably priced output devices to make those prints. While you could take a Photo CD scan and print it in a magazine, creating a digital photograph was still beyond the grasp of the majority of us.

This too began to change thanks to a technology called dye-diffusion thermal transfer, or dyesub. These printers fit on your desktop and could produce true photographic quality output. But at $10,000 or more, they were still beyond the reach of most of us.

But technology marches on

Now it is interesting when we say digital industry … ten years ago that would have meant high-end remote sensing devices, digital satellite capture systems, and maybe the occasional electron scanning microscope image. That is what was thought of by most people as digital imaging. Today you have the ability to buy a 450 megahertz processor in a machine with 128 megabytes of RAM and a hard drive the size of Montana and a scanner for $2,000 on your Sears charge. Three hundred dollar inkjet printers meet, and even exceed, the quality of dyesub printers of only a few years ago. A setup with all the power of a million-dollar imaging system 15 years ago will fit on your desktop today. And by the time you can find this book at your local library, it will probably cost half of what it did this week in our Sunday paper.

Finally, after 300 years of babystep advancements, the printing industry found a vehicle that allowed it to take giant leaps. The photographic industry, everyone from full-time professional photographers and lab operators to Mom & Dad, has taken notice and is applying the technology in even more interesting ways. We have only just begun.

Digital revolution has become digital evolution. We are beyond the airbrushing of moles off swimsuit models and have progressed (?) to putting Elvis's face on Mars and publishing it on newsstands. Closer to home, we can combine old photographs of our ancestors, finger-paintings from first grade, a love letter from college, and a digital portrait from last week into a family history that can be printed at our desk and framed, or E-mailed to twice-removed cousins overseas.

What is even more amazing is that all of this is available to nearly anyone. The prices are dropping, the capabilities are becoming more mainstream, and the world is rapidly becoming digital. Make no mistakes about it, digital pictures (and images), both still and moving, are going to be at the forefront of it all.

So where to from here? Read on.

Chapter 2
PHOTOGRAPHY

Photography has been around as long as anyone can remember and is an integral part of our lives. So much so that in times of disaster, it is often the family photo albums that are saved, or if not, often the most grieved for. Photography is a universal language and pictures speak a thousand words, no matter the dialect. To understand the impact digital photography will and can have on your world you must first understand what drives it in the first place—photography itself.

This book isn't intended as an exhaustive reference on basic photographic technique. However, knowing a few simple concepts can make a big difference in your photography, either traditional or digital. Even if you are familiar with these concepts, a refresher on them and their connection to the digital world will make your digital transition a bit less painful.

Photography is the delicate dance of light, optics, duration, amount, sensitivity, and capacity. Let's start with a typical autofocus point-and-shoot 35 mm camera. Point your camera at a bouquet of flowers and push the button. Halfway pressed, the button sends a signal to an internal light meter that decides how much light to let in and for how long. The camera takes into account the general lighting conditions it sees and the sensitivity of the film it is loaded with. This determines the shutter speed and aperture setting the camera will use to correctly expose the film.

Once the film is all exposed and filled with memories, you remove it from the camera and entrust it to a stranger who loads it into the front of a photo processing machine. After a short time, out the other end emerges your processed film and paper printouts of all, or near-ly all, of your memories. Magic? Perhaps a little but for the most part the entire process can be explained in a high school science class or two.

What makes a camera?

A camera is a box holding a lens, an aperture, a shutter, and some light-sensitive media. Until recently this media was always a roll or sheet of photographic film but today, and more so in the future, the film is replaced by a bit of light-sensitive electronics. To understand how photography works and the beginning of the process, the time of image capture, let's look at how the camera works.

The lens

The camera's lens provides a path for light to enter the camera and be precisely focused on the film inside. Most lenses are made up of groups of other lenses or lens elements. These combinations are for-mulated to enhance various lens attributes, such as allowing the lens to gather more light or to reduce distortion, the idea being to create a perfectly clean and clear path between the world and the film. Lens quality is like water quality. The purer it is the better it is.

It's when lenses are grouped together in zoom lenses—sliding tubes that allow you to vary the distances between them—that they become interesting. Zoom lenses can bring the world closer to your camera or let you capture a wide panorama. On most point-and-shoot cameras and some autofocus SLR (single lens reflex) cameras, zoom lenses are standard equipment. Following this trend, more and more digital cameras are coming equipped with zoom lenses. On digital cameras, zoom lenses have the added benefit of giving you the ability to crop within the camera before capturing an image, max-imizing those all-important pixels—spots that make up images.

On 35 mm cameras, a 50 mm focal length lens is considered normal. Fifty mm is about what you see with one eye closed. Anything below 50 mm is considered wide angle and anything above is telephoto. On 35 mm SLR cameras, the lens is interchangeable, which gives SLRs a fantastic advantage over all other cameras. You can get hundreds of different lenses for just about any model that can capture any number of views of your world.

Image quality starts with the lens. Inexpensive camera and lens manufacturers often cut corners when manufacturing lenses or choosing lens components for their cameras. Inferior lenses distort light and/or alter the characteristics of the light that passes through them. This results in pictures that are not sharp or produce washed-out colors. A basic camera with a good lens will take better photographs than a camera with all the bells and whistles that skimps on its optics.

- Telephoto lenses bring far away objects up close.
- Wide angle lenses allow you to capture a wide panorama in one shot.
- Macro lenses allow you to focus in on small objects.
- Zoom lenses do a little of everything.

The aperture

The aperture of a camera is a variable-sized hole inside the camera that controls how much light is allowed to pass through the lens and onto the film. Think of it as a blind in a window that you can roll all the way up to the top, letting in all of the light; or all the way to the bottom, letting in no light. And everywhere in between. You, or the camera, can control the size of the hole to let in more or less light during exposure. Apertures are measured in strange numbers called f-stops on a scale that only makes sense if you think backwards. The wider the aperture, the bigger the hole (blinds up), and therefore the more light allowed into the camera, the smaller the f-stop number. The smaller the aperture (mostly down), the less light allowed into the camera, and the higher the f-stop number. It's a little screwy until you get used to it.

On one-time-use cameras, the aperture is always the same size. These cameras have one lens, one shutter speed, and one kind of film in them. They use the "one over the speed of the film at f/11" as a general rule, the idea being that to get correct exposure on a sunny day without a light meter, you can apply that simple formula and be assured of fairly correct exposure. See *Useful Information* at the end of this chapter.

On point-and-shoot cameras, the aperture still adjusts, but is generally controlled by the electronics in the camera, in conjunction with the exposure system. Most camera exposure systems incorporate one or more tiny computer processors that measure light, read in the speed of the film in the camera, decide whether or not to fire the flash, then set the aperture and the shutter speed for correct exposure.

Single lens reflex (SLR) cameras and some manual point-and-shoot cameras usually allow you to set your own apertures and come with built-in light meters to guide you.

- The aperture controls how much light is let into the camera.
- The wider the aperture, the smaller the f-stop number, the more light let in.
- The smaller the aperture, the larger the f-stop number, the less light let in.
- The aperture controls depth of field (see below).

Depth of field

When you adjust your aperture, not only are you changing your exposure but your depth of field as well. Depth of field is a strange optical phenomena that changes the range of focus of a lens at any given point as related to the aperture the lens is set at and the focal length of the lens itself.

Depth of field explained

Okay, the above paragraph sounds a bit confusing but bear with us as it will soon all become clear. When you focus a camera you focus on a subject, let's say a bride and groom outside on the lawn at their reception. Depth of field (distance in front of and behind your subject that will also be in focus) is directly related to the aperture setting of your camera. So if you are using a wide aperture (small f/stop number) the bride will be in focus but Aunt Mary standing five feet behind her won't be and neither will the flower girl standing five feet in front of her. A wide open aperture, or one that lets in the maximum amount of light, allows for only a shallow depth of field. The smaller your aperture, the greater the distance in front of and behind the subject that will be in focus.

To make matters a bit more confusing, the wider a lens is, the greater its depth of field. A 35 mm wide-angle lens has a long depth of field but a 150 mm telephoto lens has far less. Not only that, the closer your subject is to infinity, the more depth of field the lens can have. Infinity is the point beyond which everything is in focus and is different on every lens. Infinity is reached when the lens is focused all the way out to its maximum point.

- Depth of field is the amount of area in front of and behind your subject that will be in focus.
- The smaller the aperture, the more depth of field.
- The depth of field increases as the focus distance approaches infinity.

The shutter

The shutter of a camera controls the length of time that light is allowed to enter the camera and hit the film. Shutters are little doors that open to let in some light and quickly close again after a prescribed amount of time and light has gone by.

Close your eyes. Open them. Close them again quickly. That's a shutter. In the old days, cameras didn't have shutters, only lens caps. To make an exposure, the photographer would take the cap off of the lens, wait a while, then place the cap back on the lens. In those days, film wasn't very sensitive to light and since exposure times were measured in minutes, if you were off by a second or two because you were fiddling with the lens cap trying to put it back on, no big deal.

Modern films are far more sensitive to light and most exposures today are measured in mere fractions of a second. Any given camera you pick up today will have a shutter that can open and close again in as little as one 500th of a second, many even faster.

Stopping motion

Shutter Speed vs. Subject Motion

Children playing	1/125
City Street	1/125
Vehicles @ 25 mph	1/250
Football/running	1/250
Vehicles @ 45 mph	1/500
Horse Racing	1/1000
Airplanes/Race Cars	1/1000

Panning is the practice of following the subject with your camera as you photograph. Stopping motion is important to help avoid motion blur. The faster your shutter speed, the smaller the slice of time you capture. Short shutter speeds stop motion but must be compensated for by opening up the aperture to let in more light. Professional digital cameras have always had variable shutter speeds and more and more "consumer level" and serious amateur digital cameras are emerging with them as well.

- Shutters are like your eyelids. They open to let light in then close again to keep it out.
- Faster shutter speeds capture smaller slices of time and stop motion.
- Fast shutter speeds must be compensated for by using wider apertures.

Exposure

Okay, so now we know how light gets into the camera and to the film and what shutter speeds and apertures do. How the heck do we know how to get them in sync to create a photograph? This can be a confusing thing, so first let's take a look at an analogy. Think of an empty bucket, a hose, and a faucet. The bucket is your film and its size is your film speed. Water is light. The diameter of the hose is your aperture and the amount of time the water is on is your shutter speed. When the bucket is full to the top, you have correct exposure. First of all, the bigger your bucket, the more water it takes to fill it. A big bucket is akin to something like 100 speed film while a small bucket is more like 800 speed film. You can fill your bucket to the top (correct exposure) in three ways. A small hose running for a long time will fill it. This is the same as a small aperture and a long shutter speed. A wide-diameter hose, running for a short amount of time, will also fill it. This is the same as a wide open aperture and a short shutter speed. And any combination of the two will also fill the bucket. The key is to find the balance that just fills the bucket without leaving any space or overflowing.

Correct exposure

Technically, correct exposure is when an 18 percent gray card, photographically reproduced, results in prints that measure 18 percent gray on a scale from white to black. So what the heck is 18 percent gray? It is a shade of black that falls between zero percent black, which is white, and 100 percent black, or pure black. Eighteen percent gray is the same shade as a concrete sidewalk just after a rain and is more or less the appearance of the patch in the middle below (18 percent gray patch). How you understand 18 percent gray affects how well your photographs are exposed.

0% White   **18% Gray**   **100% Black**

The most important thing to remember is that 18 percent gray is how the light meter in your camera judges the world. Point your camera at anything and you are telling it "this is 18 percent gray." Not a bad place to start, actually, for most general photography. Long ago, 18 percent gray was based on an average of the light falling on the world in most situations and, for the most part, it's a pretty good average. The important thing is to know which side of 18 percent gray your subject is on. A snow bunny in a white ski outfit on the slopes of Aspen on a sunny day is a heck of a lot closer to zero percent gray, otherwise known as white. Therefore, you need to override your camera's meter and overexpose by two stops or so. This is two clicks down in numbers on your aperture ring or two shutter speeds lower (or one of each) to let in more light. The more advanced automatic cameras will figure this out for you but any automatic camera worth its salt will have an overexposure button that will do the same thing. Dark subjects pose a bit less of a problem as generally we want to have the camera see them as something lighter than they are so that they hold detail.

You can purchase 18 percent gray cards (known simply as gray cards) of various sizes at any camera store. For serious photography needing exact exposure, place one in a part of the scene you are photographing, in representative lighting, to set your exposure. Point your camera at the card, note the reading, and set your camera manually to the same aperture and shutter speed. If your camera has automatic exposure, more than likely you can lock in the exposure by depressing the shutter button half way. Be careful, this also locks the focus on automatic cameras so if you are thinking of using a gray card in this case, make sure it falls within the same plane of focus as your subject.

- Correct exposure is a balance between film speed, shutter speed, and aperture.
- Film is like fruit. Not enough light and it is not ripe. Too much light and it overripens.
- Overexposing allows more light to reach the film than is needed for correct exposure, underexposing allows less.

Film

Film is at the heart of photography, both conventional and digital. Conventionally, it is the film that captures the image sent to it through the lens. Digitally, it is the level of quality to which all digital images are compared. Film in one form or another has been around for a few hundred years and is still made much the same way. Film is made up of a strip of clear, very pure polyester. Stacked on top of this base is one or more layers of emulsion made up of silver halide crystals suspended in gelatin (more or less clear Jell-O). These crystals are what make film sensitive to light and their structure and application are part art, part science. Imagine a strip of film as sort of a photographic Nestlé Crunch bar with many bits of puffed rice suspended in chocolate. This is very much how film is made. To a liquid mixture of silver halide crystals and gelatin are added various other minerals to improve light sensitivity, contrast, graininess, color sensitivity, etc. A whole host of other additives are added to the film to provide a variety of imaging characteristics, to add durability, or to achieve certain effects, and each film manufacturer has its own recipe book for making film. These recipes are more closely guarded by their manufacturers than the recipe for Coca Cola. Understanding the various characteristics of different films is key to producing good prints, or good scans, from slides or negatives. Known as "film terms," these characteristics are programmed into photographic processing units and film scanners to tell these devices how the film "sees" color.

All technical mumbo jumbo aside, today's films are pretty darn good and photographers have their favorites. Film technology is improving the quality of the film we use. And the photographic research and development labs of the world have lots of ideas for taking it further and further. We won't debate the various idiosyncrasies of one film or emulsion over another, but instead will focus (no pun intended) on a characteristic that will fundamentally affect the quality of the photograph destined to be digitized: sharpness. For this discussion, sharpness equals grain and both are directly related to film speed.

Sharpness

Sharpness is the ability for an object, let's say a black dot, to be seen at a given size. The smaller it gets, the more difficult it is to perceive until you can't see it at all. Another word for sharpness is resolution. Ahh, finally the true meaning of resolution. The sharper the image, the better shot you have at getting a good print or scan. This is an example of the burrito theory…beans in, beans out. A whole host of variables affect the sharpness of an image on a piece of film. The optics in the lens-o-matic zoom you bought at that kiosk in New York City won't come close to those in a $400 SLR, and both stand far above the plastic optics in the $10 single-use camera you picked up at the checkout stand while buying groceries. And the roll of film you got in the mail for free will not give you the image quality of a roll of Kodak Gold 100. While these factors all make a difference in the sharpness of your photographs, all things being equal, grain has the largest effect.

Film speed

Generally the faster the film, the larger the grain. The larger the grain the less sharp a film is. Film, at first, was generally the same speed, around 100 ASA. In the mid 70s, Kodak introduced Kodacolor 400, their "high-speed" film. Film speed is a factor determined by the size of the grain, the spacing of the grain, and the various salts and minerals that are added to increase sensitivity.

Larger grain particles have more surface area, increasing the chance that they will get struck by a photon of light coming through the lens. The more evenly spaced the grain particles are, the better the chance they will get struck by photons as well. And additives such as selenium, or other precious minerals, such as gold, further increase sensitivity. This is, incidentally, a major reason why 400 speed film costs more than 100 speed film. It has more expensive materials in it. Don't go wearing it as a bracelet.

In the 80s, film speed just exploded, as film technology got more and more advanced. Speeds like 1000, 1600, and 3200 were introduced, allowing us to take better photographs under adverse lighting conditions. But always there was the tradeoff; increased speed brought with it increased grain size. Today things have settled down a bit. Speed increases are coming with less grain size tradeoff.

It is interesting to see the speed progression in single-use cameras that are on the market…we will use Kodak as an example. Kodak had 400 speed film in their single-use cameras when they were introduced. Recently they have upped the film speed to 800 speed film. This is a high-speed film that has respectable image quality.

The grain is not necessarily objectionable and as the vast majority of prints from single-use cameras are of 3-1/2 x 5 inch or 4 x 6 inch size (the vast majority of prints made from all 35 mm negatives are this size) the grain is not very objectionable at all. Only a small percentage of negatives captured ever make it to anything larger than that snap-shot size.

Slides ... the first color film

The first film to make color photography really accessible to the average Joe and Jane was Kodachrome, introduced by Eastman Kodak in 1937. Kodachrome was and still is a positive, or slide, film. For years following its introduction, people shot millions of rolls of film and vainly attempted to entertain their suffering neighbors with slide shows of Grandpa Jimmy's trip to the old country.

Eventually color print film came out, which allowed us to keep our loved ones near and dear in the bottom of a purse or on the top of a fireplace mantel. The process does involve multiple generations, from film to print, which means less quality but more convenience. But for professionals, the slide or transparency was, and still is, the ultimate reproduction.

Slide film (also known as transparency film) is just like negative or print film but instead of a negative image, you get a positive one. When you get your slides back from the lab, they come mounted in individual frames and are a positive image of the scene you photographed. Hold them up to the light or pop them into a projector and they are the closest thing you'll get to the original scene.

Slide film is sharper, more colorful, and has a broader tonal range than print film and far surpasses the final print. Its tonal range also beats most digital scanners and cameras, though it doesn't come close to that of the human eye/brain combination.

Lighting ratio is the range of difference between highlight and shadow areas where details can be seen in both.

Negative and print (B&W)	5:1
Negative & print (color)	3:1
Slide/Transparency	6:1
Human eye/brain (sunlight)	125:1

Slide film is more expensive to buy but cheaper to process because the lab doesn't have to make prints. You can order prints from slides if you need to, but they are made on a special paper and are more expensive than prints from negatives.

We wish to promote a slide and transparency revolution. The highest quality scan you can get is from a film original and the highest quality film original is a slide or transparency. Therefore, if you know that your pictures are going to be digitized at some point, shoot them on slide film. With its ability to hold more information (a better quality image) you will get the highest quality scan possible. You can always make a print or have one made at your lab later.

- All film has a rated speed that determines its sensitivity to light.
- Faster film speeds (higher numbers) need less light for correct exposure.
- Faster film speeds also mean a grainier image.
- The more you enlarge a negative, the bigger the grain appears.
- Slide film has a higher dynamic range than print film.
- In general, the slower the film speed, the sharper (ability to hold fine details) it is.

Types of film formats

Large/Medium format

Large format films are meticulously crafted to offer particular characteristics. While 35 mm film needs to work in all cameras—from $10 single-use cameras to $1,000 professional SLRs—and under a variety of conditions. Large and medium format films, on the other hand, are generally used by professionals who will carefully store the film at optimum conditions and expose it carefully.

These films are also generally processed in professional photo labs that take great care with them during and after processing. As a result they don't need the same anti-scratch coatings as their amateur cousins do, which are often subjected to the rigors of processing equipment long overdue for a good cleaning and handled by novice employees with other things on their minds.

For our discussions, the most important thing about medium and large format films is that because their negatives are bigger, enlargements from them can be made larger before the grain of the film becomes too noticeable. This fact holds true no matter what imaging technology we are discussing. The bigger your original, the more you can enlarge it on a final print.

- Large and medium format films are generally used by professional photographers.
- Because they produce a larger slide and/or negative, their prints can be made larger before grain is noticeable.

35 mm

Thirty-five millimeter film makes up more than 90 percent of the film shot in the world and represents the vast majority of the 100 billion exposures taken every year. It is also the standard we will be comparing to for most of our digital camera discussions.

Thirty-five millimeter film has been around since the 30s and really hasn't changed too much since then. Thirty-five millimeter found its place during World War II when war photographers immediately saw the benefit of having a small handheld camera that also offered good image quality. Thirty-five millimeter is also a convenient format, comprising a little cartridge full of film wound on a spindle inside. Most of all it is fairly easy to load and unload. Until this time, cameras were fairly complicated. Thirty-five millimeter also offered a choice in the number of photographs you could take—12, 24, or 36 exposures, enough film to suit every situation.

Thirty-five millimeter really showed itself with rangefinder cameras, where you looked through one lens to frame your shot while a different lens exposed the film. This causes a problem called "parallax," where what you see isn't what you get. For a quick example of parallax, take a look at an object across the room. Close one eye. Open it and close the other eye. Now do it very quickly. See what we mean? The object seems to jump side to side as you switch eyes. The closer you are to your subject, the more effect parallax has on your image. This is a big problem when you hope to get from one lens what you saw through the other.

One disadvantage to 35 mm film is that your negatives are still fairly small, particularly if you are going to make any enlargements. Once you process the film, the negatives can quickly become separated from the prints. People put prints in albums and tend to put negatives into shoe boxes. When it comes time to make another copy, all they can find is a print and a copy of a print is of far less quality than a copy made from an original negative. This problem is soon to become a thing of the past as photofinishers begin digitizing every negative they process, insuring that a copy can be made at any time.

In fact, the time when the majority of people make an extra set is right at the time of processing, before they even see how their pictures turned out. Photofinishers encourage us to do this by giving cut rate prices on a second set of prints. It is also easier for the photo finisher because making another print is a simple as pushing the button twice or dialing an additional print number when printing the negative. Since additional prints are made at the same time and at the same setting, they are always an exact match, something that is very difficult to do when making another print later on.

Once your prints are developed and your negatives tucked away in a shoebox (or not—many people simply throw their negatives away!), the chances of making additional prints months or years later are mighty slim. So we have all of these pictures that we love in our albums, but no easy way to make copies to share them with friends later. There has to be a better way. Enter the Advanced Photography System (APS).

- The vast majority of film shot in the world is 35 mm.
- 35 mm is what most digital cameras are compared to.
- Soon all film processed will be digitized and stored on-line at the photo lab for later retrieval.

APS

The future of photography according to the giants of the industry is the new Advanced Photo System (APS) format. APS is the most interesting advance in consumer photography since the introduction of the 126 film cartridge in the 1960s (which coincidentally was discontinued just as APS began to gain a foothold in the market) Intended as a bridge between traditional silver halide and digital technologies, APS combines the best of both worlds. Film is still the cheapest, highest quality storage medium you can buy. There is still not a digital system available at a reasonable price that can match the quality of film.

The Advanced Photo System was introduced in early 1996 and may be one of the only documented occurrences of rival film and camera manufacturers working together in relative harmony. Kodak, Fuji, Canon, Nikon, and Minolta, meeting no doubt in some neutral place like Geneva, Switzerland, decided that they needed a way to not only boost film paper and chemistry sales but prepare for the certain dominance of digital imaging in not only photography but communications in general.

In preparing for the onslaught of digital imaging, these manufacturers designed a bridge format between the two worlds, a way to keep the inherent advantages of capturing images on film while providing an easy way to digitize the resulting photos. APS got off to a slow start but sales more than doubled in 1998 and should continue to rise as more 35 mm cameras are replaced with the new format.

The APS film cartridge is smaller than but similar to a 35 mm film cartridge. Tucked inside is a smaller format strip of film, 24 mm as opposed to 35 mm, with an attached magnetic strip running the length of the roll. The APS cassette is designed not only to hold the raw film and transport it through the camera, but also to hold the film after it has been processed, keeping the negatives protected and readily accessible. Once processed, the cartridge is returned with a 4 x 6 inch index print containing thumbnail images of each exposure. Gone is the hunting through pages of negatives, if you can even find them, holding them up to the light, trying to reverse the image in your brain to find that long-lost shot of Uncle George's retirement party.

APS also provides three image formats to choose from: C or Classic, a conventional 35 mm size; H or HDTV, a nod to upcoming high-definition televisions; and P, or panoramic, an ultra-wide format. These formats can be mixed and matched on the same roll.

One key to APS's bridge to the digital world lies in a thin magnetic strip that runs along the bottom of the film, similar to the one on the back of your credit card. This strip records and communicates a host of information from the camera to the processing and printing equipment or digital scanner. A wide range of information from the settings the camera used when the photograph was taken—whether the flash was on or not, which of the three cropping formats had been selected, and exposure information—can all be encoded at exposure, giving the output equipment at the other end some intelligence in how the photographs should look when processed.

Built into some APS cameras is a feature that allows you to record the date or encode a line of text on the magnetic strip. That information is passed on to the processing equipment. This is a step above the traditional method of date encoding, which would burn the data into a corner of the negative so it was always on the print. You could have a beautiful photograph of your daughter swimming in the pool and in orange at the bottom corner was the date it was taken. This is fine for recording purposes but it is not something you want to have on an 11x14 on the wall. By providing the ability to encode the date and other information on the magnetic strip on APS film, you choose whether to have it print out on your print (generally on the back).

The information on the magnetic strip will allows APS film to be more easily digitized because it can tell a scanner the characteristics of the film—what its speed is, for example, or what type of film it is—which determines how it is scanned and digitally processed. Every type of film has its own characteristics that determine how it captures light and forms an image. Just like every variety of apple looks a little different and tastes a little different, so too is every type of film a little different. These differences make each film scan a little differently as well. Currently, these differences are taken into account by the scanner operator, but providing that information on a magnetic strip, as APS can, will help to automate the whole process. Already supporters of the format have released film scanners for the APS format that fit right into your computer like a CD-ROM drive, making scanning your APS film at home quick and easy.

Like any emerging product, APS has suffered from slow acceptance in the market due to unavailability of film and processing sites and a 20 percent or more increase in cost of both as compared to 35 mm. In addition, the use of the new format necessitates purchasing a new camera, one that will cost more than its 35 mm counterpart. At the photo lab side of things, processing the APS format also necessitates purchasing new equipment and/or augmenting existing equipment, making its acceptance slow on the processing side of the equation. However as prices drop, sales go up, and the market begins to embrace the format, which it will, these problems will go away. Perhaps in a few years, we will look back and laugh at the problems APS is having and wonder what we would do without it just as we do with microwave ovens and answering machines.

- APS is an emerging format.
- It is a smaller format than 35 mm.
- APS has a magnetic strip that can record various forms of information.
- APS is a bridge format, helping to bridge the gap between traditional and digital.

APS to digital

APS is an excellent step between analog and digital. It is what we might call a hybrid technology, bridging the gap between traditional photography and digital photography. Being film-based, APS retains the traditional silver halide quality, but because digital information can be encoded, it can be rapidly digitized and brought into the digital realm and printed to inkjet printers or e-mailed to friends. This bridge between traditional and digital photography is sure to bring Main Street, USA, closer to digital imaging.

Companies are beginning to put APS film scanners out on the market, both for the photo lab and the folks at home with a PC. At PMA '98, a trade show dedicated to photography and photo processing, Kodak introduced the APS film drive, an APS film scanner that fits into your computer. A processed APS cartridge is slipped into a little door that sucks it into the drive, pulls out the negatives, and does a quick preview scan of all the negatives to show you what is on that roll. Then you select the image you want, crop it, frame it the way you like and click the button, scanning and digitizing the frame and putting it on your hard drive. At its introduction, the entry-level APS film drive sold for under $300, making it the least expensive film scanner on the market. When asked whether they planned on introducing a 35 mm version, which makes up greater than 95 percent of the film market, the representative flatly said no, the future is APS, the idea apparently being, "If we build it, they will come." If you have any doubt about the strategy behind that, simply look at Microsoft, one of the most successful companies in history. They sell us stuff that we aren't even sure we need. And we buy it by the millions.

APS in the next couple of years will steadily grow. It's still unclear how long it will hold off the mainstream digital evolution, but it provides a clearer film-based path to a digital world than anything else. Is APS a better format? You can make a case that it is, given some of its features and some of the abilities it affords photographers. On the other hand it produces a smaller film format, so you can make a case that it has less image area so there is less quality on enlargement.

However for most people, APS's advantages may outweigh its lesser image detail. A perfect example from history is the Beta video tape format. Beta is a superior format to VHS but VHS found more acceptance. The technology was more widely shared right off the bat and the only Beta machines you see now are either in the high-end professional video labs or at the Salvation Army.

Professional implications of APS

While the APS format may never find full acceptance in professional markets, it can fill niches where enlargements over 5 x 7 are uncommon, such as wedding and event candids, publicity photos, and real estate/insurance markets. Already APS SLR cameras are showing up in camera stores. All the advantages of a high-end controllable camera and the image quality advantages of film, married with the advantages of a fast, high-quality scanning system, are a tough combination to beat.

On the consumer side of the fence, APS is a good bet. Its ease of use, full-featured cameras, backing by heavy hitters in the industry, and increased acceptance at photo labs all pave the way for it to be the amateur film format of the future. Until digital takes over, of course. But film is not a barrier to digital. In fact it is, and will for a while be, the highest quality capture medium available. It's good, it's cheap, and it's convenient.

Film is king ... for a little while still

Film still offers photographers the best of both worlds: quality and convenience. For the majority of us, having photographs in an hour is plenty fast enough and we are still at a point, and will be for a while, where the hybrid combination of traditional film, digital scanning, and storage is a good way to go.

With a hybrid approach, you have all the advantages of traditional film technology and the quality it affords and the advantages of film scanners, which allow you to digitize that film. One frame of 35 mm film holds an incredible amount of image information, upwards of 20 mb of information; it is easy to store and, unlike a digital image, you do not need some high-tech device to use it.

The photographic market is changing rapidly and heading closer to digital every day. Film is still king. However, by the time this book has a few cappuccino stains on it at Powell's Bookstore, digital will no longer be an unproven technology. It won't be long after that before film users are considered eccentrics.

Digital is mass production. Film is fine craftsmanship. We are living in a world of rapid development. The closer the two can get to each other, the better off we all will be. There will be room for film for a while still. But the rapid digitalization of the world in general and the interconnections between people afforded by technology impact photography more so than nearly any other pursuit. Images are the future of communication and the future of communication is digital.

Photographic processing

Processing goes from film to paper, and then some.

Film is only one half of the photography story. If we're shooting slides, and few of us do, film is the whole story, but for the 90 percent of us who shoot negative film, better known as print film, there are still another few steps to go. But in any event, unless you are using an instant camera, such as a Polaroid, or a digital camera, you have to have your film processed.

Film processing

Open up the back of your camera and pull out the roll of film. Just kidding. Imagine that you have opened up the back of the camera and pulled out the roll of film. The first thing you will notice is that there is absolutely no difference in appearance between the film that has not yet been exposed and the film wound around the take-up spool that has already been exposed. The point is that until the film is processed, the images on the film are *latent*, that is they are there but not yet visible. The film is not yet processed.

Photographic processing hasn't changed all that much in its hundred and fifty year (or so) history. An exposed roll of film full of latent (invisible) images is passed through a series of chemical baths that first develop the images, then fixes them into a permanent visible state. Usually the developed film is a negative image of the original subject (hence the term "negatives") and must be printed on light-sensitive paper to be seen in its correct orientation. From the days of hand processing on the back of a wagon in the Old West to the one-hour quickie photo at the mall, improvements have been made but the basic concept remains the same.

Film processors

Film processors are made up of a number of connected tanks full of chemistry that the exposed film is either run through on rollers or dipped and dunked from tank to tank on great automated arms. First the film is run through a developing bath that transforms the latent image into a visible one. Then it is passed through a bleach/fix stage that stops the film from developing, bleaches out all of the remaining light-sensitive particles, and fixes the image into a permanent state. The film is then passed through a dryer, ready to be printed to photographic paper.

Photographic paper

Photographic paper is the second half of the photographic process and the vast majority of photos taken are printed to paper. Photographic paper is made very much like photographic film. First, a roll of paper is coated with a resin to make it stiffer and smooth. On top of that coating is spread a thin layer of color and light-sensitive photographic emulsion, similar to that on photographic film. Then the paper is given a finish, designated by a letter, that determines its surface characteristics. "F" surface is a high-gloss surface that makes a photograph really "pop" but is prone to fingerprints. "N" surface is a semi-matte surface with low gloss and good fingerprint resistance. "E" surface is textured with a stippled surface and generally not available much any more.

The paper aspect of the system can be the weak link in the chain. As the film is the original, the print is a second-generation copy. The tonalities and colors in the film are a bit muted once they are put to paper and processed, due to the paper's lower dynamic range (the ability to reproduce all the tonalities in the film). As in many things, we trade convenience for quality. It is more convenient to pass prints around than it is to hold a slide up to a lamp or drag out the projector to look at pictures of last year's holidays.

Photographs on paper permeate our lives; we see them every day. And when we talk about "photographic quality," it is really a print on paper that we are talking about. If the reproduction meets, or exceeds, the image quality of a photographic print then we can consider it photographic quality. But it is more than the look of an image that contributes to its being judged as being on par with a true photograph. An interesting phenomenon in determining what matches the quality of a photograph is it's feel. Pick up a photograph and two or three other types of paper of the same size with your eyes closed. Immediately you can tell which is the photograph. This aspect of "photographic quality" is just being noticed by manufacturers who, for example, make paper for photo-quality inkjet printers. If photographic quality is what we are trying to achieve, it is more than the way it looks that makes it a photograph, in most people's minds.

Photo paper has a fairly wide gamut; that is the number of colors it can reproduce is quite large. Photo paper is also relatively inexpensive. This fact, coupled with a highly streamlined and automated process, puts photographic labs, large and small, in an excellent position to capitalize on the emerging digital market. These labs specialize in printing color images and the media and equipment they use can produce excellent prints, quickly and inexpensively.

Printing photographs

Since we can agree that negatives are impossible to make any sense of and slides are inconvenient to look at, how do we get from film to paper?

In the old days, prints were made directly from negatives through a process called "contact printing." Contact printing is the simplest form of photo printing and involves sandwiching the paper, the negative, and a piece of glass together. The entire sandwich is exposed to a light source, which makes an exposure through the negative to the paper below, making a print that is exactly the same size as the original negative. Contact prints are still used today as a way of making a quick set of small prints in order to pick out the best images on a roll of film. Known as proof sheets, strips of negatives are sandwiched between photographic paper and glass to create strips of small images to help determine which negatives to enlarge.

Way back when, print sizes were dependent on the size of the original negative. A 4 x 5 negative produced a 4 x 5 print and an 8 x 10 negative produced an 8 x 10 print. If you look back through an old photo album or in an antique shop you'll see any number of print sizes, all made from original negatives that were contact printed.

Enlargers

It wasn't long before folks wanted to have prints that were larger than the original negatives and, as 35 mm began to take hold, enlargers became a necessity. Enlargers place groups of lenses between the negative and the photographic paper. Working like a camera in reverse, light shines through the back of the negative, through a group of lenses, and onto a piece of photographic paper, creating an enlarged image. The size of the final image is variable and is adjusted by moving the optics of the enlarger closer to or further from the paper. For making color enlargements, enlargers contain special filters that allow for precise color adjustments during the printing process.

Enlargers work fine if you have only a few prints to make, but they involve a manual process and their ability to make prints of all sizes better suits them to large prints or images that need special techniques to produce a good print.

Photographic printers

For mass production of prints, we turn to photographic printers. Photographic printers are more or less automated enlargers that blast light through a negative and focus it onto a roll of photographic paper waiting below. Photographic printers can handle a wide variety of film sizes, generally in the range from 110 to 120/220. In general, the print sizes that these devices can produce are fixed and usually range from wallet size (2-1/2 x 3-1/2) on up to 8 x 10, 11 x 14, or 12 x 18. They, too, contain color filters to control the color balance of the print and automated controls that control density. More and more photographic printers are being produced with built-in intelligence that reads a negative and attempts to determine the subject characteristics in order to make a good print the first time.

Photographic printers of this type are often separate from the paper processing units, run at high speed, and print on large rolls of paper to be processed and printed later. In general, they are found in high-capacity and/or professional photo labs that specialize in high-volume production and custom work.

Paper processing

In the case where prints are produced on long rolls as above, the next step is to process the rolls of photographic paper and cut them into individual prints. Paper processing is similar to film processing in that the paper passes along rollers as it goes through various solutions that develop the image, fix it to the paper, and wash away any remaining chemicals. The paper then passes through a dryer and is either removed to be cut by hand into the various print sizes or put through an automatic cutter that cuts, sorts, and stacks the final prints.

As in stand-alone printers, stand-alone processors are generally found in high-production labs, where they are constantly fed rolls of exposed paper to process. As digital photographic printers become more prevalent, paper processors will have even more work. If it's to be printed on photographic paper, either conventionally or digitally, it has to go through a processor, at least for a while yet.

The photographic development process does, however, use all kinds of nasty solutions, the kind that government bodies like to regulate, for good reason.

- A latent image is one that exists on film or paper due to exposure to light but isn't processed yet. It's there, you just can't see it.
- The development process makes the exposed silver visible, washes out the unexposed silver particles, and fixes the image to the paper.

- Separate photographic printing and processing units are generally found in high-speed, high-production labs.

An all-in-one solution

When George Eastman invented what is commonly known as photography he sold it with the idea of "You push the button, we do the rest." This convenience is what allowed photography to gain wide acceptance. In those days, you sent your entire camera in to have the photos developed and the camera reloaded with film. Soon it became possible to remove the film yourself and send it in to be processed, waiting weeks for your photographs to return to you. And for quite a while, and still today, sending in film and waiting for it to come back was the way we got our photos processed.

Enter the minilab

Photos in an hour

The minilab changed all of that, spawning the "One-Hour Photo" revolution. The first minilabs were named this because all of their film developing and print processing equipment fit into a storefront. Suddenly, you could have your vacation pictures developed in the time it took to do a little shopping. This changed the face of the photographic market, as anyone willing to mortgage their house could set up their own photo lab. Minilabs have been around since the early 1980s and their growth, along with the introduction of automatic 35 mm cameras, has powered the growth of picture-taking in general. In the early years, getting good quality prints from these labs was a hit-and-miss affair and even today, the quality coming out of a retail photo processor is all across the board. But, like nearly anything we touch today, the steady march of technology tends to improve quality. Today's minilab equipment is extremely automated and much easier to control than ever before. This makes it easier to get quality photo processing out the other end, regardless of the fact that the operator's girlfriend dumped him at the prom.

The modern minilab is a small self-contained film processor and printer unit, going from exposed film to finished and dried prints in an hour or less. Minilab units and their smaller siblings, the micro-labs, are all-in-one machines that process film, send the processed negatives through a printing station, make prints and enlargements, and organize everything at the back end in a nice neat pile to be priced and packaged.

Minilabs have been joined by microlabs, small units that take up as much space as an ATM machine and can sit in the corner of a gift shop on Block Island, Rhode Island, waiting to process the roll of film you just shot at your college reunion up the road. Tucked in between the shelves of carved driftwood fishermen and a postcard rack, a microlab can process 8-10 rolls of film an hour and be operated by a high school student with a nose ring.

As all-in-one photo labs become more automated, they open them-selves up to offering increased capabilities. The natural progression for this is towards digital.

- Minilabs are all-in-one film processors and photo printers. They take film in one end and return prints out the other.
- Microlabs are scaled down versions of minilabs, designed to be easy to operate, and can process and print 8-10 rolls of film per hour.

The less-than-one-hour lab

Going digital ... photographically

We have talked a lot about traditional photographic processing methods in this chapter. Later on we will discuss digital printing. Isn't there anything in the middle? There sure is, and in the photo-graphic world, the combination of traditional and digital technolo-gies, known as a hybrid, holds perhaps the greatest promise of all. After all, we are talking about putting pictures on paper and the photo world has been doing that successfully for many years. The digital revolution, while a bit slow to come to the world of photog-raphy, is rapidly moving into the world of pictures.

Digital photo printers

In the last few years digital printers that print images to silver-halide-based photo paper have appeared in professional labs and are even making their presence known in smaller retail labs. These printers have high-resolution CRTs inside of them that expose a digital image onto photographic print paper. These CRTs are basically very fancy, specialized monitors that display a negative image. The paper, expecting to see a negative, is exposed in much the same way it always has been.

Some digital printers employ LEDs (light emitting diodes) or lasers that expose the photographic paper inside of them. These printers can expose paper at higher resolutions than CRTs and in general can create larger images, not being limited to the size of a CRT.

Digital printers work very much like any other desktop-computer-connected printer does. A digital image, whether captured with a digital camera, scanned on a scanner, created in an illustration program, or a little of each, is sent to the printer, where an exposure is made on a roll of the very same photographic paper traditional negatives are printed on. Just as in a traditional photo printer, the exposed paper is then passed through a processing unit and out the other end come finished photographic prints.

Digital printers allow photographic laboratories a seamless path into the world of digital imaging. The entire process of putting an image on photo paper, developing it, and getting it out the door is something these folks have been doing for many years.

Photographic paper has the potential to create the highest quality, and least expensive, image because the equipment is run under controlled circumstances by highly skilled operators (usually). Digital photo printers hold great promise because the prints they produce are on actual photographic paper. If it looks like a photograph and it feels like a photograph then it must be a photograph … right?

The digital-enabled minilab

Things really start to get exciting when we take all of this neat technology, both traditional and digital, and combine it all together. One perfect example of this great convergence is the digital minilab.

Digital minilabs, in their initial incarnation, contain all of the parts of your everyday, run-of-the-mill minilab. They have film processors and photo printers and photo processing tanks and paper cutters in them as you expect, but they have three very important additional parts as well.

Scanners

Instead of using groups of lenses to focus light through the negative and onto the paper below, the new breed of minilabs contain digital film scanners that scan the film and translate it to a digital file.

CRTs

Once the film is digitized, the file is sent to a CRT printer that exposes the image to photographic paper. The paper is then processed in the conventional fashion, emerging as dry, cut prints, ready to go.

Connection to a computer

The feature that is the most exciting about the new crop of minilab units is their ability to output the digital file from a scanned film frame to a computer and the ability to suck a digital file in from a computer and print it to photographic paper.

These new minilab machines can take anything you can create on your PC and print it photographically. They can process color negative film, or slide film in 35 mm, APS, or 110 film for folks like your grandmother. They will accept digital files and print them at speeds of more than 1,000 prints per hour in sizes up to 8 x 10.

As these units and the technology they embody become more and more commonplace, the line between traditional photography and digital photography will truly be blurred. Eventually not a single frame of film will go undigitized and archived for retrieval at any time in the future. And as these units and the labs that deploy them become connected to digital photo networks such as Kodak's PhotoNet and Fuji's Fujifilm.net, minilabs will once again change the face of photography.

Digital minilabs are set to go one more step into the realm of the all-digital work flow. New units are emerging that do away with the photographic printing process all together. Instead these units scan processed film and print the resulting image files using an entirely digital method, such as a dyesub or inkjet printer. By eliminating the print processor and the associated chemistry, these machines cut down on environment-taxing chemicals. They also have the advantage of increased print speed and the ability to print any size image up to the maximum width of the printer they contain.

To summarize:
- Modern minilab units are coming equipped with film scanners and digital printers.
- Soon every photograph we have developed will also be digitized at the lab.
- As photo labs become more digital, it will become easier to access and share our photographs.

The digitization of photography is happening on two fronts. On one hand, digital cameras inherently digitize photos and home desktop scanners let us scan every photograph we have. On the other hand, photo labs are becoming increasingly digitally capable and can provide us with digital scans of our photographs faster than they can deliver prints from those same negatives.

Make no bones about it, the words digital and photography just go together nowadays. So let's see what this digital thing is all about anyway and proceed to the next chapter.

Useful information

Setting your exposure without a meter

The "1 over the film speed at f/11 rule"

On a sunny day or with a flash (keep in mind flash distance from the subject)

With 200 speed film in the camera:

1/200 of a second at f/11
1/100 of a second at f/16

With 400 speed film in the camera:

1/400 of a second at f/11
1/200 of a second at f/16
1/100 of a second at f/22

Get it?

Let's say that you are out on the Alaskan tundra photographing a grizzly bear when the light meter in your camera dies. Never fear. Simply use the table above to set your exposure. If the settings on your camera don't exactly match, get as close as you can. Remember, it is better to pick a slower shutter speed or wider aperture than the other way around. Color negative film always benefits from a little over-exposure.

Chapter 3
IMAGING

Now that we have talked about photography, let's make our way to the "digital" part of things. Actually it wasn't all that long ago that the digital world of computers actually began affecting the world of traditional photography, and even then it was only once the photographs were taken and sent off to be printed. Only very recently has the digital world begun to change how the actual photograph itself is captured. But before we go there we need a little history.

Color imaging in the early days (from Gershwin to Disco)

Until the mid '70s, reproducing a color photographic image meant either spending long hours in the darkroom or sending your negative to a photographic laboratory. This worked fine for a handful of photographs and enough copies to fill a briefcase, but for large quantities you needed to see a commercial printer. Options one and two were fairly straightforward and well understood by anyone with a little knowledge of the photographic process, but the third, the commercial printer, well, what he did was pure magic. Funny thing is that the man in the visor with ink under his fingernails is still the image conjured up when the phrase "commercial printer" is mentioned. Today's commercial printing operation, while leveraging aspects of the past, is light years from where it was only ten years ago.

Color "imaging" before the birth of digital

Most of what we call digital imaging is based on various aspects of commercial printing so let's first try to understand the printing of old, say ... back during the gas crisis of the seventies. In those days, and in some places still today, the heart of the color reproduction process was the process camera. Everything in the world had to be broken down, or separated, into the four colors used in the printing process: cyan, magenta, yellow, and black, or CMYK for short. This is why four-color printing is also known as process color.

Halftoning

The first step in printing pictures is to break down that beautiful color photograph with its rich saturation and tonalities into separate CMYK color plates. In the old days, the photographic print was placed on the easel of a big specialized camera called a process camera (that is, process color), over which was placed a fine screen consisting of evenly spaced lines. This screen divvied up the continuous tone image of the photograph into evenly spaced dots of various sizes. A halftone is an optical illusion. Since printing presses can only make a dot or not make a dot, they cannot actually reproduce the gradations found in a continuous tone image. Instead, halftones simulate gradations by making dots of varying sizes that trick the eye and brain into perceiving these tonal gradations. High contrast litho film, which displays only pure black or pure clear film, was loaded into the process camera and a separate exposure was made through a cyan, magenta, and yellow filter.

Halftones are dots of varying sizes

To print, we need paper (white) and ink (assumed black). So printing line work is no challenge, as it has only two tonal levels. All the white areas will be taken care of by the color of the paper, and the image areas will be printed in ink that is black in color. However, when continuous tones need to be reproduced, the photomechanical process creates a series of dots in varying sizes to simulate grayness. These varying sizes of dots create the illusion of producing tones of various shades. A cluster of smaller dots creates an illusion of a lighter gray and a cluster of larger dots creates an illusion of a darker gray.

Lets us first examine the original copy itself—the continuous tone photograph. Under a powerful microscope, not just a magnifying glass, you will see that the image in the photograph is actually composed of small grains of silver halide. More grains in an area creates a dark area and fewer grains in an area creates a lighter area.

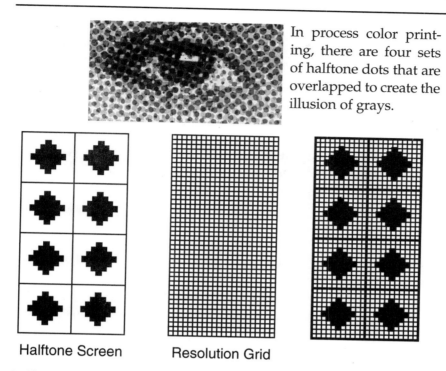

In process color print-
ing, there are four sets
of halftone dots that are
overlapped to create the
illusion of grays.

Halftone Screen   Resolution Grid

Halftone dots are based on the underlying resolution grid.

There are many ways to create various tones with a pencil; the same
is true with digital image pixels—the picture elements or spots that
make up any image. A halftone dot is one way and the most common. If we now go back to the pencil-and-paper story, we can imagine filling one grid square, in each of the top and bottom left and
right corners with black ink. The page still looks white with four
small dots in the corner. If we now start to fill in a few more of the
squares that touch each of the first four, we would now be creating
four bigger dots. If we continued, the four dots would get bigger, and
the page would look darker. Eventually the page would be filled
with black dots and the entire page would be black.

The four dots that grew from nothing to make the entire page look
dark can be called halftone dots; gray tones in an image can be sim-
ulated by assigning different values to a pixel, which can be turned

on or off. The pixels are much smaller than the halftone itself, for many of these small pixels join together and form a halftone dot. The halftone dots themselves are so small they can be seen only under magnification. An image created on the page this way can appear to be nearly equal to a photograph.

With many tiny pixels in the grid, we can print many levels of gray on paper. Please take note that in this case we used only two levels of pixels—either on or off, white or black. All we did was fill the squares (bit=1=on) or not fill them (bit=0=off). Yet we were able to create many levels of gray.

Dots refer to halftone dots

As we saw earlier, an image with grays in it that is printed on a printing press is created with halftone dots made up of spots called pixels. The task in halftone printing is to keep the size of dot as invisible to the eye as possible. Four characteristics of the halftone dot are useful to understand in order to produce good quality graylevel images. They are:

- dot size
- dot shape
- screen angle
- screen frequency

Halftone dot size

The size of the halftone dot determines the tone that will be reproduced. A smaller dot produces a lighter gray (highlight), a medium-sized dot produces midtones, and the larger dots produce the darker, or shadow, areas in an image. In conventional halftoning (photomechanical methods), the camera room technician has the skill to control the size of the dots as they were shot. By using chemicals such as pottasium ferrocyanide, they can reduce the outer diameter of the dot, thereby making it slightly smaller to give the desired detail in areas that were filled up during chemical processing. This is called "dot etching."

Halftone dot shape

A dot is usually considered to be a perfect circle. Yes, such dots are called round dots. But dots of other shapes are also used. More commonly, dots that are elliptical or diamond in shape are used. This is because the shape of a dot has an effect on the way it can grow during the printing process.

A 40% Dot On Film

The Same 40% Dot Becomes
A 57% Dot When Printed

When going from film to the printing plate or from plate to the printing blanket (to which the image is offset before being transferred to paper) there is some spread of the dot by light or by ink

The phenomenon above is called "dot gain." A round dot, especially in the shadow (dark) areas, has little space to grow, and it tends to get darker much faster. This is because the shape of the round dot permits it to grow all around its periphery. You end up printing tones that are darker than they should be. The shape of an elliptical dot is an ellipse oval. This elongated shape allows it to grow more in the elongated sides. Therefore elliptical dots are used when fine tonal renditions are desired, like reproduction of facial tones.

In the earlier days of halftoning, when a specific dot shape was desired, they were produced by using a separate screen that had the particular dot shape. Special effect screens were also used that offered dot shapes as lines, mezzo, dust, bricks, etc. In today's digital world, the screening computers in the scanners generate dots of varying shapes. Also many image programs on the desktop allow for changes in the shape of the dots. The shape of a halftone dot can make a difference in the appearance of an image. Usually a particular dot shape is chosen to make an image appear more natural, for instance, to avoid a tonal jump in flesh tones. Other times a dot shape is chosen for special effects, to make the image appear less natural.

Dot shape is very important in the printing of high-quality halftones. When printing images on newsprint, such factors as rough paper stock and less accurate presses can result in higher dot gain. A well-behaved dot and the proper pre-compensation for dot gain can result in a clean, well-rendered image instead of one that is muddy.

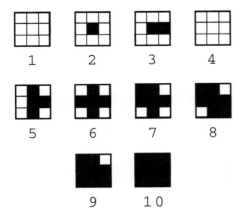

The size of the recorder spot and the number in the halftone cell determine the halftone dot, as shown at left.

A dot shape's performance is particularly noticeable in:

Highlights. Your very lightest highlights should be as smooth tonally as possible and hold a two percent to three percent dot reliably. These highlights give extra "punch" to the image. A good highlight dot should provide enough definition for the ink to adhere to the paper with smooth tones. These are the smallest halftone dots that can be printed on a printing press.

Midtones. These areas should be smooth, without perceptible tonal jumps. If this occurs, which is usually noticeable in flesh tones, shadows look filled in and gradients in skin tones look mottled instead of smooth. At the 50 percent level, some dots increase in size enough to touch. Other kinds of dots (round, elliptical, square) do not touch at the 50 percent level.

Shadows. These are the darkest areas of the image. Halftones should hold a dot without plugging or filling with ink. A fine shadow dot provides extra detail for greater realism.

In a PostScript system, the dot shape is determined by a PostScript operator called a spot function. The Raster Image Processor (RIP) calculates the dot shape based on the spot function. In one of the two types of square spot functions, halftone dots are shaped like squares throughout the tint scale. But in the other, halftone dots start out as circles, grow to squares in the midtones, and then circles again. How it works is less important than the resulting image that you can produce.

Today, most of this is done electronically through the use of scanners, computers, and imagesetters, which kick out film separations like an office copier makes overhead transparencies.

Aside from some technological advances that we will cover later, the actual printing process remains very much the same. In the most common printing process, offset lithography, each film separation negative is then used to make a printing plate for the ink corresponding to the filter used to create the separation in the first place. The plate material is exposed through the negative to create a positive image on the plate.

Once mounted on the press, the plate picks up ink and transfers it a rubber roller called a blanket, turning the image into a negative again. This rubber roller then comes into contact with the paper to create a positive image. Do it four times for each of the four process colors and you come out the other end with a process color image.

So why do we tell you about this rather arcane process of producing color images in a book on digital photography? One because this is still the way the vast majority of color images are reproduced and two, the basic process of process color is at the heart of just about every form of digital output from a lowly $100 inkjet printer to a $350,000 digital printing press.

- Printing is the act of putting dots of ink onto paper (or whatever) in a human-readable fashion.
- Halftoning simulates continuous tone images by making dots of varying sizes that fool the eye into perceiving them as continuous tone.
- While not long ago halftones and separations were produced with process cameras, today the vast majority are produced electronically.

The digital revolution

The point at which traditional printing went digital, opening the door for all-digital capture and output, began with the introduction of the electronic drum scanner. Early drum scanners scanned photographs and artwork and, under the control of a highly trained operator, separated the image into the four process colors, sending each stream of color data to a big plotter on the other side of the room or the room next door. Plotters work like scanners in reverse, writing the image file to pieces of high-contrast film, creating the separations used to make the printing plate. An entire industry segment, known as "prepress," flourished around the process of converting images, text, and graphics into film separations. But it was the act of sticking a computer workstation between the scanner and the plotter that really shook things up.

Placing a computer workstation between the scanner and the plotter resulted in the emergence of high-end digital publishing systems from the likes of Scitex and Crosfield. These systems incorporated scanners, powerful (for the time) computers, and film plotters that allowed the companies that owned them to scan in an image, manipulate it, merge it with text and graphics into pages, and output it to separated films. They also set the companies that invested in them back a million or more dollars per system.

The ability to scan in a transparency or a slide or a negative or your kid's first grade finger painting, take that image file and shoot it across the room, play with it a little, maybe even add some text to it, and send it to a machine that output pages to film separations revolutionized the printing industry. It was kind of like the kid in the Willie Wonka film, Mike TV, who stood in one box in one end and was digitally shot across the room to the box on the other end and replicated, and it turned the industry on its ear.

Services that were deeply entrenched in the printing process such as retouching images and the stripping film separations together to create finished page negatives simply disappeared as the new technology made it faster, easier, and cheaper to do them in the computer. To keep things in perspective, this is the early 1980s, not all that long ago. But pay attention, from here things change fast. Blink and you'll miss it.

A million dollars worth of junk

Enter the desktop computer and Moore's law. Moore's law states that every 18 months technology increases 2x in speed and decreases 2x in price. It has been this way for many years and it is exactly this that made the digitizing of photographs accessible for the rest of us. By the early 1990s the horsepower necessary to actually do something with a digital image became accessible to just about everyone. Until then, for most of us, a computer was nothing more than a glorified calculator and typewriter combined. Suddenly, a million dollars worth of high-end imaging equipment can be replaced by a desktop scanner, a PC, and an imagesetter for 1/50th the price.

So what the heck is digital anyway?

Analog vs. digital

We perceive the world we live in as analog, in which light, sound, taste, and smell come at us in varying degrees and intensities. There are no real delineations, just smooth transitions. An analogy we use from time to time is that of a light switch. Turn it on and it is on. Turn it off and it is off. It is either/or. This is the heart of a digital world. All things digital are made up of either on or off, yes or no, 1 or 0. This 1 or 0 choice is digital in its most simplistic form.

Now remove that on/off light switch and put in its place a dimmer switch. Dimmer switches are analog, with a varying, continuous range of values from off to on. Get a fancy dimmer switch with click stops all the way around the dial. Each click represents an intensity of light. Up a click and you get brighter, back one click and you are back to the brightness you had before. This is digital as well, but multi-bit digital, where each click represents a different intensity.

Digitized. Fancy word that one is. What it means, simply stated, is to take all of the tonal values, from the whitest white to the blackest black and every color in between, and describe them with a finite set of values. Think of it this way: You have a big bag full of marbles of every color in the rainbow but only 256 buckets, each filled with paint of a different color, that you can put them in. As you reach into the bag you have to make a choice of which bucket each marble you pull out will go into. Some marbles will be an exact match for a bucket, while some are close and some are a toss-up. The object of the exercise is to match the color to the paint.

When you are finished and you pull your marbles from the 256 buckets of paint they will each correspond to one of the 256 colors. You have just digitized the color of your marbles. The fact that each marble has been "converted" from its original color to one slightly different to correspond to one of the paint buckets is one of the pitfalls in converting from analog to digital, or in some cases from one "flavor" of digital to another. Another example of the difference between analog and digital is the difference between speech and the alphabet. The alphabet is an example of a digital scale. Every word is made up of groups of only 26 letters. Human speech, with its inflections, is an analog scale with many nuances and inflections.

Analog to digital conversion

The first step in converting from an analog signal to a digital signal is to graph the signal. The signal is sampled at specific intervals.

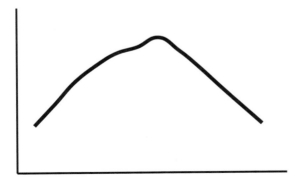

A signal is sampled at specific intervals to produce a graph as shown.

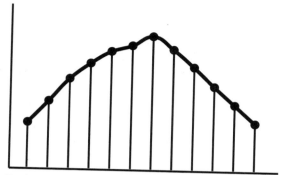

Each sample is then given a digital value.

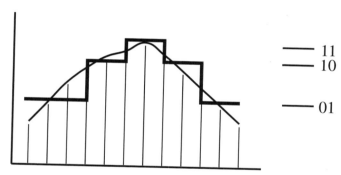

The analog image in digital form.

The result is a digitized version of the analog image. Depending on the system used to digitize the image—that is, the quality of the digital camera or scanner, the monitor, and the printer or printing press—this digital image can be a near replica or a cheap imitation. The quality of a digital image is directly related to the quality of the components used to capture and output it.

Pixels, spots, and dots

In the world of photography, analog images (photographs, pencil sketches, oil paintings, the world we see, etc.) are turned to digital images by digital cameras and/or scanners through the above process. Once digitized, images are built up of rows and rows of picture elements, or *pixels* for short. Pixels are the base unit of a digitized image and are often confused/misused by equating them with dots, spots and lines ... all themselves the building blocks of a digital image in one form or another. Let's see if we can't straighten out the differences between pixels, spots, dots, and lines.

Pixels

Pixels are the smallest spot a scanner or camera can see or a monitor can display and are the base unit of measure for a digital image. When talking about scanners, spots or pixels are often mistaken for dots as in "My new scanner can scan at 600 dots-per-inch!" A 600 dpi scanner actually captures 600 pixels per inch, which means that it has 600 light-sensitive elements along the width of the scanner. On a monitor, a pixel is the smallest dot the computer's graphics card and monitor can draw on the screen. All pixels are not created equal and just because a device touts a large number of them, it does not mean that bigger numbers are always better. It is still true that garbage is garbage and more garbage is not better. Pixel quality is dependent on the system that produces them.

Dots

A dot is the smallest point that can be made by a printing system on a print medium. When used to describe the addressability of a printing device (often improperly referred to as resolution), it is stated in the terms "dots per inch." Dot sizes differ between devices and can vary depending on the device itself as well as the paper or substrate being printed.

Spots

A spot is the smallest area that a scanner can detect or an imagesetter or printer can write. It is the basic addressable unit of resolution.

Lines

The term "lines" is generally used when describing the frequency of a halftone and the ability for a printer or printing press to hold the detail in a halftone. Measured as "line screen," it is the number of horizontal cells to the inch in a halftone screen. Lines are also used in describing the horizontal resolution of a television screen.

Typical halftone frequencies:

Subject	Lines per inch (lpi)
Laser printer	65-75
Newspaper	85-100
Time Magazine	133
National Geographic	150
Fine art reproduction	200

- The world is analog.
- Digital is a representation of an analog world.
- In order to digitize something, you sample it at specific points.
- Pixels, spots, dots, and lines are all similar, all a little different.

Image quality

Few people really understand what image quality means. The equipment manufacturers don't seem to, or at least their marketing departments don't. Numbers alone mean next to nothing. 72 dots per inch, 300 dots per inch, 1440 dots per inch, 4800 dots per inch, 200 line screen, 1.3 million pixels—without more information, they are meaningless.

All cameras, scanners, monitors, and printers are not created equal, not even those in the same price range. The number of pixels, spots, or dots is often not as important as their size, shape, repeatability, and stability. And everything can be improved through software. A basic desktop scanner in the hands of people who knows what they are doing is better than a Photo CD scan of a transparency in the wrong hands.

Raster file and bitmap file

A bitmap is a map of bits—by definition, a one-bit-deep raster file. We often think of bitmaps as the things that RIPs generate from raster and other data to send to platesetters (make plates) and imagesetters (make film). But bitmaps can be other things—for example, a common fax file (at least one without any grayscale data) is an encoded bitmap.

A bitmap is an array of spots—each spot is defined by its bit depth. It can be one bit deep (bilevel)—what Adobe Photoshop calls bitmap mode. This used to be called line art—it may or may not be in black and white (it could have been colored in QuarkXPress or Adobe PageMaker), and may or may not be at 100 percent (it could have been screened back in those applications). It can be 8 bits deep (grayscale, aka monotone or index color). It can be 24 bits deep (RGB). It can be 32 bits deep (CMYK). A CMYK copydot image, for example, has four channels, each of which is bilevel (one bit deep).

A bitmap is a type of graphics file in which a separate value for each pixel of an image is stored in a bit or group of bits. Scanned images are stored as bitmaps. The word "bitmap" is used to define an array of pixels (not bits) whose individual values are defined in bits. In prepress we use it to grasp the concept of black and white. Adding more depth to raster files, we arrive at what we describe as a "contone," or continuous tone image.

What is continuous tone?

How can something broken up into little squares be continuous tone? Continuous tone is what we usually find in original art. Contone and continuous tone actually refer to the type of original image that we are attempting to digitize, and do not describe the data itself. After all, individual pixels are squares of uniform color; the tones do not actually flow continuously from one area of an image to the next, but the squares create the illusion of continuous tone when viewed from a reasonable distance. Although in prepress we use the term "contone" for a non-halftone screened image, incorrect use of the term "non-screened" is possible. The images have a fixed resolution and are not really scalable, as one might think a true contone would be. With scalability in mind, neither is the original image—film grain and whatever. The term "contone" comes from a perfect, resolution-independent world and is being used here to describe an imperfect image.

Many of the problems that printers and their customers face are related to understanding the basic principles of how hardware, software and workflow combine to achieve results in the digital imaging process. We talk about archiving "raster images" that are one-bit TIFF (Tagged Image File Format for bitmapped images) representing halftone dots, used as instruction sets for marking engines such as platesetters. Then we hear of the benefits of Scitex workflow, where RIPped PostScript data is trapped, imposed, and stored prior to the screening process that creates halftone dots. Using the definition that says that raster images are screened instruction sets to explain the RIP process becomes problematic when also describing the imaging process of continuous-tone (unscreened) proofing systems like those required by dye sublimation printers. We use the term "raster image" and the term "screened one-bit TIFF" to describe the instruction set that drives the marking engine.

Raster is a very general term meaning data in the form of an array of pixels. It doesn't say anything about pixel depth (how many bits in each pixel), color space, composite or separated format, compression scheme, resolution, the geometry of the sampling grid (may be square but could be something else), or screening. It does mean that the data is not text or vector format. Raster data is what scanners generate. Raster data is also what you get when you "rasterize" a vector file or text—that is, toss out all that useful resolution-independent compactly-encoded information and reduce it to a grid of pixels that will serve you well if it doesn't have to be resampled, and will cost you in terms of quality if it does.

A bitmap could also be an array of pixels—each pixel is defined by its bit depth. (Wouldn't that be byte-map?) The "bit" part of the bitmap clearly defines it as bilevel, as a bit can only have a value of 0 or 1. The term "bitmap" is really a more technical description of a particular form of raster file. In prepress, we use it to grasp the concept of black and white. Adding more depth to raster files we arrive at what we describe as a contone or continuous tone image. The term "raster-image" (or raster file) seeks to clearly define the differences between various representations of graphical data. Raster data generally defines pixels, regardless of pixel-depth or order. While a bitmap is a raster image, a raster image can be more than a bitmap.

Be careful of using TIFF or TIFF/IT to describe a general data type. They are accurate only if the file literally conforms to the particular specification. TIFF by itself doesn't say anything about the data type, other than that it is a raster format. TIFF files come in various forms—bilevel and contone. Likewise, CT/LW is sometimes used as a general term, other times to refer specifically to the Scitex format.

Let's use the terms "bi-level bitmap" and "contone raster data." Some use the term "CEPS rasters" (from Color Electronic Prepress Systems) to refer to CT/LW or TIFF-IT, but I'm sure that term makes some people uncomfortable. Let's use "bi-level bitmap" to refer to separated data that is screened for output to the markup engine. Unfortunately, some will still be confused by the fact that some RIPs use intermediate formats before screening the data on the fly for output to the markup engine. There is bound to be confusion between these formats (CT/LW or other) and "bi-level bitmaps" for users who see the expression of these data sets on film or plate.

Let's make the distinction between image data and screened output data more clear. We refer to image data as a "pixel map" or "picture element map" when referring to "contone raster data" and only use "bitmap" for separated, screened, device resolution data. That way we could refer to individual elements of a bitmap as "bits" which combine to make various shaped "screen dots."

Beyond bits

People could be confused between binary "bits" and screened data "bits." The terms "contone" and "continuous tone" actually refer to the type of original image that we are attempting to digitize, and do not describe the data itself—after all, individual pixels are complete squares of uniform color; the tones do not actually flow continuously from one area of an image to the next, but merely create the illusion of continuous tone when viewed from a reasonable distance.

Camera operators use the term "contone" to distinguish original art from halftone film or repro. An extension of this logic to the digital age allows us to use the term "contone" to refer to any unscreened image data types, including (but not limited to) CT/LW, TIFF, GIF, etc. The term "contone raster data" is specific to digital images, where "contone" can refer to either digital or analog image data.

Before Adobe Photoshop, the term "bitmap" was widely used in the graphic arts industry to represent any file made of individual pixels, whether those pixels were only on and off or capable of multiple shades. Only after Adobe took the very literal translation of bitmap as being a map where only a single bit controls the value of a pixel did this new definition sweep the land. The term bitmap is commonly used in both manners, and we should clarify what we mean by "bitmap" when we use the term.

The contone raster image contains many pixels of various shades; these shades are used to determine the size of the post-screening halftone dots on most devices, but are used to directly drive the marking engine on continuous tone proofing devices such as dye sublimation printers.

- For data which is already screened, and at device resolution, the term "bi-level bitmap" is descriptive and unambiguous.
- For data which is unscreened, "contone raster data" is my preference.
- For two-component formats, like TIFF/IT-P1 or Scitex CT/LW, various terms are used: "compound raster," "dual raster," "multi-resolution," etc.

Image quality above all is subjective. Subjective image quality tests undertaken at the Rochester Institute of Technology's Research Corporation show that what people perceive as image quality does not always coincide with physical measurements of image quality. Many things affect our perception of image quality, including the experiences we bring with us. When it comes to digital output, for example, the feel of the paper an image is printed on can affect its perceived image quality, particularly if asked "Overall, which image do you prefer?" What one person perceives as good will not always coincide with another's. Some people prefer high-contrast, snappy images; some prefer more muted tones. Some people prefer images that have a particular color bias. Asian cultures, for example, prefer cooler tones and higher contrast than Westerners. In the United States we tend to like our photographs a bit warmer.

Image quality is relative. National Geographic and the Sunday color comics are both produced in the same way through relatively the same process. One looks a lot better than the other, however.

- Image quality is a relative thing and is dependent not only on the system that produces the image but the system (person) that evaluates it.
- "Photographic quality" means that an image when printed is virtually indistinguishable from a photograph.

Getting to digital

Once you have a print of something, an old photograph or your son's finger painting or a slide from the 1964 World's Fair, how do you get it into your PC and how does the whole process work anyway? Your best bet is to scan it.

Scanners

A scanner consists of a light source, optics, and a sensor. Light is passed through, in the case of a slide or transparency, or reflected off, in the case of a photograph or flat art. An original is detected by a sensor that converts analog image data to a digital signal. Scanners have been around a long time and can be found not only as stand-alone devices but as part of office copiers and fax machines. In fact, a combination of an office fax machine and a fax modem in your PC set to receive will allow you to scan an image into your computer. Useful in a pinch. Reversing the process also allows you to print a document in a pinch as well.

Drum scanners

Drum scanners are the granddaddies of all scanners. Still considered the highest quality scanning path available, they are being given a run for their money by emerging high-quality, easier-to-use flatbed scanners. Introduced in the 1960s, drum scanners soon became the de facto way to prepare images for the printing process. But it was the introduction of high-end digital publishing workstations that made high-quality desktop scanning truly possible. Drum scanners employ photomultiplier tubes (PMTs) as imaging sensors and use very focused, very controlled light sources, usually a laser, to illuminate an original. PMTs are extremely sensitive capture devices that scan an image by capturing light reflected off a photograph or through a transparency. Because they are very accurate, they are used when color fidelity and image quality are of the utmost importance.

Drum scanners are also difficult to use and not particularly fast. For this reason, highly trained and skilled operators are employed to operate them. As a result, many companies are looking toward the emerging high-end flatbed scanners, which are increasing in quality, dropping in price, and becoming easier to operate.

Flatbed scanners

Flatbed scanners are the easiest, least expensive, and most accessible way to digitize your photographs. Flatbed scanners are basically the top half of copy machines, copying what you put on them to your hard drive instead of to paper. The basic flatbed scanner consists of a light source, a light-sensitive scanning CCD (charge coupled device) array (hence the word "scanner"), and a glass top that holds the original to be scanned.

For home users, flatbed scanners are one of the easiest and least expensive ways to get involved in digital imaging. For a few hundred dollars, one can be had that is more than sufficient for scanning photographic and printed pieces for output to desktop printers or for creating web pages. Models that include transparency adapters are also available that will allow you to scan your negatives and/or slides as well, although at the consumer level, their limited resolution won't allow you to enlarge the image more than a few hundred percent.

There was a time when flatbed scanners were thought to be insufficient for professional-level-quality scans. This is no longer the case. Again, it is the use of your image that dictates the kind of image quality you need to have. For office documents, newspapers, or catalog use, excellent quality flatbed scanners can be found for under a thousand dollars. In fact, there are a number of flatbed scanners that rival all but the highest level drum scanners, cost far less, and are easy to operate.

Film scanners

Film scanners bridge the gap between flatbed scanners and drum scanners. While unable to scan reflected art, they excel at scanning negatives and transparencies. Today, good quality, small format film scanners that accept 35 mm and APS film originals can be had for a little over $500. Excellent models are available for just over $1,000. Given this price point, the sensitivity, resolution, and image quality afforded by desktop film scanners make them an attractive alternative to digital cameras altogether.

We will go so far as to suggest that many photographers, particularly if all they shoot is 35mm, should forget the idea of buying a digital camera at all. Adding a desktop film scanner to your digital darkroom provides a host of benefits. First and foremost, you can still use every piece of photographic equipment you have ever owned. (Maybe not that disc camera in the back of the junk drawer in the kitchen, but we're not telling anyone about that camera.) In addition, the resolution and image quality achieved from a good desktop film scanner rivals that of a digital camera costing almost ten times as much. File storage is smaller and cheaper to boot. A typical 35 mm film frame can hold 50 million pixels of information (an average culled from various sources). A drum scan of this frame results in an image file of more than 175 megabytes. A scan at this size is overkill unless you are making wall-sized prints to be viewed close up.

Hybrid scanners

New scanning technologies are finding their way into the market that combine the ease of use of flatbeds with the image quality of drum scanners. The FlexTight Precision II scanner by Imacon is a hybrid scanner that offers the benefits of both. It can scan transparent and negative images as large as 4 x 5 inches and reflective originals as large as 8.5 x 12 inches. The FlexTight scanner captures 16 bits of RGB information per pixel at 5,600 dpi in a single pass and boasts a dynamic range of 4.1. It also features an adaptive light source that automatically adjusts light intensity based on the original image's brightness to capture more detail in shadow areas, according to the scanner's manufacturer.

The FlexTight also has a built-in light table, a vertical design, and a magnetic holder that flexes originals around an internal drum and the CCD, which is stationary. According to Imacon, the design keeps the original in constant focus and eliminates distortion and noise.

- Drum scanners scan originals at high resolution and with high color and image fidelity. Only originals that are flexible enough to be wrapped around the drum can be scanned.
- Flatbed scanners scan originals that are placed on their platens, or glass surfaces. Anything that can be placed on the glass can be scanned.
- Film scanners scan negatives and slides either individually or in strips.
- Hybrid scanners hope to offer all of the above.

Photo CD

Photo CD is not so much a technology as a collection of them with a name. It is a combination of photographic original, film scanner, file format, compression scheme, and storage medium. We include Photo CD here because it is the most accessible form of high-resolution image capture out there, serving the lowest common denominator of the PC world, the CD-ROM drive. Anyone with a PC made within in the last few years can have large digital photo files at their fingertips.

The Photo CD format is the Tolstoy novel of the digital world, a case of good and bad. Its introduction in 1989 coincided perfectly with the emergence of CD-ROM drives as standard equipment in PCs. It holds 100 images, at five resolutions, for output from on-screen thumbnails to 11 x 14 color photographs and costs a buck or two a scan. All this at a time when a desktop PC had the horsepower of a pocket organizer, 8 megabytes of RAM was more than enough, nobody knew what a color copier was, and few people had ever heard of an inkjet printer. Despite this cosmic event in the history of imaging, the inventor, Eastman Kodak, marketed it to people in their living rooms as a new spin on the old slide show. Though criticised on various fronts, the growing popularity of WebTV and introduction of HDTV shows that Kodak wasn't wrong, just far too early.

The market that stood to benefit the most, and still does today, was the desktop printing and publishing industry. Even today a Photo CD is the fastest, easiest and cheapest way to get a high-resolution photographic image into your PC. Photo CDs are as easy to have made as reprints. The images are fairly secure and stable (though recent reports indicate not nearly as well as thought earlier). A CD of 100 high-resolution photos holds as much space as a small hard drive and takes up as much space as a Sinatra album … err … CD.

Photo CDs have gotten a somewhat undeserved reputation as not suited for commercial printing. Nonsense. While they are not equal to a drum scan, with a copy of Adobe Photoshop and some simple image processing techniques, they are just great. For home and office use, they are far more image than you'd ever need.

Picture CD

Picture CD is a development spawned by a partnership between Eastman Kodak and Intel. While seemingly a freshly painted version of Photo CD, Picture CD takes the concept one step further and a step closer to acceptance by consumers.

Picture CDs are made at the time your film is processed. For a small fee (under $10), you get back with your prints a CD of the same images, ready for loading and display on your PC. Where Picture CD goes a step further than other forms of digital picture offerings is that the software needed to enhance, enlarge, and crop your images is included on the CD as well and orchestrated to make working with your images an easy process. *Photo CD and Picture CD are storage formats for digitized slides and negatives.*

Capturing images

There are three basic ways to capture image data. Any or all of them are used in digital cameras, scanners, and anything that uses a scanner such as a copier or fax machine. The most prominent is the charged coupled device or CCD.

The CCD

The charged coupled device (CCD) is essentially reusable "film" and is the digital in digital camera. Invented in the early 1970s, CCDs are the most common form of light sensor found in digital cameras and have been used in video cameras, facsimile machines, and desktop scanners for years.

CCDs are available in two flavors: either stacked in a straight line, known as linear arrays, or in a specific matrix of rows and columns, known as an area array.

Linear arrays are moved, or scanned, slowly across the image plane to capture an image.

This scanning action allows for the capture of only still objects and as such, linear array cameras have quickly lost ground to area array cameras.

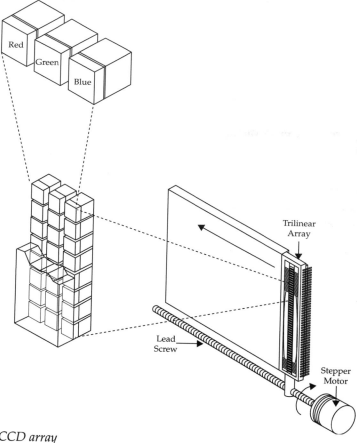

A CCD array

In an area array camera, the CCD is an array, or group, of light-sensitive semiconductor squares arranged in rows and columns like a window screen. Each hole in this screen is between 5 and 25 microns (millionths of a meter) in width and is known as a picture element or pixel. The camera's lens focuses light on this array just as it would a traditional film plane, exposing each pixel to an amount of light. As light strikes the pixel, it releases electrons.

The more light the pixel is exposed to, the more electrons are set free. After exposure, the electrons that are freed from each pixel are read row by row into the camera's memory as an indication of the amount of light each pixel has received.

CCDs are monochromatic. Color images are created in one of two ways. In most handheld digital cameras and all consumer-level digital cameras, each pixel is covered with either a red, green, or blue filter. These filters make the pixel sensitive to only one color. Algorithms then use the values of colors at neighboring pixels to determine the value of the other two colors at that pixel location. This is known as color interpolation.

Three-shot systems

The second way to create color images with a CCD is by capturing the same scene three different times, once each through a red, green, and blue filter. While this technique makes capturing objects that move even slightly impossible, it does take full advantage of each pixel in the array for each color.

After capture, the three filtered images are merged together to form a complete, full-color image file. These three-shot cameras are becoming less prevalent as single shot cameras increase in resolution and image quality.

The output from each pixel is transmitted through various signal conversion, signal processing, and memory circuits on its way to memory storage. This tangle of circuits boosts the CCDs cost. CCDs are difficult, time-consuming, and expensive to manufacture and require hundreds of steps over several weeks. In the end only one in every 100 chips is flawless and able to be used. In addition, CCDs have a voracious appetite for energy and go through batteries faster than a hot knife through butter. In their quest for a lower cost, more efficient solution, nearly every major CCD manufacturer has been experimenting with alternative light sensor technologies.

In any event, trilinear arrays are found in copiers, desktop scanners, and some digital cameras. They are more or less horizontal bars with three rows of imaging sensors.
- One row has red sensors that see the world in terms of red light.
- One row has green sensors that see the world in terms of green.
- One row has blue sensors that see the world in terms of blue.

Capturing an image with a tri-linear array is accomplished by scanning the array across the image area. If you take a piece of paper and cut a slit in the middle of it and hold it up to your eye, you have to move it across what you are trying to see in order to see the whole image. It paints a line of image data onto the CCD array.

When we say grayscale, don't get wrapped around the word gray. A grayscale or monochromatic imaging center doesn't see colors, it sees tonalities. In order to make color, you need to filter those tonalities through one of the three filters; then when you put those tonalities together and mesh all three layers together, you come up with an RGB image that covers a full tonal range that the image sensor can capture.

When we say that color has grayscale, we mean bitdepth—each of the colors has some tonal value, from, for instance, bright red to pale red and all the shades of red in between.

Tri-linear arrays

The advantage of a tri-linear CCD array is that it can be fairly high resolution because you can pack a lot of imaging sensors in that array and then all you have to do is move that array across the image. As you move that array across and capture data, at the same time you can download the data from the array that you just captured. You scan, capture, download, scan, capture, download … moving the array between each capture.

A common example of a tri-linear CCD array is in a desktop flatbed scanner. You can see how they move as well in copiers. They just zip across underneath the glass and, strip-by-strip scan the image. The disadvantage of a tri-linear CCD array is that you need to have a stationary subject. If you put a piece of paper down on a copy machine and move it while it is being scanned, the copy is blurred. That is the same with a desktop scanner. There are also scanning tri-linear CCD array cameras and camera backs. They capture images the same way and they are also not appropriate for moving subjects. They are high-resolution, they capture a lot of image data, but they have to have a fixed subject.

Three-shot area arrays

The second form of capture technology is the three-shot CCD area array. An area array is shaped like a window screen. You see rows and columns and there are little squares that are called pixels. Each one of those squares can capture a spot of data, a spot of an image. Rows and columns together make up the entire image area. A three-shot array is monochromatic. It captures images in grayscale. Color is produced by placing a filter wheel with red, green, and blue filters in front of the array and capturing it three times.

Capture once through the blue filter, download the information from the processor to the array, capture again through the red filter, download the information, capture again through the green filter, download the information.

The advantage to a three-shot camera is that you can capture high-resolution images because the full array is used for each of the three colors. The disadvantage is that three-shot arrays are not appropriate for stopping motion or for subjects that move. Each separate capture is taken through a different filter and then put together later. If the subject moves between the filter captures you have a mis-registration. However, if you are only concerned about capturing a grayscale or a black-and-white photograph, these arrays can be used as a single-capture camera, capturing a greyscale image in one shot.

Single-shot area arrays

Single-shot CCD arrays are built the exact same way as a three-shot CCD array but instead of having the array only sensitive to tonalities, different areas of the arrays, pixels, or squares are colored with either red, green, or blue filters. Therefore, they can capture a full RGB image in one shot. However, they have one-third the resolution of a similar three-shot array. They have to build up colors all at once and each pixel is either a red, green, or blue pixel. In some cases, there are even two green pixels for every one red and blue pixel. This is because most of the image detail is seen through the green filter and, therefore, camera manufacturers tend to over-compensate for green so as to boost the perceived sharpness in the image.

Single-shot area array sensors are the vast majority of imaging sensors in digital cameras today because, for the most part, people want to capture motion and have the freedom to do so. As the technology and CCD array manufacturing progresses, the arrays become larger and more sensitive, and the disadvantage of having to capture all three colors at once, therefore capturing at a lower resolution, really becomes a non-problem.

Analog video cameras also have CCD single capture arrays inside of them. In fact, a lot of technological advances in CCD technology have been made through the explosion of the camcorder market. That technology has trickled down or laterally to the digital still camera market.

Digital camcorders also use single-shot arrays. They capture at a lower resolution than their single-shot camera brethren. They have to, because they have to capture at rates of, for example, 30 captures a second. Current technology can capture at those rates but not at exceptionally high resolutions. This is not a big problem for digital video because in most cases these images are being shown on a computer monitor or, at the least, a TV screen whose resolution is far lower than even the least expensive computer monitor on the market today.

CCD technology has been around quite a while and it is well understood. Manufacturers are continually pushing the limits on yield but even today only a few out of every 100 CCD chips is actually deemed marketable and therefore able to be put into a digital camera. While advances in CCD technology benefit the digital camera world, the emerging technologies are being looked at as ways to decrease the cost and increase the speed and increase the yield of digital camera sensors.

- CCDs are the heart of the vast majority of camcorders, copiers, scanners, fax machines, and digital cameras.
- CCDs are the electronic "film" in a digital camera.
- Linear arrays make one pass for each red, green, and blue capture.
- Tri-linear arrays capture red, green, and blue all at once in one sweeping pass.
- Area arrays are like light-sensitive window screens; each cell is light sensitive.
- Single-shot area arrays have alternating red, green and blue sensitive cells and capture full-color images in one shot.
- Three-shot area arrays capture images in three shots through color filters, one each for red, green, and blue.

CMOS

One alternative to CCD technology that has received attention in recent years is the Complementary Metal Oxide Semiconductor (CMOS). The CMOS sensors are not very light sensitive (a definite drawback when it is light that you are trying to capture!) and their signal-to-noise ratio is low. The signal-to-noise ratio of a device describes the purity of a sensor's signal. Think of it as the amount of hiss you hear in the background when you are listening to your favorite cassette. As is the case in every technology-related frontier, progress is being made rapidly. Amplified CMOS arrays are arriving on the scene that magnify the light sensitivity of the sensor and specialized digital signal processor (DSP) algorithms are being employed to filter a great deal of the noise that has plagued CMOS technology.

CMOS technology has some definite advantages. CMOS chips contain virtually the entire camera's capture technology on a single chip. Because everything exists in one place, data from each pixel does not have to be shuttled to and fro through a maze of wires, greatly increasing the capture speed. In addition, CMOS chips have a much lighter appetite when it comes to power, using about one-eighth the amount of juice their CCD cousins do. CMOS chips are less complex to manufacture than CCDs and, as their acceptance increases, economies of scale afforded by large production runs will eventually drive their price below that of CCDs. While CMOS is not yet the Holy Grail of capture technologies, the smart money is behind them for the long run.

Most digital imaging companies are banking on CMOS technology. Lucent Technologies, for example, has licensed camera-on-a-chip technology that offers effectively all the capabilities of a digital camera in a space about the size of a marble. Now it is easy to imagine digital cameras being placed in cellular phones, in laptop computers, in cars, in house plants, or in your dog house, if you want. The miniaturization of these digital cameras will be boons to upcoming applications such as video conferencing and various security methods.

Currently this camera-on-a-chip technology is somewhat less than the quality of a home video recorder but it will not take long before it is photographic-quality ready. Certainly the advances made in miniature cameras can be applied to larger arrays, increasing their quality and decreasing their cost as well. Because all of the image processing and capture overhead is built onto a single quarter inch of silicon, these cameras can be placed virtually anywhere.

- While CMOS sensors are not yet at the quality level of CCD sensors, they are catching up.
- CMOS sensors hold promise as they contain the capture and image processing functions on one chip.

Hybrid sensors

Some companies are utilizing the best of both breeds by combining CMOS and CCD technologies, utilizing the high-resolution capabilities of CCDs and the image processing speed of CMOS. In early 1998, Intel released a camera kit that incorporated hybrid sensors for use in manufacturing entry-level (under $300) consumer-level cameras. California-based Suni Imaging Microsystems introduced a hybrid camera in the professional range based on similar technologies they have developed for the medical and aerospace industries.

We anticipate this to be a step above currently available hybrid sensors due to the company's past track record. In Suni's hybrid camera, 2,048 x 4096 pixel chips are the main imaging sensors used in the world's largest and most famous digital camera: the Hubble Space Telescope. Hybrid sensors attempt to combine the advantages of CCD and CMOS sensors.

Bit depth

Resolution alone is not enough of a factor to describe image quality. Not only can a pixel be on or off, it can be somewhere in between. This is known as "bit depth."

Each pixel (or spot or dot for that matter) is a digital value described in terms of a one, a zero, or any combination of the two. For example, a one-bit image is like the light switch in your bedroom. It is either on or off. One or zero. The bit depth number describes the range of possible values for each pixel, which corresponds to the number of colors, or shades of gray, that pixel can represent. The higher the bit level, the greater the range between on and off the pixel can represent. This is the difference between having an on/off light switch or having a dimmer switch. You can have a little bit on, a little more on, and a little bit more on until you hit full power.

A two-bit image gives you four possible combinations for each pixel (00, 01, 10, and 11), and four possible colors or gray levels. Eight bits give you 256 possible values; 24 bits gives you more than 16 million possible colors, etc. This can get somewhat confusing. Remember that the total number of bits is divided by the number of channels in the image. For RGB digital camera, scanner, or monitor images, 24-bit color means 8 bits for each channel.

So what does all of this mean anyway? If the imaging application you are going to use to manipulate images supports only 24-bit color, and frankly that's more colors than anyone can discern anyway, why would you even bother with 30 bits or more from a digital camera or scanner? Good question.

Bit depth describes the density of a spot or dot between all the way off and fully on.

Resolution and file size

Digital camera and scanner resolution is measured by the number of pixels in the array, first horizontally, then vertically. A 640 x 480 array has 640 pixels across by 480 pixels down. This also gives us a convenient way to calculate the resolution of any given CCD simply by multiplying these two numbers together. Therefore the above array will give us a captured image 307,200 pixels in size. This is the camera's optical resolution. Software can be employed to increase the size of the file and the perceived resolution of the image by averaging the values of neighboring pixels to form new pixels. This is known as image interpolation, and depending on the technique used, can have varying effects on image quality. Knowing the size of your CCD array will also help you determine the file size of an uncompressed image. Multiple your resolution by three and divide by 1,048,756 (the number of bytes in a megabyte) to determine the file size of your captured image.

Image quality is very much related to the size of the camera's sensor array. Think of a pixel as a grain of silver halide in the emulsion of a frame of film. Film grains are approximately one micron in size while pixels can be between 5 and 25 times that size.

Like film grain, the larger the pixel, the less magnification it can withstand before it becomes visually objectionable. The larger the array, the more information that can be gathered. A digital camera with a 640 x 480 (.3 million pixels) array cannot be enlarged as much as one with a 1152 x 864 (1 million pixels) array. Luckily, digital camera resolution is ever increasing.

In 1996 493 x 373 was the standard. Within a year this had increased to 640 x 480. In 1998 the standard had grown to 1280 x 960. This size is significant, as resolutions of this size are in the "megapixel" range and sufficient for many print applications. Until the end of 1997, consumer-level digital cameras were relegated to capturing images destined for on-line viewing or low-quality newsletters and brochures. By mid-1998, megapixel sensor cameras became the norm and their prices dropped well below the magic $1,000 mark, sparking a marked increase in digital camera sales at the consumer level.

Professional-level digital cameras have employed sensors of very large sizes for the past few years. Though some professional photographers are using cameras with as little as 1.8 megapixels of resolution, high-end reproduction dictates resolutions of five to fifty times or more resolution than that. Professional-level digital cameras tend to output files with sizes ranging from 15 to 100 megabytes per image, allowing these cameras to truly compete head-to-head with film.

- In general, more is better when it comes to resolution.
- Consumer-level digital cameras typically have resolutions below two million pixels.
- Professional digital cameras tend to have resolutions above five million pixels.

How much is enough?

Let's take a minute or two to get ourselves a dose of reality, or at least practicality. Just because you can capture a million and a half pixels of information, do you really need to? (This question also applies to scanners.) Images take up space and grow exponentially as resolution increases. Memory prices have dropped like a stone in recent years and are sure to continue the trend as memory costs less and less per megabyte, so this becomes somewhat of a convenience issue. Smaller files mean fewer trips to the PC to transfer images from the card to your hard drive, freeing up space to keep shooting. Image size is a tradeoff between the resolution you need to do the job and the amount of space you can afford to allot to each image.

The first thing you have to decide is the way you will be using your images. Are you photographing houses for on-line viewing? Then you do not need the full 1280 x 960 resolution your camera may be able to capture. Consider that a 640 x 480 image will fill the entire screen on a 14" monitor at 72 dpi screen resolution and take up 1/4 the storage space of the full-resolution capture. The same image printed at 5 x 7 on a 600 dpi desktop inkjet printer, however, will look pixelated and blurry.

The idea that bigger is better does have some merit in this case. If the shot you are taking is a once-in-a-lifetime opportunity, or at least enough of an opportunity that you wouldn't want to go through the trouble to set the whole thing up again, you should consider capturing the image at full resolution. This is especially true if you will be using the image from time to time, making it serve double duty for on-screen presentation and print output, too.

This does not mean that your full capture at 1280 x 960 should be used for both your website and your newsletter. Always adjust your image's resolution for your output. But remember, you can always throw away information to decrease an image's resolution. You will have much less success making an image's resolution higher.

One of the best investments you can make in your digital camera is to buy as large a removable memory card as you can afford. Bigger is better in this case.

- More is not better sometimes. Capture only the data you need for your required output when you are certain it will only be used in that circumstance.
- When in doubt, capture more in case you need to enlarge or repurpose an image.

Video cameras

When we start talking about ways to digitize images, you may not realize that you might already have a digital camera of sorts, your home video camcorder. In most cases these are analog capture devices but converting the images to digital simply involves having a video capture card or device attached to your PC.

Camcorders, particularly Hi-8 models, effectively act like low resolution digital cameras with super fast motor drives working at 30 frames per second. Simply dump the video footage into your computer (be careful, video files take up lots of room) take a frame out, and e-mail it or print it, simple as that.

If your computer doesn't come equipped with video capture built in, you can buy an external capture device that sits between your computer and your camcorder that will do the job. You are limited to the resolution of your camcorder, generally around 500 x 480, but for images to be printed at small sizes or displayed on a monitor, this is just fine. More importantly, this is a great way to experiment with digital images before plunking down hundreds of dollars for a digital camera.

The way a video camera captures images is very much like the way a cassette recorder captures sound and very much like the way a camera captures film. Light comes through the lens and it falls on a CCD, which is the same sensor that exists in a digital still camera. The sensor array in that camcorder is just like a window screen made up of little squares that are sensitive to light. Each one of those squares has an electrical charge in it. As they are struck by light, they give off electrons in proportion to the amount of light that strikes them. Those electrons then are read by a little wire that goes back to a processor in the camcorder that says this is the value that I saw, recording that data to videotape.

In situations where multiple images must be captured over time, particularly short spans of time, video cameras and camcorders are an excellent route.

Camcorders are following the path of traditional cameras in that they, too, are going completely digital. Digital camcorders are basically the same idea as traditional camcorders except that instead of recording to an analog recording medium like a tape, you are actually recording to a little mini hard drive in the camcorder or to a digital tape. This not only increases the ability of the camera to capture higher resolution but multiple resolutions as well. Even at 30 frames per second, digital camcorders are beginning to surpass the quality of their traditional brothers and sisters. At still capture rates, digital video cameras beat the image quality of traditional video cameras hands down. Their use of sophisticated electronics and elimination of bulky analog reading and writing heads and video tapes makes them much lighter and more compact as well. With the emergence of High Definition Television (HDTV) and the increased use of digital video on PCs, the digital camcorder sits poised to enjoy enormous growth.

An image captured with a digital video camera and one captured with a digital still camera of the same price will not match in terms of quality. A still camera will be the higher quality. It only has to capture one image every second or so.

The other end of digital photograph is outputting digital images to film. Capturing images digitally, eliminating the camera, is all well and good, but what if you need to go the other way? What if you have a digital file and need to make a hundred photographic reproductions of it? Even though digital printing is making great strides in the printing and publishing world, there are some advantages to going the photographic route, particularly if you are making big enlargements or are dealing with a printer who prefers a real piece of photographic film to work from. Not to worry. Not only can you capture a traditional image to a digital medium, you can write a digital image to traditional film.

Film recorders

The emergence of desktop digital imaging prompted the photographic market to look for ways to recreate their images in higher resolution, more approaching the quality they were used to. One of the first, and highest-quality, ways to do that is through the use of a film recorder. Film recorders work sort of like a scanner in reverse, writing digital files line-by-line to a piece of film.

One of the first systems to do this somewhat affordably was the Kodak Premier system introduced in the late 1980s. The Premier system, for the investment of a few hundred thousand dollars, allowed you to scan a photograph or transparency at high resolution, bring it into an imaging workstation, make whatever corrections, additions, or subtractions that you wanted, and send it back out to a high-end, high-resolution film recorder that then produced a digital negative or transparency, which was virtually indistinguishable from one taken traditionally. The resulting piece of film could be printed photographically just like any other.

Systems like Premier could output photographic-quality resolution on film sizes up to 16 x 20. These devices were employed by photo studios and photo labs in large markets for the composition of images to be printed in magazines or catalogs.

Technology like the Kodak Premier system began to trickle down to systems like Apple Macintosh and Windows-based systems as they became faster, giving them the horsepower, the storage space, and the communications throughput to accept high-end digital files, which run in excess of 100–125 megabytes to print 8 x 10 transparencies.

On the lower end, 35 mm film recorders began to emerg as ways to produce slides for corporate slide shows. Much like the higher-end systems, these devices accepted computer files and wrote them to 35 mm film for high-quality presentations. They found a lot of success in that market but lost footing as people began to use less 35 mm slide presentations and more easily accessible presentation printing systems, such as overhead transparencies produced by technologies such as color laser printing or inkjet.

In the early 1990s, the industry experimented with putting negative film in a 35 mm slide recorder, after much coaxing of the device's owner who only reluctantly agreed. The resulting digital negative cost ten times less than one produced on a high-end film recorder, was printed on common minilab processing equipment, and produced 4 x 6 inch prints virtually indistinguishable from those made from the original negative. Soon after, many photo processors embraced this technique for bringing the digital world into their labs.

Advances in lower-end digital film recorders and their subsequent drop in price allowed more and more photographers the ability to take their photographs, scan them into their PCs, manipulate them, and write them back out to film to have them reproduced on photographic paper.

The size of the negative you are writing to directly influences the size of the digital file you need to send it to. The higher the resolution of the film—that is, the larger the film size, given the same film speed, the more information it can hold. The more you want to enlarge that negative, the more information you have to write to the film negative in the first place. While a five-megabyte file on a 35 mm transparency or negative will give you enough information to print a snapshot-sized print, you are going to need closer to a 20-megabyte file to make a 8 x 10 print from that same negative.

Large-scale professional photographic laboratories soon realized the advantages of being able to produce large, high-quality transparencies and negatives from digital files and began to purchase high-end film recorders. Their advantage? They have made their business out of producing photographic prints of all sizes and configurations from any size and type of film on the planet. Film recorders allow these labs to still leverage their equipment and processes while fully embracing the digital revolution. As a result, the photographic industry stands to have an easier transition to the digital world than the printing industry has had.

- Film recorders work like scanners in reverse, writing digital files to traditional film.
- Film recorders are a bridge technology, bridging the gap from the digital world to the traditional photographic world.

Helpful information

Dynamic range

Dynamic range is the difference between white and black that your camera or scanner can discern. It is also sometimes applied as a measure of the values between the darkest shadows and the lightest highlights. It is logarithmic, that is one .1 of a unit is an increase of 100x. So every little bit counts.

Device	Typical dynamic range
Drum scanners	4.0
High-end flatbed	3.6
Midrange slide scanner	3.4
Midrange flatbed	3.3
Low-end slide scanner	3.0
Low-end flatbed scanner	2.2

Typical halftone frequencies

Subject	Lines per inch (lpi)
Laser printer	65-75
Newspaper	85-100
Time magazine	133
National Geographic	150
Fine art reproduction	200

Photo CD File sizes and use

Size	Use
192 x 128	Thumbnail images
384 x 256	Small monitor display
768 x 512	Large monitor display, small prints
1536 x 1024	Medium size prints
3072 x 2048	Enlargements

Uncompressed 24-bit color (file size in Kbytes)

DPI	2 x 3 in	3 x 5 in	4 x 6 in	5 x 7 in	8 x 10 in	11 x 14 in
72	91	228	365	532	1215	2339
100	176	439	703	1025	2344	4512
150	396	989	1582	2307	5273	10151
200	703	1758	2813	4102	9375	18047
240	1013	2531	4050	5906	13500	25988
300	1582	3955	6328	9229	21094	40605
320	1800	4500	7200	10500	24000	46200
400	2813	7031	11250	16406	37500	72188
600	6328	15820	25313	36914	84375	162422
1200	25313	63281	101250	147656	337500	649688

Chapter 4

DIGITAL CAMERAS

Why use digital cameras anyway? Digital cameras offer three advantages not afforded by traditional cameras. speed, convenience, and cost savings. The first two of these are tough to dispute. Push the button, wait a few seconds (or longer depending on the camera and the size of the resulting capture file) send it to a printer (via a computer or not) and presto! . . . pictures, fast and convenient. The cost savings afforded by going digital, on the other hand, depend very much on how you use photography. For professional photographers taking many images in a session, the savings in film and processing alone can often justify the purchase of a digital system. The ability to provide clients with preseparated CMYK files, ready for the printer, is a definite advantage. Given the adage "time is money", the speed and flexibility digital photography affords equates to dollars and cents as well. If you are a professional and burn film in quantity or depend on tight deadlines, the switch to digital is hard to fight.

For home and small business users, the cost savings are less clear. Digital cameras are still relatively expensive as is the cost of consumables from inkjet printers, the most readily available output device for home and small business users.

For home users, the draw to digital cameras lies in the ability to capture and interact with images. If you are the type who enjoys the creative aspect of photography and will enjoy the freedom to play a little with your photographs, then digital may be for you.

Small business users lie somewhere in the middle. If your business uses images in newsletters, flyers, product brochures, catalogs, or on the Internet, then digital photography is just what the doctor ordered. In fact, it is in the insurance and real estate markets, big users of photography, where digital photography found early acceptance and has enjoyed strong growth.

Regardless of the category you are in, sooner or later digital photography will be a part of your life. That's why you picked up this book in the first place. Digital cameras are destined to be just another peripheral like an inkjet printer or a disk drive.

Digital camera technology is rapidly catching up to conventional image quality levels. A few things to keep in mind: any camera that is a megapixel or more (a million pixels of information) will provide acceptable quality for making snapshots and small enlargements up to 5 x 7. If you approach 1.5 million pixels or more, you can make 8 x 10 enlargements with few noticeable quality problems. The vast majority of all photographs produced fall between snapshot size and 8 x 10, with the scale heavily weighted at the snapshot end. Given that the difference between printing a 4 x 6 of an image or an 8 x 10 can be as simple as a few mouse clicks, not to mention the ability to print out an image of any size or shape in between, digital print size may not parallel that of conventional photography.

Most desktop inkjet printers top out at 8-1/2 x 11, anyway, so there is really no need, from a consumer perspective, to produce an image that can print much larger than that. The rise in the resolution of consumer-level cameras is a clear indication of how rapidly digital photography technology is advancing.

What happens when you push the button?

In most digital cameras, as the shutter is depressed, a light sensor inside the camera reads the amount of light falling on the CCD array. If you have a built-in automatic flash, it determines whether or not the flash needs to go off. If yes, it sets the camera's aperture, flashes the flash, opens the shutter, and exposes the CCD array to the light coming through the lens. If no, the same thing happens, minus the flash.

Each little square in the CCD registers the amount of light striking it. Once fully exposed, these values are read off of the CCD line by line and passed down thin wires to the camera's processor. Once at the processor, basic image processing takes place—a little sharpening, a little exposure compensation, and, depending on the type of camera, a good deal of interpolation, or making pixels where none exist to round out the data captured by the CCD. Compression, if selected, is applied, and the whole image is then sent to the memory card (the internal memory) or, in the case of a camera tethered to your computer, downloaded to the PC directly. The whole process takes anywhere from a second or two to a minute or two, depending on the final image size.

We think there is a misconception among many photo finishers and other people whose livelihood depends upon traditional photography that if people are capturing digital photos and can view them on their little LCD screen on the back of the camera and can decide "that is a good one," or "no, that is not a good one" and then throw that image away, then, over all, people will be taking fewer pictures because they edit them on the fly. If you are at Disney and your granddaughter is meeting Mickey for the first time and she is not bursting into tears like the last kid who just met Mickey, you are quickly snapping off photos, you are not stopping off to edit them along the way. If anything, because digital cameras allow you to capture more images on a film card than perhaps you could get on a roll of film, maybe you are taking more pictures.

Once you get home, you may not be inclined to try and download 60 separate shots of your granddaughter with every Disney character since Steamboat Willie. You may not be inclined to download all those to your computer and send them to your inkjet printer and wait the 6 days it will take for those to print. You might drop your disk off at the photo finisher and have them take care of it for you. Digital photography does not necessarily mean the demise of photo finishing as we know it. For that reason, photo finishers may be inclined not only to embrace digital but also to think of new and creative ways that they can take your digital photos and print them out on their equipment.

Compression, squeezing more pictures into the camera

Digital camera files are memory hogs and most cameras offer a choice of compression alternatives to be applied as images are captured and sent into memory. Generally, there are two kinds of compression for digital cameras: JPEG and FlashPix, although FlashPix is really a file format that uses a form of JPEG as its compression scheme.

Compressing an image is very much what it sounds like. It's kind of like compressing the garbage. (We are not editorializing on your photography skills here.) Compressing your garbage involves squeezing out the air information and jamming the garbage information closer together. Image compression works in a similar way. We squeeze out the redundant information in the image and squeeze the important image information closer together, sometimes even replacing some of it.

Compression is very image-dependent. That is, the type of image you have will directly affect your ability to successfully compress it and not come out the other end with a picture that looks like small children have fingerpainted on it. Busy pictures, those with patterns and subjects that break up large flat areas of color, tend to compress best. Images with large areas of flat color or gradations, like sky, will show compression defects quickly.

But image compression is a necessary evil and until memory drops substantially in price, and the electronic processors built into digital cameras increase substantially in speed, we must compress image files in most cases.

There are a few things you need to know:

JPEG

JPEG is known as a "lossy" compression. It makes image files small-er by throwing away some image information. Depending on the amount of JPEG compression you apply, image quality will suffer. In general the more compression you apply, the poorer the resulting image quality will be.

JPEG compression is by far the most used compression scheme in digital cameras today. The options on most digital cameras fall into three categories: low, medium, and high (or best, better, and good).

Low compression

Selecting low JPEG compression offers some gains in decreased file size with little or no noticeable loss of quality. When memory and file size aren't an issue or when your images need to be printed out in the highest quality possible, select low compression. Surprisingly, low JPEG compression does do a good job of squeezing file sizes down without losing image quality.

Medium compression

Medium JPEG compression is usually a good middle-of-the-road choice, balancing file size with image quality. For quick prints that are not for display, or for images that will be viewed on-line, medi-um compression is probably a good bet.

High compression

Use a high compression setting only after having experimented with it a little. Depending on the subject of your image, high compression can make it look lousy. But the compression ratios achieved by high JPEG compression can be quite dramatic, particularly if image qual-ity is not of the utmost concern.

FlashPix

The other compression type that is finding favor in the digital photo world is FlashPix. FlashPix is a consortium, begun by Kodak, Hewlett-Packard, Microsoft, and Live Picture. What they came up with is a compression format and a file format that is very similar to

Photo CD in that you have a hierarchical image structure for each image (each file associated with a particular image is a larger version of the one that comes before it) and the FlashPix compression is similar to JPEG compression; depending on how much you compress, you may give up some image quality. But the advantage of FlashPix is not just a compression scheme; it is also a file format that wraps it all together nicely in one package. There are more and more image processing programs accepting FlashPix formats so it is anybody's guess which compression scheme will win out. They will probably co-exist peacefully.

More compression
Resolution and compression are the two most important choices you can make. There are two ways that you can affect the quality that comes from your digital camera. One is by determining how much compression is applied to the image, anywhere from no compression to maximum compression. The other factor that you can have control over is the actual resolution the camera captures in the first place. Most megapixel cameras will capture an image that is perhaps 1280 x 960, the resolution of the actual CCD, as well as a lower resolution that might be 640 x 480 and one quarter the file size of full-resolution capture.

If all you are going to do is print your images at business card size or display them on the computer monitor, you don't need to capture the resolution at the highest quality anyway. And if each image takes up one quarter of the space, then you can put four times as many of them in memory than you could at the higher resolution. Knowing the final destination for your images will help you make these compression and format choices.

We'll use the PixelPerfect 9000 (yes, we made that up) as an example, but the concepts hold true for all digital cameras. Beginning in 1998, the PixelPerfect 9000 was one of the highest quality consumer-level cameras on the market. It is a megapixel camera, capturing 1152 x 864 pixel resolution, providing a file suitable to print a 5 x 7 photograph that, for all intents and purposes, is near photographic quality.

The PixelPerfect 9000 is a typical megapixel camera, megapixel being defined as any camera that can capture more than one million pixels per image. Let's look at the tradeoffs between compression, resolution, and file size. The 9000 ships with a 4 megabyte compact flash memory card. It captures at two resolutions, a "high" resolution mode of 1152 x 864 and a "standard" resolution mode of 640 x 480. The PixelPerfect also offers three compression settings of best, better, and good (low, medium, and high compression). At high resolution (1152 x 864) and minimum JPEG compression applied, a four-megabyte card will hold 13 images.

Maybe you are just going to print the images out on a desktop inkjet printer for reference only and are most concerned with getting more pictures on the memory card. If you decide that you can get away with a few artifacts (image imperfections), you can choose medium compression, or what the manufacturer calls "better." The same full resolution capture with medium compression applied, using the "better" compression option, will fit 19 images on a 4-megabyte card. The same resolution captures when set to compress under Pixel-Perfect's "good" setting (maximum compression) will squeeze 31 images onto our 4-megabyte card. These images will also show signs of artifacts from high compression.

We can also make tradeoffs in terms of capture resolution. If our needs are not great, that is, if we know we are not going to print these images out at 5 x 7 on a photographic quality inkjet printer at home, instead intending to display them at full screen size of 640 x 480 on a website, we have the option to choose standard resolution, which on the 9000 coincidentally happens to match the monitor's 640 x 480 resolution. Perhaps there will be a "smart" resolution that adapts itself to the intended use, but today you must make that decision.

By capturing less information, we can better leverage the compression afforded by PixelPerfect's JPEG compression. A standard capture with little compression or the "best" setting will now fit 28 images on our 4-megabyte card as opposed to the 13 high-resolution images stored at the same compression before.

Staying with our standard resolution and playing with compression a little bit, we now take our standard 640 x 480 and compress it with "medium" compression, using PixelPerfect's "better" setting, fitting 38 images on a 4-megabyte card. Compressing a standard-resolution image at maximum compression using PixelPerfect's "good" setting squeezes out every last bit out of the 4-megabyte card by jamming 59 images on to it at 640 x 480 under high compression. These images will only be suitable for display on a website or for printing out at small sizes.

Playing with the variables of capture resolution and compression we have gone from 13 images at full resolution with little compression, to 59 images at standard resolution with high compression. These are tradeoffs that you have to make that are dependent upon the image you are capturing and the medium you want to display or print it on. Those 59 images captured at standard resolution with high compression under the good setting will be a far cry, in terms of image quality, from the 13 high-resolution images we captured under the "best" setting.

- More compression makes smaller file sizes but poorer looking images.
- Compression is image-dependent; some images can undergo more compression before looking bad than others can … experiment.
- For images going to print, use no compression or very little.
- For images to be viewed on a monitor (that is, on screen presentations or via the Internet), try a little more compression.

As good as film?

Any of those compression and resolution settings, even at the highest resolution and the lowest compression ratio and, therefore the highest quality image that the camera can capture, is still a way from the image quality 35 mm film and silver halide prints can capture. We are still far away from a consumer-level digital camera matching the quality of a 35 mm camera. But this blanket statement should be viewed through the lens of reality. If you digitally capture and print a 4 x 6 photograph that looks the same as a 4 x 6 print from your conventional camera, is it not as good? Even though the 35 mm print has the potential to have more resolution in terms of having more information there, if your eye can't see it, then the question is, is it better? Frankly, no. Studies have shown that prints at 4 x 6 size from a digital camera and photo-quality inkjet printer are often preferred over 4 x 6 prints of the same image captured conventionally and output from a one-hour processing laboratory. No doubt the printer's ability to enhance certain aspects of the image has this effect.

Despite the relative similarity at snapshot size, as soon as you take both images and blow them up to 8 x 10, the advantages of the 35 mm are apparent. But, given the fact that the vast majority of people never make a print bigger than the 4 x 6 that comes from the photo lab, image quality is a relative thing.

Quality and features increase, prices decrease

Our PixelPerfect 9000, which sold for $1,000 at the beginning of 1998, by the middle of 1998 had dropped to $700 and is replaced as the "flagship" consumer-level camera by the PixelPerfect 9001, which coincidentally, or not, is released at $1,000 ... $999.00 to be exact. This is the magic $1,000 barrier. The kiss of death for consumer-level digital cameras is considered to be the $1,000 barrier. Go above this and no one will come. Get significantly below with high resolution and important features and the market is yours.

The Kodak DC 260 broke new ground for a consumer-level camera, blurring the lines between what is "consumer" and what is "professional." With its 1.6 megapixel resolution and professional features ,this camera can serve the needs of both worlds. Look for other manufacturers to follow suit. The DC 260's larger LCD panel, extended range flash, and flash sync all speak to a user with more professional photographic goals in mind. The flash sync in particular makes this "consumer-level" camera ready to play in the big leagues, making it the first camera in its range with the ability to utilize off-camera flash and/or professional studio strobes. At 1.6 megapixels of resolution, this camera also has what it takes to print out respectable 8 x 10 and excellent 5 x 7 photo images. For less demanding printing applications, such as catalogs, brochures, newspapers, and on-screen presentations, a camera with these features is a definite winner.

The other feature that the DC 260 has, and which we will see in more cameras, is computer scripts which allow the camera to do certain things. One of the scripts included allows you to program the camera to take a picture at certain intervals—seconds, minutes, or even hours. You can take a picture of an event unfolding over a half a minute or over a half a day.

Another script that ships with the DC 260 is one that allows you to squeeze one more photograph onto the memory card. For those times when you run out of space but just need one more photo, this feature is a godsend. The ability of a digital camera to be scriptable opens up the potential of a whole host of features we probably have not even thought of yet.

In 1997, digital cameras outsold 35 mm single lens reflex cameras. Twice as many digital cameras were sold in March of '98 than were sold in January of '98. Sanyo estimates that by the year 2000, four million digital cameras will be sold. The growth curve points up and it is steep.

So far, the growth in digital cameras is more a result of the demand from real estate agents, insurance professionals, marketing departments, and the like, rather than from from people like my father, who wants to take pictures of his grandkids. These professional users of digital cameras are looking at the devices in terms of speed and convenience. There is still not a high-volume infrastructure to support the output of those images.

For the most part, these users are stuck printing out images themselves. As more digital captures occur, there will be a growing need for professional organizations or commercial entities to output those digital files, and whether it be to traditional photographic paper or to some other digital media such as inkjet or dye-sublimation printer, this will be a growing market.

The Fuji 500 is an example of the new breed of highly portable digital cameras

Camera features

Resolution

Here, bigger is always better. As resolution directly relates to image quality in terms of how much a digital camera image can be enlarged, this number is very important. For desktop publishing applications and digital snapshots, do not even consider purchasing a camera with any less than 1 million pixels. These megapixel cameras, virtually non-existent in 1997 and earlier, were considered in 1998 to be mainstream offering. During the summer of 1998, 1.3 megapixel cameras were commonplace. By early 1999, 2.0 Megapixel cameras will show their faces. And in every case, prices will drop like a stone as newer models with increased resolution and more gee-whiz features are introduced to the market.

Buy the highest resolution camera you can afford.

Zoom

Zoom lenses are self explanatory. They zoom the image closer, as if you have walked closer to your subject, filling more of the frame with it. Common in point-and-shoot 35mm cameras, this feature is extremely important to digital cameras. Zoom lenses originally evolved to allow the photographer the ability to have a different vantage point from where he stood without having to move his camera. In digital photography, this benefit still exists, but the ability to zoom in closer to the subject is key.

The sensor arrays that exist in digital cameras are of limited size and resolution, far smaller than film, at least for the near future. The ability to fill as much of the frame as possible with the thing you are trying to photograph cuts down on the image enlargement you will have to do on the back end of the process once you download the image to your PC. CCD arrays are like urban real estate in Tokyo, limited in available space. Zooming helps pack important data into them right up front.

The above holds true for zooming that is optically done. Optical zooming actually repositions the elements in the lens to increase or decrease the angle of view that the CCD array captures. Starting from the widest angle of view for the camera's lens (generally a 35-40 mm equivalent in the 35 mm world), the zoom feature enlarges the image that falls on the camera's sensor.

Digital zooming is an entirely different matter. A digital zoom is accomplished entirely within the camera's electronic circuitry. Digital zooming is the same as using the magnify tool in an image editing tool, enlarging the size of the pixels. This gives the illusion that the subject is closer to the camera. A digital zoom is like sitting closer to the TV.

There is a difference between digital zoom and optical zoom. Optical zoom actually enlarges the image falling on the camera's sensor; digital zoom enlarges the pixels once they are captured.

Accessory lenses

Accessory lenses were somewhat popular when 35 mm point-and-shoot cameras were first introduced. Digital cameras that accept accessory lenses have threads at the front of their lens so the accessory lenses can be screwed in. Fish-eye or wide-angle lenses show an incredible field of view, usually in the 100-180 degree range. Their drawback is that they tend to drastically distort the image they capture. This can be an interesting effect.

Another accessory lens available for some digital cameras is the telephoto lens. These work like zooms but are not variable in their ability to enlarge the image presented to the camera's sensor array. They do not affect the view seen through the optical viewfinder of the camera, so you will need to make an educated guess as to their field of view. Their effect can be seen on the LCD panel, if the camera has one. Telephoto accessory lenses are add-ons so their image quality does not match that of a comparable zoom lens that has been designed as one integrated unit; still they can offer better image quality than digital zooming affords.

Accessory lenses fit onto the front of your camera's regular lens and add wide-angle or telephoto capabilities.

Filters

The same threaded mounts that allow a camera to accept accessory lenses also allow it to accept filters. Some manufacturers make filters that can screw onto the front of the camera lens, but most of these threads are small, making the variety of the filters available for them somewhat limited. One way around this dilemma is to buy a step-up ring that screws into the threads on the front of the camera lens and accepts filters of a larger, more available size. This instantly opens up the possibilities for using a host of creative and compensation filters on a digital camera.

The single most prevalent use for filters on 35 mm cameras is to protect the front element of the camera lens. A skylight or UV filter is usually the choice in this case, providing the added benefit of filtering out some amount of ultraviolet light, keeping it from striking the film. While digital camera sensors are not plagued by the same UV problems as their silver halide cousins, the protective benefits of a filter over the lens of your fancy new digital camera cannot be over-stated. Speaking from experience, it is a far more pleasant experience to watch the large rock you just dropped your camera on break a $10 piece of glass than it is to kiss goodbye to the actual business end of your megapixel camera.

One thing to remember when using filters on a digital camera is that they do not necessarily give the same results as they do on 35 mm cameras. Experiment with their effects before you decide to use them at your daughter's kindergarten graduation.

- A UV or skylight filter will protect the front of your lens. If your camera accepts one, use it.
- Filters work a little differently on digital cameras than they do on conventional cameras. Experiment.

LCD

The Liquid Crystal Display (LCD) panel is one of the most important features on a digital camera. The LCD functions like a built-in monitor allowing you to view an image after it has been captured. It is also the place where more and more camera controls are being placed. As a mini-monitor, the LCD panel is useful for cropping images, checking for people who blinked or were making a funny face, checking exposure to some extent, and reminding you what you have photographed already. Because the LCD panel can display any kind of data, many of the pre-exposure controls, such as exposure compensation, timer, exposure number, compression amount, and battery life, have found their way onto it.

LCDs, as seen above, are very convenient but use up a great deal of battery power. Use them sparingly.

Optical viewfinder

The downside to LCD displays is their voracious appetite for power. LCDs go through batteries faster than a barfly goes through beer nuts. It is wise therefore to use them sparingly, relying on the camera's optical viewfinder for pointing the camera and framing images. Save the LCD for viewing and erasing your images once they have been captured. Parallax, the difference in point of view between what you see through the viewfinder and what the lens sees, works the same as it does on traditional cameras that use a separate lens to point and frame from the one used to expose the film. The further the optical viewfinder is away from the capture lens, the larger the effect parallax will have on your photos. Parallax is a non-issue when your subject is more than 20-30 feet away, but becomes a bigger problem the closer you get to your subject, being downright screwy when using the camera's macro setting.

The further the optical viewfinder is away from the capture lens, the larger the effect parallax will have on your photos. To better understand the parallax factor of a given camera, take a variety of images at various distances from 20 feet to the minimum focus distance the camera can handle on its macro setting. Pay attention to subjects at the edges of the frame of the viewfinder, comparing them to the image displayed on the camera's LCD. This will give you a feel for the effect of parallax for your camera.

Optical viewfinders help save on batteries by supplementing the LCD. Use them as much as possible for framing your photographs before capture. Shown: MegaVision.

Flash

A flash is one of those features that seems like a natural. "Of course you need a flash!" you might say. Time was when a flash was considered an extra, but more and more nowadays, flashes come standard on traditional point-and-shoot cameras, even all the way down the line to the single-use cameras. Flashes create light, that's their job. But not only do they create light, they create the right kind of light: daylight. In traditional photography, the light a flash creates is daylight balanced, matching the color of sunlight.

Digital camera sensors are more forgiving than their film cousins and can be balanced internally to the type of light they are used under. This adds a great deal of flexibility so you can shoot under various lighting conditions. Where most digital camera sensors fail is under low light conditions. Digital cameras are notoriously bad at capturing printable images in poor light. This is where the flash comes in. As long as you stay within the flash's range (usually 3–12 feet) the sensor has enough light to capture an image with a full range of values. Also, images captured under flash conditions will not need any additional color correction before printing.

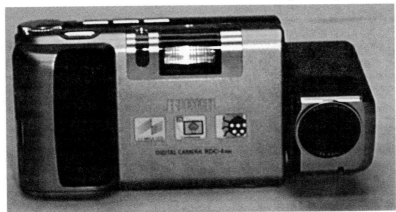

Ricoh has a built-in flash

Flashes do have their drawbacks though. Built-in flashes are generally underpowered for all but a fairly close range and the light from them is very directional, straight on. Flash photos are characterized by harsh, inky black shadows directly behind subjects. Light from a flash also drops off dramatically. While your intended subject may be correctly exposed, objects closer to the camera receive more light, making them overexposed and washed out. Objects past the subject fall into deep shadow, eventually disappearing the farther away they are. As in traditional cameras, the internal settings the camera defaults to when the flash is selected are usually suited to flash exposure only, negating the effect any natural light may have on image capture.

"Red-eye," the effect that manifests itself by making the people in your photographs look like extras in a B horror movie, plagues digital cameras as it does traditional cameras. Red-eye is caused by the light from the flash being reflected back to the camera by the retinas of the people in the photographs. What you see are the actual blood vessels that make up the retina. People with light-colored eyes are more prone to the effect and the more dilated the iris (that is the more open it is) the greater the chance red-eye will occur. The iris of your eye works like the aperture of your camera. The less light available, the more it opens to gather additional light. Turning room lights on will allow the iris to close, lessening the chance of red-eye.

- Flash is a necessary feature; unless you are using hot lights in a studio, you don't want a camera without it.
- Flashes use a lot of battery power.
- When photographing outdoors under strong sunlight with dark shadows, your flash can help even out exposure—turn it on.

Flash Sync

Professional digital cameras generally do not come with built-in flashes. Handheld models based on traditional 35 mm camera bodies have hot shoes, brackets that hold a flash unit, linking it to the camera's internal circuitry. This feature allows you to choose from a wide variety of flash selections. These cameras will set themselves automatically to the necessary shutter speed for flash, known as the flash sync, if desired, or they can be set manually to any shutter speed, allowing you to combine a mixture of flash and available light for your shots.

Professional handheld and single-capture professional digital studio cameras also have a flash sync jack, allowing them to connect to off-camera or studio flash units. This feature is not limited to high-end cameras. The recently introduced Kodak DC 260, a consumer-level point-and-shoot camera at less than $1,000, also includes a flash sync feature.

If you are buying a digital camera for professional use, make sure it has a flash sync.

Memory

All consumer-level digital cameras and the majority of professional cameras have storage memory of some kind to hold images once they are captured. For some cameras, this memory is of a fixed size, usually a few megabytes, and hard-wired into the camera. The amount of internal memory varies from camera to camera and, in the case of a cameras like Sony's Mavica line, internal and external memory are one and the same. Mavica cameras use standard floppy diskettes for image storage and transfer.

Memory cards

The more removable memory you have, the more you can shoot before having to head to your PC to load, and image size does matter. The higher the resolution of your images, the larger a print you can make with acceptable quality, but the more storage space the image will take up. If you have the space available and want to use an image for printing, capture it at the largest resolution you can. If you know you'll be only using it for reference and aren't too concerned about image quality, capture at a lower resolution.

Removable memory

If you are capturing a lot of images at anything above monitor resolution (640 x 480), you're going to need some form of removable media to hold them all until you are ready to download them to your PC. Digital camera files take up space and unless your camera is tethered to your computer, as some studio cameras are, you will run out of space fast.

The good news is that removable memory cards are becoming the norm, even in some mid-priced consumer cameras; 8-megabyte cards come included.

Floppy disks

Only one camera manufacturer uses diskettes for image storage—Sony. While this may seem like an inspired choice for image storage, it does limit the ability to hold high-resolution images in any number. And while the choice of a diskette instantly makes every computer since 1990 a candidate for viewing those images, if Apple Computer's iMac, with its lack of a diskette drive, is any indication, floppy drives will soon go the way of the eight-track tape.

Micro disk drives

A constant in anything electronic is that things will get smaller. Such is the case with the rapid miniaturization of hard disk drives. IBM announced in late 1998 a tiny disk drive that fits into the Type II memory slot of a PC or digital camera. Weighing a little more than 1/2 ounce, the first drives will hold either 170 megabyte or 340 megabyte of data and will transfer at a rate of 32 to 49 mbps (megabits per second) making them super fast.

Other removable storage

Iomega, developers of the Zip disk (the diskette of the future?) introduced in early 1998 a smaller version called the Clik! Holding 40 megabytes of data and not much larger than half of a credit card, the Clik! holds great promise as a small, inexpensive removable storage medium. As of the end of 1998, no devices had yet been released with Clik! capabilities and we hope that we do see such storage and transfer technology from the innovative little storage company and even other developers. But nature abhors a vacuum and no doubt we will see similar offerings from other removable storage manufacturers.

- Get as much memory as you can afford with your camera or make plans to buy more later. You'll use it.
- Memory will drop in price, just like everything else.

Timer

Self timers were originally invented as a way for photographers to get into their own pictures, and serve equally well on their digital counterparts. Here, a tripod or some other stable platform is in order to keep the camera level and steady until the shutter trips. Traditionally, self timers give you eight to ten seconds to get out from behind the camera, sprint across the room, and join the rest of the people in your photo. We have seen many photographs of photographers who did not quite make it into place before the self timer tripped the shutter, freezing them in time a few steps from their place in the group.

To improve on the self timer concept, some cameras have evolved to the point where their "timers" are actually remote control units. This makes the whole job of including yourself in your own photographs that much easier, allowing you to trip the shutter remotely from your place in the photograph whenever you are ready to shoot. Same effect, much more convenient, and no more racing to beat the ten-second timer. The real benefits of a remote control unit make themselves apparent when you want to take pictures of things you can't get to. A remote control will allow you to fire the camera from anywhere within the remote's range (usually up to 30 feet away.) The remote's ability to allow you to put the camera in one place and click the shutter from another opens up a host of opportunities for remote photography.

Traditional cameras have the disadvantage that you still need to be able to put your eye up to the viewfinder to compose, and, in some cases, focus your image. Digital cameras offer a few more convenient ways to capture remote images. Cameras with LCD panels allow you to see image composition without having to have your eye pressed to a viewfinder. Some cameras swivel their viewfinders separately from the lens, or separate viewfinder and lens altogether, making composition in tight spaces a breeze. Depending on how far you need your camera to be from you, a video-out jack on your camera will let you see on a television where your camera is pointing.

Timers and remote controlled shutter releases let you get into your own picture or take a picture where you (and your head) might not be able to go.

Multiple photo capture

Timer functions on digital cameras really show their stuff in the case of multiple photo capture, a feature that is being found on more and more cameras. The multiple photo feature lets you preset an amount of time for the camera to capture successive images. For James Bond wannabes, this feature lends itself to any number of surveillance opportunities. Find out just who left the cap off of the toothpaste or win that bet on who will break their diet first, going for that last piece of chocolate cake.

A great use for the multiple photo feature is time-lapse photography. Time lapse is a technique employed by every science class film production company wanting to show how a flower blooms, a thunderstorm rolls in, or a caterpillar turns into a butterfly. If your digital camera has a multiple photo feature, you can do the same thing—capture a handful of images (here a tripod is essential) at prescribed moments in time and save them to a folder on your PC. Use Quick-Time or Animated GIF-enabled software to turn your images into mini movies that can be played on your PC or shown over the web. Another twist on the multiple photo feature is the ability to capture multiple frames quickly. This is the old motor-drive feature found on higher-end 35 mm cameras. As with their older brethren, many digital cameras now come with the ability to capture multiple images as long as the shutter button is held down. The resolution of the captures and their rate is very much dependent on the data transfer rate of the imaging system itself. For now, figure on a frame or two a second, at 640 x 480 or so.

- Multiple photo capture features are a low-budget time-lapse feature, allowing you to capture images over time.
- Multiple photos can be stitched together in an image program to create mini movies.

Audio annotation

Add sound to your images! The voice annotation feature is a great way to capture audio along with your images, linking pictures of your daughter's birthday party to snippets of her friends belting out "The Birthday Song" in those adorable five-year-old voices. It's also a great way to send digital postcards with a quick voice message to friends and relatives via e-mail. The sound is saved in AIF or a similar audio format and is attached to your image.

For business uses, this is an extremely valuable feature. Real estate agents can dictate features of a property. Insurance adjusters can dictate particulars that the image alone can't show. If a picture is worth a thousand words, a picture plus a few words is worth even more.

- Audio annotation gives an additional dimension to your photographs. Use it when a picture alone is not enough.
- Narration will remind you of details that are associated with an image but not visible.

Text annotation

Text annotation serves much the same purpose as audio annotation, with one added benefit. You don't need a computer to get the message as it prints right out on the print. Of course, you miss hearing your spouse singing in the shower, but you shouldn't be taking those pictures anyway.

Text annotation lets you attach information directly to your images as a reminder or to add additional information to the photo. Shown: Sound Vision.

Crop

Some cameras allow you to crop your images right on the LCD panel. While this feature has some file size advantages, we are proponents of framing correctly in the first place. For the most part, cropping is better left until your images are right up in front of you on your monitor; however, we do see advantages in being able to do some light cropping to photos once before sending them directly to a printer. For more on direct-to-printer capabilities, read on.

Cropping of photos while still in the camera saves storage space, saving only the part of the image that you really want.

Macro

The macro feature is another of our favorites. Push the button and you can focus in on objects mere inches from the front of the camera, adding a whole new perspective to your photographs. The macro feature has dozens of uses from getting REALLY close to the ones you love to documenting valuables like jewelry and coins for insurance purposes. In fact, if you ever even think that you will need to take a photograph of something smaller than a breadbox, you will need a macro setting on your camera.

Because the macro setting allows you to get in very close to your subject, it also changes the relationship between the optical viewfinder and the lens, increasing the incidence of parallax (that what-you-see-is-not-what-you-get effect where the viewfinder sees one view but the lens itself sees a view that is slightly shifted to the right). To combat this problem, rely on your LCD display if you have one. It shows exactly what the lens sees.

Along the same lines as the increased parallax problem is the offset flash problem. Depending on how close you are to your subject, say a half a foot or so, your flash may not even illuminate the scene you are trying to capture. For good macro images, either light with alternative light sources such as an off-camera strobe or incandescent lights or get outside or near a window where good old Mother Nature can help you out. Have on hand a variety of reflectors as well to bounce light just where you want it. A tripod is handy, too, to hold the camera while you futz with the lights.

Use the macro setting whenever you need to get close to a subject to see detail or when your subject is small.

Video-out

Video-out gives brand new meaning to the term slide show and is a high-tech way to bore your friends with your vacation photos from Mud Hollow, West Virginia. Video-out capabilities are a great feature if you want the ability to show your photos anywhere to anyone. Well *anywhere* is one of the many millions of televisions out there on which to show your work.

Many digital cameras have an RCA or S-video-out port that connects to the back of a TV via a cable. This provides a quick and easy method for seeing what you've got quickly and showing it to others. Remember that the resolution of the television is, in most cases, far less than that of the camera.

In any event it will look better than the kid's well-worn Barney video. For another good use of the video-out feature see the next entry: video-in.

Video-out also allows you to record slide shows of your images on your VCR or add still photos to your videos.

- Video-out capabilities allow you to show your photos anywhere there is a TV.
- Video-out also lets you record your photos to video tape.

Video-in

The video-in feature rates high on the coolness scale. Some digital cameras actually allow you to upload files to them, storing them in your camera's memory to be played back later. This feature is ideal for anyone who stands in front of a room to give a presentation. Simply use your PC to create your presentation in PowerPoint or an illustration program. Throw in a few digital photos and load the files (in order of presentation) into the camera.

When you get to your meeting, plug a cable into the video-out port on your camera and into the video-in port on the projection system or television in the room. Voila! You have just traded your five-pound laptop for a half-pound presentation unit you can slip into your pocket.

Video-out and video-in capabilities allow you to transfer presentations and graphics to your camera, turning it into a mini presentation system

Direct to printer

There exist two camps in the digital camera world. Those that feel the future is in the ability to download photos to a PC, play with them a little, and then print them out and those who think that it will be a simple point, shoot, and print world, leaving the PC out of the process. We fall somewhere in the middle. Currently, few photos taken by digital cameras are good enough to send straight to a printer without some tweaking and, besides, half the fun is adding stuff to the photo before printing it out!

Yet there are a whole host of people out there that either do not own a PC or don't want to fool around with it just to get out a few pictures. And digital camera sensors and algorithms are becoming more sophisticated, providing printable images right off the bat. Some cameras also include some simple cropping and print size options, making direct-to-printer an easy operation to perform.

The most seamless direct-to-printer capabilities are afforded by manufacturers who market digital cameras as well as printers (for instance, HP, Epson, and Canon). This doesn't mean that you are limited to these companies alone for such capabilities. In fact, a handful of digital camera manufacturers, knowing full well that there are bags full of money to be made in printer consumables, are marketing small printers to go with their cameras.

As standards emerge, more and more digital cameras will interface directly with printers marketed by other manufacturers.

Direct-to-printer capabilities free you from your PC to make prints, given a direct-from-camera-capable printer.

Tripod mount

We had thought that the tripod had all but gone the way of the 8-track player for everyone but pros and serious amateurs. The digital camera clamors for its return. For higher-end scanning cameras and backs and three-shot cameras, a tripod is a necessity to hold the camera perfectly still during the long capture cycle. Pick one that is very sturdy, as it will be asked to hold what is sure to be a heavier load than a typical 35 mm camera. If you are using a medium- or large-format camera with a digital back, your tripod had better be able to support a small house.

Film is stationary during an exposure, making it at least a little bit forgiving of camera shake, depending on lighting conditions and the focal length of the lens. Digital capture adds a few more variables to the mix. In the case of a scanning back, camera shake will cause different effects as the frequency of the shake and the progression of the scan change. The result is different areas of the sensor capturing different amounts of camera shake. You can't do much to fix that one.

For three-shot cameras, the above applies as well. Different amounts of shake during each exposure results in quite a mess when the three planes are glued together to form a color image. You're not fixing that one either.

For handheld, single shot cameras, camera shake becomes a problem only at the lowest shutter speeds. The old adage is that you can safely handhold your camera at a shutter speed equal to or greater than 1 over the lens's focal length. For most handheld digital cameras at the "normal" zoom setting, this is about 1/40 of a second. Consumer-level digital cameras rarely go below a shutter speed this slow, so your best bet is to have a firm grip on your camera, cradling bottom and lens in your left hand, gripping the right side in your right hand.

A tripod is also highly useful when exercising one of the many cool features listed on these pages. Tripods help when using the macro setting and are essential when using the self timer or remote capture features. In these cases, you may find that a small portable tripod and some stationary object with a flat top, like a table or bookcase, is better suited to your needs.

- Use a tripod if you have a scanning back, scanning camera, or three-shot camera or slow shutter speeds.
- Use a tripod for self timer, multiple photo, or remote capture.
- Consider a tripod when using the macro setting.

Image size options

Digital photo files take up a lot of space at high-resolution and any more than a handful of them soon uses up the available space on all but the largest memory cards or hard disks. While bigger is better in terms of resolution, if you know right off the bat that the photos you are taking are intended for a laser-printed newsletter or for display as 2x2 photos on a website then there is no need to capture at the highest resolution available. Most cameras offer a selection of capture resolutions to choose from. Unless you know that you will be using your photos for some other purpose, consider the fact that an image at 640 x 480 takes up one fourth the space of one captured at 1280 x 960.

- When space is an issue, capture only at the resolution you will need for your final output.
- A 1280 x 960 image is four times as large as a 640 x 480 image (at the same compression ratio).

Compression

Another factor that influences the amount of space an image takes up is the compression ratio that is applied to it. JPEG is the most common form of compression used and the ratio used directly impacts the image quality of your photos. Compression ratios in the 1:4 range usually have little noticeable effect on image quality, while higher compression ratios result in smaller files but poor image quality. Compression is half science, half magic and is very much dependent on your image content. Some images can handle a great deal of compression while others far less. As in all things digital, don't be afraid to experiment.

- Use minimum compression when image quality is more important than file size, as when printing digital photos to paper.
- Use more compression when file size is more important than image quality, as when using images for reference only.
- Experiment with a combination of the above when creating photos for the web.

Rechargeable battery

If your camera doesn't have rechargeable batteries then get some for it. Zoom lenses, LCD panels, flashes, and CCDs go through batteries faster than a 1974 Plymouth Fury goes through gasoline. If you don't want to be spending your camera's worth in alkalines, you will want a couple sets of rechargeables. As the drain of the above components is strong, particularly when they are all used together, have a set in the camera, a set in the bag, and a set on the charger. Rechargeables are cheap when compared to the amount of single-use batteries you will go through, and they last longer.

Some cameras do come with rechargeable batteries but most of them do not. Time was when rechargeables didn't last as long as alkalines, but advances in battery technology have reversed the course. The good news is that while digital cameras do go through batteries quickly, advances in their technology have lessened their appetite for power a bit.

Buy rechargeable batteries for your camera if they do not come included. Buy a spare set too. All digital cameras, as with this Fuji model, have many features—all dependent on battery power.

The first practical battery is believed to have been developed in the 1790s; it was first documented in 1800 in a letter to the Royal Society in London. A chain of advances in battery technology in the 19th century yielded zinc-carbon batteries. These batteries, cheap and low-powered, are still in limited use (and likely to come in devices that are sold with batteries included). Zinc-carbon batteries have given way to alkaline batteries; they use an alkaline electrolyte, which reduces corrosion and gives a longer life.

Contrary to popular belief, batteries do not store electricity. They store energy, which is translated into an electric current when a device is turned on and an electrical circuit is completed. Over the years, the chemical reactions in the batteries have involved substances like manganese dioxide, zinc, nickel, lithium salts, hydrogen-absorbing alloys, and potassium hydroxide.

Improvements have been mostly made in small steps, not big leaps, in the chemistry that underlies the battery's power. Changes in materials—new combinations of more refined chemicals—have made battery components lighter, thinner, and more efficient. That has resulted in stronger and longer-lasting batteries. Here are the most common today:

Nickel-Cadmium, or Nicad. These are the most common and most durable batteries. The basic technology dates to developments made in the electrical systems of America's first manned space flight programs. The battery charges quickly and works well in extreme temperatures. It can take 700 to 750 charge-and-discharge cycles before petering out. These batteries are, however, subject to "memory effect," which can severely shorten battery life.

For example, if a four-hour Nicad battery is repeatedly recharged after only one hour of use, it will eventually run for only an hour before it needs to be recharged. The memory effect can be substantially erased by draining the battery completely before recharging.

Nickel-Metal-Hydride. These can run 75 percent longer for each charge than Nicad batteries. They are less likely to suffer the memory effect and pose less of an environmental problem than Nicad batteries. The life expectancy of a nickel-metal-hydride battery may be 500 to 1,000 charge-and-discharge cycles.

Lithium-Ion. These batteries are the newest on the market. Depending on how they are used, they can run longer on a charge than comparable-size nickel-metal-hydride batteries. They are not prone to the memory effect and will last for about 400 charges. A lithium-ion battery can cost as much as four times what a Nicad battery would cost. It requires a special recharger.

There have been significant advancements in some batteries, especially in alkalines, the most popular type, and in the newer types of rechargeable batteries, including some alkalines. The industry has $4.3 billion in annual sales in the United States.

Modern batteries, whether disposable (called primary batteries) or rechargeable (called secondary), generate electricity through electrochemical reactions. A battery has two electrodes—one positive (a cathode) and one negative (an anode)—in a material called an electrolyte, which carries the flow of energy between the electrodes. The electrolyte can be a liquid, as in many rechargeable batteries, or a solid, in the case of dry cells. The anode and cathode go through electrochemical changes as the battery produces electricity. A battery runs down when they reach a state in which they can no longer pass electrons between them. The voltage drops and the battery dies.

The common AA alkaline battery, the kind that would commonly power a portable cassette player, contains more than two dozen components and materials, requires 40 manufacturing steps to assemble, and involves more than 15 different chemical and electrochemical reactions to produce one spark of electricity. And the rechargeable batteries are even more complicated.

Computer-like circuitry is showing up in some batteries, particularly high-end rechargeables for laptop computers, digital cameras, and cellular phones. These so-called smart batteries started coming into use in the mid-1990s. The electronic circuits perform a range of duties, like keeping the battery from being improperly charged or reporting its energy levels.

Battery manufacturers often speak of a battery's capacity in terms of voltage and milliampere-hours, measures that are meaningless to most consumers. Sometimes battery potency simply comes down to a marketing claim like "longer lasting." Batteries that can produce a lot of power, like Nicad batteries, are best suited for short bursts of energy. Nickel-metal-hydride and lithium-ion batteries are best for more sustained power. Variables affecting the length of a battery's life are the design and efficiency of the device being used and the conditions under which the batteries are used. Heat is a well-known slayer of batteries and digital cameras have earned a reputation for quickly depleting batteries because of their demands for power.

Users of digital cameras should use nickel-metal-hydride or high-capacity Nicad batteries and save money by recharging them. Alkaline and lithium batteries, especially lithium batteries, should be kept as emergency backups because they maintain their charge for many years when they are not in use, unlike rechargeable ones.

There are at least two significant developments on the horizon. One is a variation on lithium-ion batteries, the most sophisticated and expensive of the rechargeables, called the lithium-ion-polymer rechargeable battery. The zinc-air-cell battery is lighter and has a higher energy density than the lithium batteries.

Positionable lens

A few of the major camera manufacturers have added a swivel lens design to their cameras. This feature, pioneered by camcorder manufacturers, allows you to position the lens in a plane different from that of the LCD panel, enabling you to see what the lens sees without having to hold the camera to your face. This is perfect for taking pictures of subjects when you don't want them necessarily to know.

The Nikon has a swivel lens.

At least one manufacturer allows for the complete removal of the lens. The Minolta Daimage V has a removable lens attached to a three-foot tether. Hide the lens in a potted plant or peeking out of a handbag and you're an aspiring James Bond. Just keep it legal. A detachable lens allows you to take photographs around corners or above your head in crowded locations. Look for more cameras to offer this feature in the future.

- A lens that can swivel gives you freedom to point the camera in a direction where you are not necessarily able to press your eye to the viewfinder.
- A detachable lens system allows you to shoot above crowds and from behind obstacles.

Image transfer

Okay, you've filled your camera's memory with photos—now what? Luckily the ways to get images out of your camera are numerous and most manufacturers afford a variety of paths from your camera to your computer. Let's start with "direct connection," the most basic.

Direct connection

Nearly every camera on the market allows you to connect it to your PC with a cable. Depending on what operating system your PC runs, this more than likely will be a serial cable. Plug it into the camera, plug it into the back of your PC, fire up the transfer software (included with the camera) and transfer images to your PC. In some cases, this connection allows you to "mount" your digital camera as if it were just another hard drive.

Just showing its face on the market is the Universal Serial Bus (USB). Still more the exception than the rule, soon USB connections will dominate the PC market as the primary way to connect any peripheral. USB is true "plug and play" and is up to 40 times faster than serial connections. Both Apple Macintosh and Windows-based systems will soon widely support USB.

Removable media transfer

While a serial connection is the most prevalent way of connecting to your PC, it is also pretty slow and a bit messy as you struggle to remember where you put the cable and reach back behind your computer to plug it in. Luckily, many digital cameras come with some form of removable media that can be popped out of the camera and popped into a reader of some kind at your PC.

The easiest method of transferring images is afforded by Sony's Mavica line of digital cameras. The Mavica uses plain old diskettes for both storage and transfer. This is mighty convenient but limits you to a rather small amount of storage space (1.4 megabytes), even with compression.

Most digital cameras use digital "film" in the form of small removable media cards. These offer by far the fastest transfer of images to your PC. A few use Type II PCMCIA cards that then plug directly into a PCMCIA slot in your PC or laptop. These cards, while able to hold large amounts of data, are expensive. More widely used are the CompactFlash and SmartMedia mini cards. These can be popped into a PCMCIA adapter card that will plug directly into a PCMCIA slot on your PC or laptop. Mini card readers are also emerging on the market that plug into the serial port (and eventually USB) on your PC and work just like any other removable media drive.

Olympus

Perhaps the most innovative and universal solution is presented in the SmartMedia diskette adapter marketed by Olympus, Fisher, Fuji and Toshiba. Winning kudos for its straightforward approach, this device is the same size as a 3.5 inch diskette and contains a slot that holds a SmartMedia card. Slide a Smart-Media card into the slot and the entire unit into the diskette drive of your PC and you're on your way. Try this little device once and you'll never go back to your old serial cable connection again.

- Transferring images is an important aspect of using a digital camera. For fastest (and most convenient) transfer, get a memory card reader of some kind for your PC.

- Look for the Universal Serial Bus (USB) to become the standard method for image transfer over a wire.

Manual exposure/bracketing

This feature, generally found on professional digital cameras, has crept into the top-level consumer digital cameras as well. Instead of automatically selecting exposure parameters for you, a digital camera with manual exposure control allows you to adjust for things like depth of field and freezing motion. This also affords you greater creative control over the way your images are exposed. Professional digital cameras offer extensive control over these parameters while all but a few consumer-level cameras offer more limited control.

For most consumer-level cameras, exposure control is limited to plus or minus a stop or two—actually more a bracketing feature than exposure control. But as the lines blur between what is consumer-level and what is professional level, full manual control is beginning to be offered on cameras below the $1,000 threshold.

Manual exposure options let you decide how your camera should capture an image, compensating for challenging lighting conditions or subjects.

Scripting

The ability to script various camera functions is an interesting innovation introduced to the digital camera market by Eastman Kodak, borrowing from the PC world where nearly every action or group of actions can be linked together in a script that can be played back. Scripts allow you to capture images over a specified span of time or squeeze one last picture into the available space on your memory card. Look for this feature to expand and be included on more digital cameras.

- Scripting automates various digital camera tasks.
- Scripts can provide functions not built into the camera at time of manufacture.

Digital cameras: the future of photography?

Yes, and no. Eventually all images will be captured digitally, but when is anybody's guess. Eventually we will all fly to work, too. In the meantime, traditional photography will be augmented in all areas by digital technology. The good news: If you have or are considering buying a digital camera, the technologies necessary to capture, share, and output your photographs have now reached Main Street, USA. You can buy them all at your local WalMart. More good news: If you refuse to give up your Nikon SLR for one of those fancy digital cameras, you are OK too. Film still beats digital for consumer image quality and is only partially challenged for professional image quality, particularly on a cost-of-use basis. And you can still take advantage of all the gee whiz digital toys to scan, transfer, share, and print your film-based images.

Digital camera of the year … the Barbie digital camera

In early 1998, Mattel introduced the Barbie digital camera at an unheard-of price of $69.95. This silver and pink no-frills camera holds six exposures, includes a self timer and, according to Mattel, doesn't have a flash because it doesn't need a flash. Best of all, unlike every other Barbie accessory ever made, it's life-sized.

If you've long dreamed (or long ago dreamed) about sharing adventures with Barbie while she frolicked along the beach in front of the Malibu dream house or cruised to Alaska in her motor home, then your dreams have come true … in pictures anyway. Simply grab your Barbie digital camera, have your best friend take your picture, and, with a few mouse clicks, you have a digital photo of you seated next to Barbie in her pink Corvette as the two of you head towards the coast. If you have an inkjet printer, you can even print out snapshots to show your friends. As far as digital cameras go, the Barbie digital camera offers the fewest capabilities of nearly anything on the market. But, for an eight-year-old girl awash in a sea of electrons all aimed at the boys, this is a fantastic way to explore her creativity, have a lot of fun, and improve computer skills, all at the same time.

Chapter 5

IMAGE MANIPULATION

Although many digital cameras allow you to send your images directly to a printer for output, half the fun is dumping them into a PC and doing things with them. There are two camps in the industry, one that says "people don't want to mess around with the whole digital thing, they just want to shoot and print," and another that says "Digital cameras are peripherals and people are going to want to play with images before printing them out." Our money is on folks playing with their photographs on their computers.

So once you've taken photos to your heart's content, how do you get them into your PC? And then what do you do with them to make them view or print properly?

Connect your camera

The easiest way to get images into your PC is through a physical connection—a cable. All digital cameras can connect via cable to the back of your computer, whether it's a Macintosh or an Intel-based PC. In fact, some high-end digital cameras must be tethered to a PC at all times for them to work, due to the size of the image files they capture. You can spot the photographers who use these by the laptop that they trot around. But even this is changing as removable flash card storage is becoming larger in capacity and hard drives are becoming smaller in physical size.

Many digital cameras let you record on a removable medium that you can then insert into your computer to transfer images.

There are more or less four ways to connect your camera to your PC with a cable.

- Serial connection.
- Parallel connection.
- SCSI (Small Computer Systems Interface).
- USB (Universal Serial Bus).

Serial

The serial port on your computer, also known as the COM (communications) port on Windows machines, is a way in and out of your PC. Serial ports communicate pretty slowly and are generally used for connecting modems, joysticks, and other devices. On the Macintosh, two serial ports are all you get, one for the printer or built-in AppleTalk networking and one for a modem. Serial connections send data one bit at a time, one after the other, making for slooooow data transfer. But it works, and on a Macintosh sometimes it's your only choice.

Parallel

Parallel communications are standard on Windows machines and used mostly for communicating to scanners and printers. Instead of transferring data a bit at a time, the data is sent a byte (8 bits) at a time, in parallel. This makes parallel communications eight times faster than serial communications. Still not speedy, but, given the fact that Windows machines all come with parallel ports, chances are this will be the easiest way into your PC from your camera. Most consumer-level cameras can interface via the parallel port. Parallel is still a pretty slow way to send data, particularly if you are transferring large files, which opens the door for the next three choices.

SCSI (Small Computer Systems Interface)

SCSI is the speedy way to communicate between devices, comes standard on the Macintosh, and can be used in Windows machines with the installation of a communications card. SCSI connections are very fast and are a preferred method for getting large image files out of professional digital cameras.

USB (Universal Serial Bus)

The Universal Serial Bus (USB), found on many Windows machines and now on the Macintosh, promises to simplify the camera-to-PC problem. The USB lives up to its name in that it is universal, making plug-and-play a reality, and it is much faster than any other tethered connection method except for SCSI.

But what if you don't want to mess with cables and besides, it's dusty back there behind that PC—then what? A host of products are emerging to help bridge the gap between camera and PC.

Don't connect your camera

Most cameras sold today feature removable flash memory cards that hold between 4 and 64+ megabytes of data. These are evenly split between the CompactFlash variety and the SmartMedia type. These cards at least get your images out of the camera, but how about into the PC?

Both varieties of flash memory cards can be plugged into PCMCIA card adapters found on most notebook computers. PCMCIA readers are also available for desktop systems. Similar readers are available that can read CompactFlash cards directly. Perhaps the most interesting and convenient transfer option is offered by Toshiba and a few other companies. It is a device that looks like a diskette, the memory card fits into it and then fits into the diskette drive of your PC, transferring images that way. Neat idea.

Image compression

In imaging, size does matter. The bigger your file, the longer it takes to transfer from one place to another, the more memory and power you need to work with it, and the longer it takes to print. And when it comes right down to it, you may not need all of that image information anyway.

Ask yourself, "What am I going to do with the image?" Are you printing it at a large size? Don't compress at all or compress very little. Are you showing it on a monitor or TV? Compress moderately.

Are you printing out thumbnails to e-mail to a client to peek at before output? Compress a lot and warn them that the final prints will look better.

How compression works

If you have ever tried to pack your car for a long trip then you understand the need for image compression. Sometimes what you need to take with you just won't fit into the space you have to fit it in. A suitcase here, a sleeping bag there, all packed tightly themselves, are wedged into every available nook and cranny. While you may like to have all of the comforts of home with you, smaller versions of your things get packed because they take up less room.

Compression is divided into two categories, "lossless" and "lossy." Both refer to the effect a particular method has on image quality.

In order to standardize on a method of compression for still images, a committee of the International Standards Organization (ISO) developed the Joint Photographic Experts Group (JPEG) compression scheme. JPEG is what is known as a lossy compression method and is the compression type you will most often be faced with because it offers the greatest file size economies, yet can allow for the preservation of image quality through various settings.

Compression is a double-edged sword, in which you balance how much space you want your image files to take up against how much image quality you need to have. If all you want to do is to display the images on a computer monitor and you have to send it to that monitor via the Internet and a 28.8 baud modem, and you may be willing to give up some quality in order to make the file nice and small. Besides, if you are only displaying at 72 dpi, which is the resolution of most computer monitors anyway, you don't need all that quality in the first place.

Lossless compression

Lossless compression looks for patterns in an image and substitutes mathematical codes for these patterns. Then, once the image is played back, the decompression algorithm substitutes back in the actual values for the coded ones.

For example you might say: "I graduated from the Rochester Institute of Technology with a Bachelor of Science in Information Technology. By interacting with Rochester Institute of Technology alumni, I soon landed a position as Director of Information Technology for International Business Machines in the United Kingdom. Once you caught your breath, it would be much faster to say, "I graduated from RIT with a BS in IT. By interacting with other RIT alumni, I soon landed a position as Director of IT for IBM in the UK." Same road, shorter distance.

Examples of lossless compression are LZW, named for its inventors, used in TIFF and GIF, and run-length encoding, used in PICT and fax.

Lossy compression, the JPEG story

Lossy compression methods, of which JPEG is by far the most widely used, are so named because, after a round of compression and decompression, the image loses a little something in the process. Although you can compress an image to nearly 1/10 the size of the original file, you can also make it look like it was run over by a car. Lossy compression is a give-and-take proposition. The more you compress an image, the worse it will look when you decompress it and view it or print it. You can control the amount of compression an image receives, trading file size for image quality. The less you compress a file, the more space it takes up, but the better it looks.

JPEG compression condenses files the way Lipton makes Cup-A-Soup. Start with soup and then reduce it by taking all of the water information out (that is, compress), leaving the soup and spices information in a very concentrated form. Once the water is added back in (that is, decompressed), the soup resembles its original form. We say "resembles" because we all know that despite the best efforts of instant soup manufacturers, once soup is dehydrated and rehydrated, it isn't quite the same. JPEG works in a similar way.

Lossy compression can shrink file sizes far more than lossless compression, but does so at the expense of image quality. Lossy compression looks at an image and decides what information can, depending on the quality settings, be discarded while retaining information important to the overall image. Using our example above, you might say: "I got an IT job at IBM overseas, thanks to a fellow RIT alumni." The idea is there but, depending on how you structure the words, a few to a lot of the details are missing.

Lossy compression schemes are very image-dependent. Noisy or busy images tend to hold up better than those with fine details or large areas of smooth gradations. The key to image quality when using lossy compression schemes is to play with the settings a bit until you are happy with the results.

File formats

Once images are captured or created electronically they must be stored as a digital file. Digital files come in many flavors, known as file formats, and some are more suited to particular uses than others. Some file formats are universal, such as TIFF (Tagged Image File Format) or EPS (Encapsulated PostScript), which allow them to be shuttled between various applications and across different platforms. Other file formats are proprietary, or "native."

Native file formats are unique to a particular application or device and often contain image- or process-specific information that is applicable to, and readable by, only tthe application or device that created them. If the file is destined to be shuttled to an imaging or desktop publishing application, it must be converted to a more universal format. Often this will result in the loss of image- or device-specific information. If you will need to interact with the file again, it is often better to do so in the application's native application, exporting a copy in a universal file format for transfer to another application or use.

This approach allows you to go back to the "original" image if need be. All digital cameras export their images in at least one universal file format.

Converting between formats

Most imaging applications support a number of file formats in addition to their own native format. Adobe Photoshop, for example, supports more than 15 file formats in addition to its native Photoshop format. Photoshop can be useful for converting from one image file format to another.

Applications such as Equilibrium's DeBabilizer and Graphic-Converter exist solely to convert image files from one format to another. Both support a host of formats, some rather obscure, and are a godsend when you are faced with a file that refuses to be opened by more traditional imaging applications. GraphicConverter has the extra advantage of being shareware and available to anyone with an connection to the Internet or one of the major on-line services. Remember to pay the modest shareware fee if you use Graphic-Converter; it is worth it and has saved our bacon many a time.

Native formats

Most digital cameras and their accompanying capture software operate in a native file format mode. One reason for this is that, for high-end cameras, a greater number of bits of information per channel is captured (that is, 30 bits or 36 bits) than can be used by most image editing software (24 bits). By capturing and manipulating a high-bit image, intelligent choices can be made by the photographer and the capture software as to various image processing routines to use, white and black point settings, and histogram modifications, working at the fullest bit depth the camera can capture.

Once finished, the photographer, using the native capture application, can then intelligently discard bits when converting to a universal file format for manipulation in an image editing application.

Imaging applications also use a native format as the highest level starting point for image creation and manipulation. Native formats here preserve particular features such as transparency, layers, masking channels, etc. Once converted to a universal file format, most of these features are lost—yet another reason to leave an image in its native format if these features are to be used and export a converted copy when it comes time to move the file.

TIFF

TIFF files are versatile bitmaps. The Tagged Image File Format is the most commonly used format for storing bitmapped or picture images in various resolutions, gray levels, and colors. It does not store object-oriented (vector) images. TIFF was created specifically for storing grayscale images, and it's the standard format for scanned images such as photographs—now called TIFF/IT. TIFF files have different levels based on the number of colors or grays they can contain. It is a composite format.

Monochrome TIFF stores one-bit images, but the black and white pixels can be dithered in a variety of patterns to simulate grays. Dithered patterns limit the degree to which you can edit and scale an image. Grayscale TIFF typically holds 256 grays. It's the best choice for graphics used in page layouts, because most page layout programs can adjust the contrast and brightness of grayscale TIFF images.

Color TIFF handles 16.7 million colors. With EPS, it is one of the top two formats for images that will be color separated. Some programs save TIFF images with subtle variations from the norm, but TIFF/IT has changed that.

Tag Image File Format for Image Technology (TIFF/IT) is an ANSI standard that builds on the Aldus 6.0 version of TIFF (Aldus came up with the idea) and carries forward the work done on DDES (Digital Data Exchange Standards) and IFEN (Intercompany File Exchange Network). TIFF/IT provides an independent transport mechanism for raster images and integrates high-end and desktop publishing formats. In practice, TIFF/IT should make it easier to exchange data between high-end and desktop environments.

TIFF is a format for storing and interchanging raster (as opposed to vector) images. This usually refers to data that comes from scanners and frame grabbers, as well as photo-retouching and paint programs. TIFF describes images in a number of formats and also supports several compression methods. It is not tied to proprietary products and is intended to be portable. It is designed so that it can evolve as new functions become necessary. It is the tags from TIFF which made the format attractive to the supporters of DDES. Because TIFF has been designed to evolve, it is possible to create new tags for TIFF/IT to satisfy requirements of high-end systems. The tags describe each pixel in terms of color, graylevel, and other attributes.

By August, 1986, the first version of TIFF was approved. Microsoft played a role in the drafting of TIFF, and later formally endorsed TIFF for Windows. This helped establish TIFF in both Macintosh and Windows applications. While Aldus was finalizing the 6.0 specification in 1992, the IT8 committee of the American National Standards Institute (ANSI) was working on TIFF/IT, which was approved in 1993. The TIFF/IT format is made up of three primary components; only the first component (CT) is actually part of the TIFF specification:

- Contone image (CT)—Each pixel is described by four bytes, one for each of the four process colors: cyan, magenta, yellow, and black (CMYK). This format is equivalent to the TIFF CMYK previously known as TIFF s (separated TIFF).
- Linework image (LW)—High-resolution, multi-colored contone, graphic, and text elements described as run-length compressed data. LW is superimposed onto CT during color separation. While LW pixels may be assigned a color, they may also be assigned to be either opaque (to block out the CT below) or transparent (to let the background CT show).
- High-resolution contone image (HC)—Run-length coded format that is commonly used for masking or trapping. The resolution of this format must be high to avoid stairstepping at the edges of masked images.

Use the TIFF format if you are using your images for high-quality printing.

EPS

EPS (Encapsulated PostScript) files use the PostScript page description language to describe images. While most often used to export vector-based files to desktop publishing applications, it can also be used to store images, though this greatly increases the file size. Because PostScript describes images in terms of vectors, mathematically described lines, the resolution of the image is dependent on the resolution of the output device. EPS files also embed image information such as halftoning method, screen ruling, screen angle, and dot shape. EPS files are also cross-platform compatible.

JPEG

While technically a compression scheme, JPEG (Joint Photographic Experts Group) has become an image file format standard for consumer-level digital photography and photographic images destined for the World Wide Web. JPEG is known as a lossy compression, which makes files smaller at the expense of throwing away some image data. The greater the amount of compression, the greater the effect on image quality. Low compression settings offer some gains in decreased file size with no noticeable loss of quality. High compression settings afford very small image files but often of poor quality. As in many things, the effects compression will have on image quality are image-dependent.

Experiment with various compression vs. quality ratios to better understand the tradeoffs. JPEG-based image files are best suited for low-end applications and consumer-level digital photography, rarely for high-quality print work. JPEG has also found favor as a de facto standard for Internet-based photographic images due to its ability to highly compress image data and hold 24 bits of information.

GIF (Graphics Interchange Format)

Originally developed by CompuServe for their on-line data delivery network, GIF has become the universal standard for non-photographic-based color images for the entire Internet. The GIF format is an 8-bit format (256 colors) that is excellent for graphic type images such as logos or solid areas of color. Due to its limit of

256 total colors, GIF is not particularly suited to photographic images.

GIF is best suited to web graphics with well defined, solid areas of color such as headers and logos.

FlashPix

Created in mid 1996 by a consortium consisting of Kodak, Hewlett-Packard, Microsoft, and Live Picture, FlashPix is a multiresolution file format that allows you to make changes to an image at a lower resolution that are applied to higher resolution versions of the same image, greatly speeding real time image manipulation. Flashpix also offers built-in compression options as well, based on JPEG. Like JPEG images, FlashPix-based image files are best suited to low-end or consumer-level imaging situations or on-line viewing. Given its backing by the heavy hitters in the consumer imaging world, it will be interesting to see its acceptance as a consumer imaging standard.

FlashPix uses a hierarchical image structure that allows the user or device to make adjustments to an image on a low-resolution version and apply them to the higher-resolution version all at once.

We repeated some of the storage and transfer information to emphasize how important these decisions are in moving images around a system. Now we move on to the issues involving image manipulation.

To print and beyond

By now you have successfully taken a picture or two with your digital camera, and you want to know what needs to be done next. Ask yourself the question "what is the ultimate use for this image?" This may seem obvious, but it is often overlooked.

Is this a picture of a house that is going to be e-mailed to a prospective real estate client who is moving into the area? Is this an image of your family that will be used to print the family holiday card? Or is this the picture of the CEO that is going into the company's annual report?

Just as you choose your digital camera for a specific purpose, the handling of the image depends on the final use. Each use is not mutually exclusive, so let us stress the importance of keeping your originals intact and working on copies. Nothing will make your blood boil faster than working on an image, losing it to a crash, and finding out that it was the only one you had.

The examples that follow relate to Adobe Photoshop, a professional level imaging application that you should have if you will be doing any serious digital photography and image editing. If the idea of spending $600 on a piece of Imaging software to work with a handful of birthday party images leaves you cold, take heart. The examples we use hold true and should be implementable at some level in most imaging applications.

Different versions of Photoshop have different features. This is the version that we are referencing in this chapter.

Our use of Adobe Photoshop is a reflection of the industry and the product's dominance as the leading image manipulation application, not an endorsement of a product. There are many different packages of imaging software available; one may have even come with your camera. Many of the options shown here are similar to those in other packages; they might have different names.

Preparing an image for e-mail or display on a monitor

Our first scenario involves preparing an image to be displayed on a website, in a multimedia presentation, or to be e-mailed to a friend, relative, or client for on-screen viewing. First, let's discuss a few things that we know about e-mail: the larger the file size, the longer it takes to upload from the sender and the longer it takes to download for the end user (causing many people to reject large e-mails). And since it is for viewing on a monitor, speed often beats out quality as the top concern (not that it should be disregarded). If the image is to be looked at only on screen, then it only needs to be 72 pixels per inch, the standard for on-screen display.

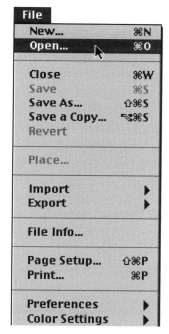

Bringing the image into Photoshop.

The first step in the process is to open or acquire the image. This process depends on the type of camera that you are using and the software that came with it and involves either copying the image onto the hard drive from a diskette, PC, or flash card, or transferring it from the camera via a cabled connection. Once transferred, go to the File menu, choose Open, find the image on your hard drive or removable disk, and open it.

If you have one of the more sophisticated cameras, you may acquire the image directly through Photoshop using the special acquisition software that was bundled with the camera. If you have a camera like this, choose Import under the File menu and find the image file you want to work on.

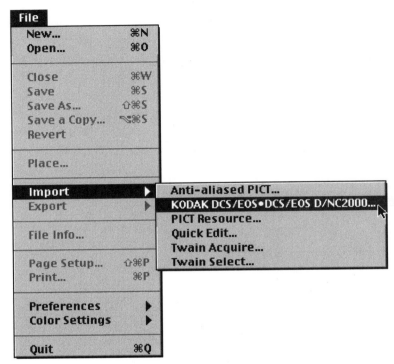

Importing an image from a high-end camera.

Let's say that you have decided that this image's final purpose is for a web page but you need to E-mail a copy of it to a client as well. Given those parameters, our most important issue is probably file size. Even today the most common size screen is 15 inches at a resolution of 640 x 480 (pixels down x pixels across.) Viewing size is an important consideration. Anything more than the actual size of the image at 72 dpi will be wasted information.

The image is viewable in the program's window.

Depending on the the speed of the viewer's Internet connection, any additional bits and bytes will just choke the system, slowing transfer to a crawl. Figure that a 56 Kbps modem (the fastest modem using phone lines available at this time) at top speed can transfer a one-megabyte image in about three minutes. Our goal here will be to get the image size down into the neighborhood of 100K. There are a few different methods of achieving this, but we will show a relatively simple one, using features already built into Photoshop.

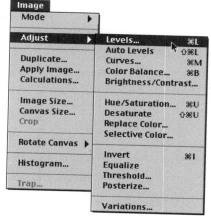

Accessing Levels.

The first step is to set the correct highlight, shadow, and midtone of the image. The idea here is to get the same thing that you want from a good laundry detergent. You want your whites white and your colors clean and bright. This is accomplished by going into the Image menu, choosing Adjust, then Levels. The window that opens looks like the one below.

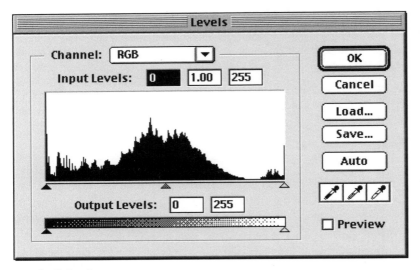

Levels dialog box.

Highlights. The light areas of an image. A good highlight should provide enough area for the ink to adhere to the paper with smooth tones. These are the smallest dots that can be printed.

Midtones. These areas should be smooth, without perceptual tonal jumps. If this occurs, which is usually noticeable in flesh tones, shadows look filled in and gradients in skin tones look mottled instead of smooth.

Shadows. These are the darkest areas of the image. A fine shadow dot provides extra detail for greater realism.

In the Levels dialog box you will see a histogram of all the densities that are contained in the image. A histogram is a graphical representation that shows the number of grey or color levels in an image. Looking at the histogram of the image above, you can see that there is a lot of information in the middle tones, hence the big hump in the middle of the graph.

Beneath the histogram are three sliders: a white one, a grey one, and a black one. These are for setting white point, midpoint, and black point of the image. Setting the sliders is an image-dependent operation and their settings will vary from image to image. These three sliders basically define the density range or the curve characteristic of an image.

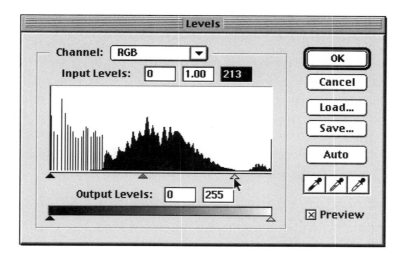

In general, you want to start with the white slider to adjust the highlights in the image first. Make sure that the preview box is checked so that you can see the changes you make in real time. Every move of the white slider to the left makes the whites whiter and overall lightens the image until the image is totally washed out.

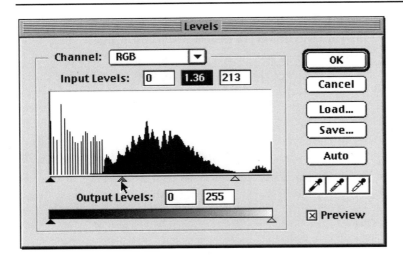

The grey slider is used to either expand or compress the highlight to midtone range. If moved to the right, the range is compressed and if moved to the left, it is expanded. The settings for this slider are also image-dependent and are generally set according to the key of the picture. If the picture is of a white cat in the snow, you may want to expand the range so that more detail is visible in the whites. Conversely, if the image were of a black cat in a coal bin, you would want a compressed highlight to midtone range, so that there would be more detail in the shadows.

Since this scenario calls for the image to be displayed on a monitor, we can interactively adjust the sliders until we get the range of values that make the image look its best. As in all things digital, do not be afraid to experiment.

Saving

Since the purpose of this image is to go to the web for on-screen display, there is no need for a large file size. To save on space, the first thing to change is the image size. It is under the Image pull-down menu and it brings up a dialog box like the one shown next.

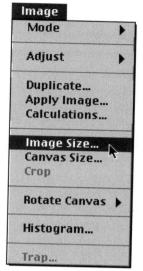

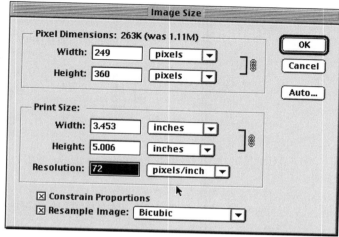

Because we want to change the size of the image, make sure that the Resample Image Checkbox is checked (this will allow the image file to be made smaller). The first change is to set the resolution at 72 pixels/inch, since that is the maximum most monitors can display.

As can be seen in the dialog box, that reduced the size of this file by 75 percent (from 1.11 M to 263 K). Now the image is 249 x 360 pixels, roughly 3.5 x 5 inches on a 640 x 480 monitor. Click on OK.

Now with the image as it is, you are just about ready to save the image in a format that will decrease the file size by compressing the image information. Here is where we will make some compression choices between lossy and lossless. Lossy compression is a way of throwing out redundant information during storage, making a file very small. When the image is displayed again, the missing information is replaced in a way that attempts to trick your eye into believing that all the original information is there. Two very common examples of lossy compression used on the web are JPEG (Joint Photographic Experts Group) and GIF (Graphics Interchange Format).

The other kind of compression technology is called lossless, meaning that no information is lost. The file is stored in such a way that all the redundant pixels are mapped and stored, but in a simpler format, making the file slightly smaller than the original. When the image is displayed again, all the information is still there, simply a little rearranged.

An example of this format is TIFF (Tagged Image File Format). One of the best formats to use on photographs for the web is JPEG because it was specifically designed for use with photographs and depending on the quality level you select, it does a fairly good job of preserving image quality. To save the file as a JPEG, go into the File menu and choose Save As.

Save As selection under File.

Choose JPEG in the format pull-down menu (you can see JPEG and Photoshop in the Format section in the illustration below) and be sure to add .jpg to the end of your file name so that web browsers can recognize that the type is JPEG. Click the Save Button.

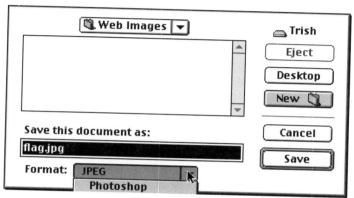

The Format area is a pull-down list of file formats.

In the next dialog box you see, you will have to decide on how much compression is desired. Because our image is for monitor display only, we choose 3, which is towards the low end of the quality scale. You will want to experiment with a few different settings so you can see what kind of difference each setting makes.

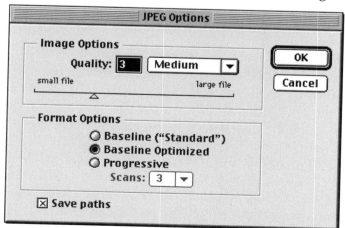

JPEG options dialog box.

The lower the number, the greater the loss of information, but the smaller the file size. Compression and image quality is very image-dependent. You will want to experiment with a few different settings on your own to find out which amount works best for any particular image.

At the settings shown, the file in its final format ends up being only 48K. That is small enough to e-mail and download at the other end without taking too much time.

- E-mail is still pretty slow; for images that are to be transferred over standard phone lines, squeeze the file size as much as possible at an acceptable quality level.
- For images to be displayed on-screen, remember that 72 dpi is all you need and that you can compress the image more than if it was going to be printed.

Preparing an image for color desktop printing

For this example we want to create a greeting card that will be printed on a desktop inkjet printer, using an image of your family dog (a black dog on dark green grass). Using a typical megapixel (million pixel) camera, the average image size is about 1240 x 980 or equivalent to 3.4 Mb image file. These cameras capture enough data to make a post card or greeting card for your family and friends, but are not yet at the quality level to replace your high-quality 35 mm film-based camera. Yet.

The image preparation process is much as our earlier example. Open/Import the image so you can see what you have to work with. In our dog image, we notice that there is little distinction between the dog's face and the dog's eyes. We want to be able to see some detail there, so open the Levels dialog box and lighten the image in the midtones by adjusting the midtone slider towards the right to bring out more detail in the face.

Our image. Note the file name, percent of enlargement, and color model.

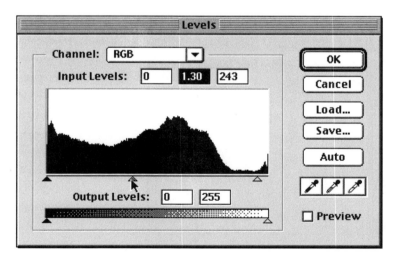

The histogram gives you the feedback you need, as above.

While doing that lightening, you have lightened the green grass too much, so Choose Edit, Undo to revert back to the unchanged picture.

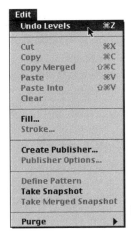

Undo is in the Edit menu.

Now go back into Levels and and lighten the image slightly.

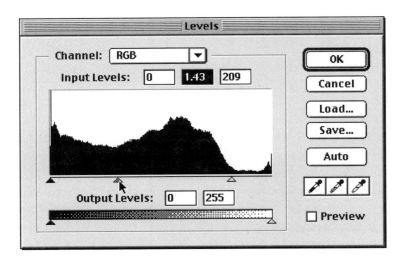

The dog's face is still not perfect, so we have a second tool that we can use, Selective Color. Now open the selective color dialog box under Image, Adjust, Selective Color.

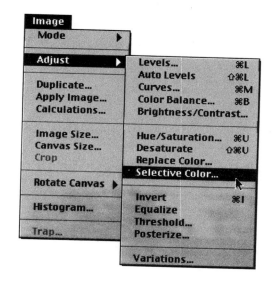

Selective Color dialog is in Adjust in Image.

In this dialog box, you can selectively adjust one color, or group of similar colors in one image, at a time. This is a great tool for removing color casts and color shifts in images, or for selectively bringing out more detail in one particular color.

The slight level adjustment we did earlier brought out some of the whites in the image, but did not bring much more detail in the blacks (you still could not see the dog's eyes because they blend in with the fur). Because the dog is black and the rest of the image is mainly other colors, we can select Neutrals and remove some of the black component that is making up the neutrals. We have effectively lightened up the face of the dog without washing out the rest of the image.

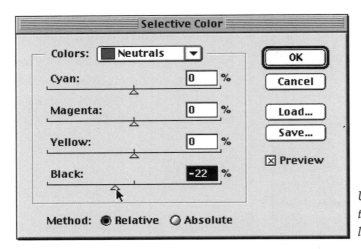

Use Selective Color to reduce the Black in the Neutrals to lighten a background.

We are now are ready to print the image. Choose File/Print and print out your cards following your inkjet manufacturer's directions, or the instructions that came with the paper. Remember, paper quality is everything. In general, the better the paper, the better your images will look when printed, and the more they will cost per print.

Print is in the File menu.

For photographic images, we recommend using a resin-coated Photo Glossy inkjet paper or a Photo Glossy Film. The imaging characteristics of these papers help insure that the image you get from your desktop inkjet printer is of the highest quality.

- Subtle image manipulations may look different in print than they do on-screen. Get as close as you can on your monitor, then print a test print on the paper you will be using for your final print.
- The more experience you have with your printer, the better you will be at determining what effect changes on screen will have on the final print.
- Desktop inkjet printers are high-quality printing devices; for photographic printing, choose a high-quality paper for your final prints.

Preparing an image for the printing press

Imagine that you are Snaps McFarland, photographer to the stars, and you have just been assigned to take a photograph of the CEO of a large corporation to appear in *Time* magazine at 4 x 5 inches. You already have a high-end digital camera and have taken the pictures required. You now need to know how to prepare the image for a four-color offset web printing press.

The first steps are the same as before. Open or Acquire the image. Now you need a bit of information about the printing setup before you start any manipulation. One thing that a printing plant can supply you with is a printing profile for their press. This is a small file that programs such as Apple's ColorSync or Microsoft's ICM (soon to be released in an improved version) use as a lookup table to convert a RGB image into a CMYK image. We prefer to bring the image into a professional publishing program for separations to be output.

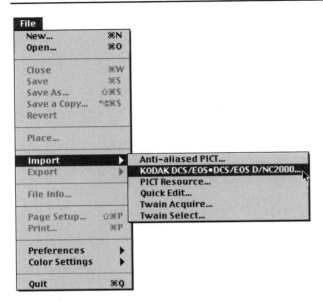

Import is in the File menu.

Let's say that the typical image file from your professional-level digital camera might be 16 megabytes. This factors to 2100 x 2700 pixels, and will produce a 6 x 9 inch print at 300 dpi. This is a pretty large file to be working on, but if you can, resist the urge to immediately reduce it to the client's final print size. Yes, it will be a smaller file and quicker to work on but remember that for each manipulation you do, the application throws away a little (or a lot) of data.

As our goal is to produce a high-quality image for magazine reproduction, we want as much information as possible to work with during the process, resizing only as a final step. In fact, it is often better to leave the image a little larger than the final size, so the graphic designer who has to lay out the page has more image to work with, allowing he or she the freedom to use the image at a little larger size or crop it a little differently.

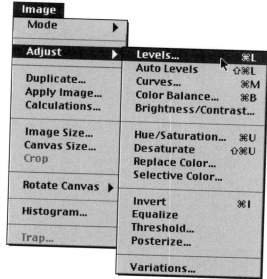

Image/Adjust/ Levels.

Once again, start with the levels adjustments—Image/Adjust/ Levels. Now you can set your highlight, midtone, and shadow points correctly.

Looking at the image, you realize that it just does not look that crisp (clean edges around the subject as best the monitor can display). This problem can be corrected by using the Unsharp Mask filter. Unsharp masking is a technique that was first developed in traditional film separation as a way of affecting the contrast between objects of different tonal values in an image, simulating sharpness. It basically adds a darker line around the edge of the darker of the two adjacent objects and a halo around the lighter object. If it sounds like this effect has the potential to produce bad results, it does, and very easily. Just think "subtle is better."

Once again a little experimentation will go a long way. The fact is, nearly all images captured from a digital camera or scanner can often benefit by a small amount of unsharp masking.

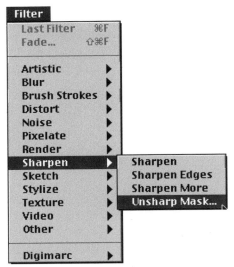

Unsharp Mask is in Sharpen in the Filter menu.

When using unsharp masking, there are three variables you need to worry about: Amount, Radius, and Threshold.

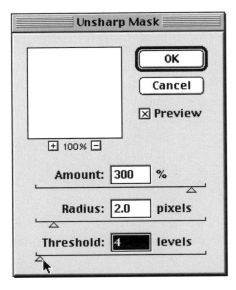

Unshark Mask dialog box.

The first variable, Amount, adjusts the intensity of the black and white that are added between the objects. Simply, it says how white to make the halo and how dark to make the outline.

The second adjustment is the Radius, which affects the width of the halo and outline. The number in the dialog box is not a direct relation to the number of pixels that are affected. You need a light and a dark pixel to produce the effect, so the number is a relative number. Usually lower numbers are better, because the higher the number, the more pronounced the effect. Too much Radius will produce a more pronounced and unnatural result.

The third adjustment, Threshold, is the minimum difference in values between light and dark that need to be affected. For example, the digital count scale goes from 0 (black) to 255 (white). A value of 10 in the Threshold dialog box will not affect any shade variations that are less then 10 values apart. Let's say that you photograph a grey car with some diffuse highlights (not fully white) placed in front of a bright white background. You want to have a little more separation between the car and the background, but you like the highlights where they are (not washed out). Use Unsharp Mask with a high Threshold of 20 or more. That way, the areas where the car and the white background meet are affected, but the areas where the car has a lighter grey highlight are not.

Back to our original image. For a portrait, we want the subject to look as natural as possible, so we do not want a strong separation between light and dark areas, only a slight one to give the image a bit more clarity. Start with the Amount set at 200 percent, the Radius around 0.8, and the Threshold at 6. This gives only a slight correction, a sample of which you should be able to see in the window in the dialog box. If these setting are not enough or too much, we can vary them until we get the desired effect.

Once we have the sharpness taken care of, we can undertake any other image manipulations necessary. We now need to save the file for the printer/graphic designer. They will need the image in a format that is not the Photoshop native format (unless they are doing the separations). Our advice here is to call the person who will be receiving the file and ask them what format they would like it in. Chances are that format will be TIFF (Tagged Image File Format), the de facto cross-platform standard for continuous tone images such as photographs.

Color images need to be converted from the RGB of the camera or scanner to the CMYK of the printer or output device in order to be printed correctly. If the printer gave you an ICC (International Color Consortium) Profile, you can use a conversion program such as the Colorsync export module or a similar plug-in from another company to produce a CMYK TIFF file specifically for the output device you are going to. The export plug-in is an external conversion table that is specific to a particular printer. To use this feature, go under File/Export TIFF with ColorSync Profile. From there, you can choose the profile to use. This will create the CMYK version of the photograph to deliver to the client or the printer.

Selecting TIFF with ColorSync Profile.

Some clients and/or printers will prefer to receive a RGB file from you so that they can separate it themselves for their output path. This can potentially save you a lot of headaches in the long run, as it relieves you of the responsibility for producing calibrated output for a system you may not have very much knowledge about. In any event, a good working relationship with your clients and their printing vendors is a key part of a successful relationship and quality color printing.

High-end color printing is an involved process. Work closely with the people who will be printing your images.

Recommended refresh rates by tube size

The computer monitor is a key element in digital photography. It should be large enough to show you the image and all the associated menus and dialog boxes for the image manipulation program. Screen size and resolution and price are inter-related.

Tube Size (inches)	Maximum Usable Resolution	Recommended Refresh Rate
14"	640 x 480	75Hz
15"	800 x 600	75Hz
17"	1024 x 768	75Hz
19"+	1280 x 1024+	85Hz

Bit level	Number of levels of brightness
1	2
4	16
8	256
16	65,536
24	16,777,216

Failure of the number 8 to be divisible by 3 is overcome by allotting 2 bits to the blue channel instead of three because the human visual system is less sensitive to blue than to red and green. Your television uses a similar technique.

Place your monitor in a position so that its viewing position is similar to the way you would read a book, reading with a downward gaze. A study conducted on computer users shows that a lower monitor position results in a lower Heart Rate Variability (HRV) reading than a monitor placed at eye level. The HRV Index reflects the activity of the nervous system and is used as an effective method of evaluating mental strain. The lower your HRV, the better. You've got enough to worry about.

Look for a dot pitch of no more than 0.28 mm, or .26 mm on monitors using Trinitron picture tubes.

Weight of 15" CRT Monitor	40 lbs (88 kg)
Weight of 15" LCD Panel	12 lbs (26 kg)

Resolution vs. video memory RAM (Mb)

Resolution	16 (4-bit)	256 (8-bit)	65 K (16-bit)	16 M (24-bit)
640 x 480	.5	.5	1	2
800 x 600	.5	1	2	2
1024 x 768	1	1	2	4
1152 x 870	1	2	4	4
1280 x 1024	1	2	4	4
1600 x 1200	2	2	4	8

Below are some sample resolutions, print sizes, and monitor sizes for a typical digital photograph

JPEG Resolution vs. print and monitor size

Resolution Level	Quality (1-10)	File Size	Print size at 300 dpi	Monitor at 72 dpi
1600 x 1200	10	1.1 MB	4 x 5.3 in.	Full Screen 32"
1280 x 760	10	945 K	4 .25 x 3.2 in.	Full Screen 21"
1024 x 768	10	662 K	3.4 x 2.5 in.	Full Screen 20"
640 x 480	10	315 K	2.1 x 1.6 in.	Full Screen 15"
360 x 270	10	126 K	1.2 x .9 in.	4" x 5"

- For photographic quality printing, always use the highest compression quality (10) possible.
- 300 dpi is usually enough resolution for printing to a photo-quality inkjet or thermal printer.
- 72 dpi is the standard resolution for display over the Internet.
- 360 x 270 displays at approximately 4 x 5 on a monitor, approximating a 4 x 5 print size.

JPEG compression ratio vs. file size

Print and monitor size remain the same as above.

1600 x 1200	7	378 k	
1280 x 760	7	347 k	Medium-quality desktop printing
1024 x 768	7	221 k	High-quality monitor display
640 x 480	7	126 k	
360 x 270	7	63 k	

1600 x 1200	5	221 k	
1280 x 760	5	189 k	Low-quality desktop printing
1024 x 768	5	158 k	Medium-quality monitor display
640 x 480	5	95 k	
360 x 270	5	63 k	

1600 x 1200	3	158 k	
1280 x 760	3	158 k	Low-quality monitor display
1024 x 768	3	126 k	
640 x 480	3	63 k	
360 x 270	3	63 k	

- Quality is also dependent on the image itself. Some images compress and look good, some not very well at all.
- At some point you just can't make a file any smaller.
- Use the above as guidelines, your mileage may vary.

Chapter 6

STORAGE & TRANSFER

All of the digital files you have or are soon to have will soon become the equivalent of a digital shoebox, overflowing with files of different sizes and types all scattered about. The nice thing about a real shoebox full of photos is that you can sit down for a few hours and take a trip down memory lane as you look for that picture you think you remember having from six years ago. Or was it seven? "Let's see, we were living at the old house and Jennifer had just graduated from school so it was May, maybe June, which means that it should be in this shoebox here, unless we took it out to give to her fiancée for her 30th birthday party collage...."

You get our point. The shoebox effect gets even more maddening when we are talking about digital images, files you can't see unless you open up each and every one on your PC. It is very easy to just dump your files into the "My Computer" folder on your PC where they will pile up like garbage in the church basement in Arlo Guthrie's Alice's Restaurant, soon overtaking your computer's hard disk.

So now that you are making digital photos, let's talking about housing them.

Physical space ... your digital filing cabinet

Despite what you may think, digital files do take up physical space, albeit a mere fraction of what the comparable amount of photographs, slides, paintings, and prints take up. Take your average 50-page photo album, for example. Fifty pages, times two sides, times four photos per side equals 400 photographs in one book. A comparable digital file for one 4 x 6 photograph takes up about a megabyte or so depending on how you compress it (your mileage may vary) which means that twenty of those big albums will fit on your average computer hard drive nowadays, leaving plenty of room for a few games and other assorted files. That's 8,000 photographs ... enough to fill your bathtub if they were all printed out.

So why even worry about storage if you can fit a bathtub full of pictures in your computer? Three reasons: space, disaster, and sanity.

First, you will run out of space. Did you hear us?

YOU WILL RUN OUT OF SPACE.

Images multiply like rabbits and before you know it, you've photographed and/or scanned just about everything you can think of. In addition, there are many things that compete for space on your computer's hard drive. A huge space hog is the operating system (Windows 2000 or Macintosh OS 9.9) and all it needs to run your PC. Others are the various applications, browsers, games, and e-mail jokes we all seem to collect over time. Besides, keeping all of your images on your hard drive is the proverbial eggs-in-one-basket.

Second, disaster will strike. Not only will you run out of space, your hard drive will decide one day to just lose/erase/discombobulate any and/or all of your files at some time. Allows us to reiterate. Your computer will mangle files sooner or later ... the proverbial tape deck eating your favorite tape. This is called a disk crash. If your disk crashes, you may still be able to recover your important images. But they better be REALLY important because, depending on the cause of the crash, it may be cheaper just to fly the entire family back to Disney World and take their picture again.

Disks crash, files go bad (kind of like digital milk), images get lost. We don't always know why. We regular people, that is. Techies can go on for hours about why you lost your files and what an idiot you are for not having duplicates stored away somewhere. You're better off having a second copy of the important things, somewhere separate from your main storage. This is called a backup. If you lose your images you can get them back.

Third, sorting through a bathtub of pictures to find a photo from Earth Day 1992 will make you insane. As soon as you start accumulating images, start deciding on a file system. You have a wide range of choices, from programs that may come with your camera to systems you can put together yourself with your favorite database. Having every picture your family has ever taken is great until you have to look through a few hundred of them to find the one you want, or attempt to decipher the two word name you gave it a year ago.

Hard drives

You cannot buy a computer today without a hard drive and today's hard drives are enormous compared to those of only a few years ago.

Your hard drive is just like the filing cabinet in your office. All it does is hold bunches of files, in no particular order, and in fact in one big heap if you aren't diligent about where you store things. Once you start taking digital photographs, plan on having at least one folder or directory on the hard drive of your PC dedicated to holding them. If you are a professional user, make even more related directories or folders, one for each subject, or job, or salesperson, etc.

Remember what we said about disks—they crash. So it is important that you have some kind of removable storage to not only transport your pictures to and fro but to have an extra copy of them in case you find smoke emanating from your hard drive some day. Don't laugh, we have seen it happen … personally, it's not funny.

Removable disks

If you plan on giving your images to other people to print out, the easiest way is to put them on a disk (or some other form of removable media). A picture is worth a thousand words and takes up 100 times as much disk space. You'll need a way to get them out of your PC and onto something to keep them safe or take them places to share with other people or to have printed professionally.

Small size

The lowly diskette. Diskettes have been around since the early days of personal computing. In fact, back then all you could get was a computer with a really floppy floppy disk; hard drives were pretty rare and very expensive. Today, diskettes are the equivalent of a digital penny, you always seem to have a few lying around and there isn't a whole lot that you can do with them.

While it looks as if computer manufacturers are beginning to abandon the diskette entirely, there is still a little life left in that 3 1/2 inch piece of plastic. Sony, for example uses diskettes both as internal memory and removable storage media, not a bad idea considering this makes images from their digital cameras readable on almost any PC in the world.

The main drawback to using a diskette to hold and transfer images is, of course, its limited capacity. At 1.3 megabytes per disk, you aren't going to fit a whole lot of images on one. At nearly 1 megabyte per image for photographic-quality images printed at snapshot size (4 x 5 at 300 dpi), you get one image per disk.

Diskettes also die. We are talking about some pretty old technology that has gone through far fewer changes than the VW beetle ever has. Don't keep your photos on a diskette for too long if they are important to you. Despite their shortcomings, diskettes are a very inexpensive, nearly universally acceptable, and convenient. Though not glamorous, they are often your best choice for one or two images.

Iomega Clik!. The Iomega Clik! disk and drive, while not yet available at the time of writing, promise to be a welcome addition to the digital photography world. Clik! disks are about half the size of a credit card and hold 40 megabytes each. At a selling price of just under $10 per disk, Clik! could be the reusable digital film at a reasonable price we have been looking for.

Iomega's plans call for digital camera manufacturers to build Clik! drives into their cameras. If Clik! finds the widespread acceptance that Iomega's Zip disk has, it should be a huge success, spawning Clik! drives in any number of digital products. Already Iomega has set its sights on Personal Digital Assistants (PDAs), mobile computers, and other small devices that have a need for inexpensive removable storage.

Medium size

We categorize medium-sized storage media as one that holds between 100 megabytes and 1 gigabyte (1,000 megabytes). These drives are generally inexpensive and may come already built into your PC. Medium-size media can be used for backing up files or transporting them.

Iomega Zip. The Iomega Zip disk is a great example of an excellent product targeted just right. Zip disks are just about the size of two diskettes stacked together, yet hold 100 megabytes of information. At under $15 each for the disks and just over $100 for the drives, Zip disks have become the de facto Super Floppy of the digital world. Iomega's announcement of Zip drives for other digital devices such as printers and TV set-top boxes will enable digital images and other data to be shared from device to device without the intervention of a PC. This means that a Zip disk full of digital photographs could just be inserted into a printer and the images printed out automatically.

Nearly every computer manufacturer includes a Zip drive as an option and many as standard equipment. This universality makes a Zip disk a necessity for anyone who will be storing and transporting large numbers (read more than ten at once) digital photographs.

Imation SuperDisk. The challenger to Iomega's Zip disk is the Imation (formally 3M) SuperDisk, holding 120 megabytes of data at a cost about the same as a Zip disk. Imation, too is aligning itself with computer manufacturers who will offer its drive as a built-in option. While off to a slow start, time will tell if the SuperDisk will find the same favor that the Zip has. A distinct advantage to the

Imation SuperDisk drive is that it also accepts traditional 3.5 inch diskettes, allowing it to serve a dual purpose. As computer manufacturers phase out diskette drives, this ability will make SuperDisk drives a welcome peripheral to anyone with boxes of diskettes full of old files.

CD-R/RW. Holding roughly 65 megabytes, Compact Disk-Recordable (CD-R) and Compact Disk Rewritable (CD-RW) disks are both versions of the traditional compact disk. CD-R drives not only read CDs but can write to them as well (known as "burning"). While additional files can be added to a CD-R, up to the disk's capacity, once burned they are forever there. Burning CDs yourself has become easier and less expensive in the past year or so, with drives dropping below the $300 level. Blank CDs will run you a dollar or less each, depending on the quantity. Most of the drives available can burn an entire CD in about 20 minutes.

CD-RW drives are a little different from CD-R drives in that they can be written and rewritten a number of times. The drives are more expensive than CD-R drives but can write both CD-RW disks and CD-R disks. You can label your CDs with a permanent marker to keep track of what is on them or a better option is a CD labeling kit. These kits come complete with templates, self-adhesive labels, and an applicator that allow you to produce professional-level labels on your inkjet or laser printer and apply them flawlessly every time. If you plan on mastering a larger number of CDs, CD label printers are available for around $1,500 that print your text and graphics directly on the CD itself, making your CDs stand on par with anyone's. Special blank CDs are available with ink-friendly white or silver matte coating.

The advantage to CD-R and CD-RW disks is that they hold a large amount of information in a very compact form and can be read on nearly every desktop PC made in the past five years. CD drives come standard in all PCs and their replacement, the DVD drive, holding four to eight times as much information as a CD, can read them as well.

Large size

We categorize anything that holds more than 1 gigabyte of data as large-capacity media. These drives and disks are mostly suited to backing up or archiving large numbers of files and can hold hundreds, even thousands of digital photographs.

Iomega Jaz. Iomega soon followed their success with the Zip disk by releasing a version with ten times the capacity (one gigabyte) and soon after, a drive with 20 times as much capacity (the Jaz 2 at 2 gigabytes). At $250 for the Jaz and about $100 more for the Jaz 2, Iomega has priced the drives at a level that is affordable by almost anyone. As with the Zip drive, Jaz drives are also being offered as options by many PC manufacturers. Cartridges for the Jaz drive retail for around $100 and the Jaz 2 for $125. The popularity of the Jaz drive also means that many service providers, copy centers, and digital photo labs will have a drive that you can use to transfer files as well.

SyQuest SparQ. SyQuest is the granddaddy of removable media, pioneering the removable disk market with its original 44 megabyte disks and drive in the late 80s at a time when 44 megabytes was considered large for a built-in hard disk.

Though recent years have seen SyQuest lose ground to rival Iomega, they have seen competitors come and go and remain making removable disks. The SyQuest SparQ drive continues the tradition by offering disks that hold 1 gigabyte and that retail for around $50 with a drive that costs about $200.

SyQuest SyJet. The SyQuest SyJet is another offering in SyQuest's removable line. With a capacity of 1.5 gigabytes, a disk that retails at $80, and a drive that sells for $300, the SyJet is priced to compete with Iomega's Jaz drive. It is puzzling, however, how SyQuest plans to split the market between two drives, their SyJet and SparQ, with similar capacities.

DVD. The Digital Versatile Disk (DVD), with a capacity of 2.6 gigabytes per side, is touted as the Super CD for the next millennium. Marketing prose to be sure, but its speed and capacity firmly cements it as the high-capacity, high-speed storage media of the near future. By the end of 1998, DVD drives were appearing as replacements for CD drives on newly build PCs. In addition, stand-alone DVD devices are emerging that will play the rapidly growing number of movie titles that demand the speed and storage the DVD provides. This convergence of computers and entertainment at the consumer-level means that we will soon see DVD drives built into a whole host of digital appliances.

For users of digital photography, a DVD drive can not only hold an entire year's (or decade's) worth of pictures but can read regular old CDs as well, making it backward compatible with the millions of CDs currently on the market.

- You will need some form of removable storage for archiving images and transferring them.
- Before you settle on one type of removable storage, check to see what your friends, family, associates, and service providers (photo lab, copy shop, printing company) use. Using the same type will save headaches.

Organizational space—finding a needle in a haystack

Not only do you need a place for your images (storage), you also need every image in its place (cataloging). Storage is only half the battle of keeping your digital photos; you also need to catalog and organize them so that when you need to find a picture of young Joey's bar mitzvah or that construction project you worked on three years ago, you can do so quickly. The way to do this is to catalog all of your images (or any document) in some sort of database or image storage program.

Unlike your file cabinet in your office, alphabetical filing just doesn't cut it. Take a picture of the kids sledding during the holidays. How do you catalog it so you can find it years from now when they are married? File it under kids? Sledding? Christmas/Hanukkah/Kwaanza? Winter? The date? Any and all of the above. That's the beauty of a database—you can apply any and all of those terms to the image and go back later to search for it with any of them. You may get thirty pictures of sledding (maybe you live in Buffalo, NY) but you'll at least know that the one you want is in there. Once you've a place for everything and everything in its place, you can search through your collection all kinds of ways. Searching is the neatest feature of databases and once you get the hang of it, it's pretty neat.

Digital cameras and the software associated with them have gotten more and more advanced in just the few years that they have been available. It is not hard to imagine in the near future that the images you take with your camera will automatically have the date they were taken applied to them as well as the file name and a few other references that you may add when you take the picture. Future image cataloging programs will suck them out of your camera and automatically catalog them for you. But no matter how sophisticated these systems get, you will always have some sort of manual input. After all, you are the one who has to find those images five years from now, not the camera.

For storing and retrieving your images you have a couple of options.

Image capacity by media type

Media	# of monitor-quality images at 4 x 5 (approx. 360 x 270) Quality level 5	# of print-quality images at 4 x 5 (1600 x 1200) Quality level 10
Diskette	20	1
Zip Disk	1500	100
CD-ROM	10,000	600
Jaz (1 gig)	15,000	1000
Jaz2 (2 gig)	30,000	2000

- The above numbers are averages and represent typical digital photograph files.

- The above media is typical of what you will find in many PCs, copy shops, and printing companies.
- Use small files for e-mail or to transfer images via the Internet.

Professional-level image databases

Image databases for the professional market have been around for a while and are generally used by companies who use a lot of images in their regular work, such as catalog producers, digital studio photographers, color separators (middlemen between clients and commercial printers), or commercial printing houses. These folks store tens or hundreds of thousands of images for themselves or their clients. Because they deal in such a large number of images and related files, used in any number of different jobs, their needs dictate very large, very powerful database systems.

The folks that use these large image databases also use them to track images and related files throughout the production of a print job. Putting together a full-color 112-page catalog, for example, takes more than just finding a picture of the red cable knit fisherman's sweater. It also involves matching the picture with the most recent version of the description of that sweater, the most recent photo of that sweater, and the version and page of the catalog it is in.

As a result, most professional-level image management programs also tend to encompass the various related aspects of an image's use. Most of these systems are very comprehensive, pretty expensive, and take a bit to master. If your business revolves around a large number of image files and being able to not only locate them but make sure they get to the right place, then these systems are for you.

Consumer-level image databases

Until recently, home users had to either try to find some stripped-down version of a professional image management system or create one themselves with the help of a commercially available database such as Access, ClarisWorks, or FileMaker Pro. While the latter option is still a good way to go, consumer-level image cataloging programs are beginning to show themselves.

As digital cameras become more widespread, count on more and more of these applications becoming available. Many digital cameras and some desktop scanners come bundled with image management software that will get you up and running right away on organizing your images. If yours doesn't or you don't like the one that came with your device, there are other choices available with more on the way.

Creating your own image management system

We've discussed off-the-shelf cataloging software. In the professional market there are quite a few choices; in the amateur or consumer market there are not as many choices, but that will soon change. In both cases, the available software tends to lock you into particular description fields, keywords, organizational styles, or even look and feel.

Most of these applications do allow you some flexibility. In some cases you can create your own fields or the program provides blank fields that you can name yourself. In general though, you are stuck with the layout they come with, which may or may not suit your own style of organization. This is kind of like walking into somebody else's office and having to use their filing system instead of your own. We all tend to use our way of filing things and looking things up. Because of this, one good way to catalog images is by utilizing a standard computer database.

Most of the computers you can buy come with one database or another for storing and retrieving information. The nice thing about them is that they really don't care what form that information is in. Pictures, graphics, text, and numbers are all just digital files to most databases. The best part is that generally those databases come with templates, predesigned forms, or layouts that you can use to get you going instead of having to start from scratch. Templates exist for most common databases for anything from recipe files to address books to personnel records and image files, where you can build your own picture management system.

Because the existing templates are built on a common database, you can pick exactly the fields and the layout you want to use and customize them to suit your own style. More importantly, three years from now when you decide that there are a couple more descriptors you want to add, you can put them in, instead of starting from scratch. If you are at all computer inclined, we encourage you to seriously look at what database software is available to you. Building your own image database is easy and you can download different templates from the Internet or off the manufacturer's website to get you started.

Designing your own system also allows you to catalog your images in a way that works the way you work, making it more intuitive for you. Going this route is also less expensive because chances are the database software you will use comes prepackaged with your computer anyway. By leveraging an existing database application to build your image catalog, you will also be able to take advantage of any upgrades that become available as well. And you can always find more templates to increase your catalog to include your cassette tapes, your CD-ROMs, address book, spice rack, etc.

- Image cataloging applications usually come bundled with digital cameras or scanners; try those first to see if they suit you.
- Look to any current database applications you may already have. Chances are you can find templates for them that will get you started on an image database.

Understanding how to use a database

Databases are the key to not only digital image cataloging but digital printing, websites, and just about anything done on a computer that holds information. More and more, databases are becoming the key element to these digital repositories of information. Understanding how databases work and interacting with them is very important. Now that you've filled your catalog with images, how do you get them back out?

The reason you put all these key words and descriptor fields in is so that you can go through and search along various parameters. The neat thing about databases is that they all pretty much work the same. This makes them easy to search through if you remember one simple technique. Pretend you are at the local Burgerama, ordering a hamburger.

Search engines use Boolean logic which means that doing a search is just like ordering a hamburger at your local burger joint. You walk in and you say "I want a hamburger WITH swiss OR provolone AND lettuce AND tomato, NOT onions, NOT mayo." Eventually you will get the hamburger you exactly want. So, if you are searching for Timmy's birthday party picture from a few years ago you say, "Find Timmy AND birthday, NOT Christmas, NOT 1998." What this does is focus your search to bring you just the images that are related to those keywords you put in. Incidentally, this is exactly the same way search engines for websites on the Internet work.

Building your haystack

In order to find a particular image you need to build your image catalog according to a few simple rules. Whether you build your own or buy a preconfigured image database, these rules will generally hold true.

1. Fields. Fields are what the descriptor parts of the database are called and can contain just about any type of information. Some of the most important fields in an image database are the filename the computer knows the image as, the filename you know the image as, and the date it was taken. Filename is the name the computer itself uses to find a file. This can and probably should be different from the name you want to give to the image; both are important. A picture of Timmy on his birthday may be called Timmy.tif to the computer. You may want to also give it a name in the database of "Timmy's 8th Birthday." This way you are not limited to the naming convention imposed by the PC you work on. The "date taken" field is important because we take photographs over time. The beginning of the roll is always from a span of time before the end of the roll and this tends to break up our photo albums chronologically as well.

Depending on how you set up your image catalog, you can add any number of fields. Design them according to how you currently collect and organize your photographs. Do you organize them by event? Create an event field. Do you organize by person? Create a family member or salesperson field. Don't know? Don't sweat it, if you decide later on that you want to organize images a particular way, simply add another field.

2. Keywords. Technically, the keyword field is just another field but it can be the most powerful. In fact a database of just keywords alone, while simple, is very powerful when it comes to searching for things. Keywords are simply words you would use to describe the subject matter of each photograph.

Even though the image may have a title you put to it—"Tim's first birthday" or "Red brick house on Maple Drive"—generally you will also want to associate other words with it. Timmy's first birthday might also have the associated keywords "birthday," "Timmy," "party," "1982," etc. And the red brick house on Maple might have associated keywords such as "Maple," "brick," "fireplace," "garage," etc. You can generally have any number of keywords you want. The advantage of keywords is that three years from now you might not remember what you called that picture but you knew something about a birthday party and you knew that Timmy was in it but you did not remember the filename so you can search in the keyword field for "birthday party" and you might get every birthday party from 1976 on, but somewhere in there will be Timmy's birthday party.

Now creating a database does involve some time and effort on your part. You have to put these words in. Some of the catalog programs allow you to designate a folder or a directory and say, "catalog all of the images in this folder." Then, it goes through and dumps all of the images in the folder into the catalog. This gets everything organized and even the filename your PC goes by is put into the catalog, but you still need to add your own keywords and titles. No small job, particularly if you take a lot of photographs and/or have decided to digitize every picture since the one of your grandmother sitting on a pony at age three. But the time and effort is worth it. Once finished, you can call up images in any number of ways, along any number of search terms. Find all of the pictures of Timmy since he was born to embarrass him at his high school graduation party. Or call up all of the weddings in your family to begin making a family tree, the key to it all being the database.

- Don't worry about including every category field you will ever need when building an image database. You can add others later.
- Keywords should be words that come to mind to describe each image subject; they will make the images easier to find later.

Sending your images here and there

Sneakernet. Sneakernet is the oldest, lowest tech method of image transfer around. It involves simply copying your files to a disk, removing the disk from your PC and carrying it or mailing it to the place it needs to go. The sneakernet method of transfer, while not very flashy, is often the easiest and most reliable. Sending a disk full of pictures across the country to a family member is simple and does not rely on data communications equipment, network protocols, software compatabilities, alignment of the planets, or any of the other various aspects of digital transfer that can thwart digital files trying electronically to get from one place to the other. As long as the person on the other end can access the disk you send them, you're in business.

Sneakernet is not very fast, limited to the delivery speed of whoever you use to physically deliver the package your disk is in, but it is inexpensive. If you are sending megabytes or even gigabytes of images, it is the only way, next to shelling out big bucks for a dedicated digital system. Keep in mind that disks do fail; disks sent through the mail or other carrier can be subjected to all kinds of nasty things (though rarely), so they can fail. Use special disk envelopes available at office supply stores to help protect them in transit. And never send your only copy of an image this way; always keep a backup just in case. We repeat: always keep a backup and never trust your only copy to anyone.

E-mail

Electronic mail (e-mail) is probably the easiest and most convenient digital way to send digital pictures to someone. Including an image or two as an attachment is as easy as clicking on the "attachment" button in your e-mail application and telling it which file or files you wish to attach. When you send your message, a copy of the files you attached goes with it.

Your e-mail software offers you a choice in the way it will encode your digital images. Multipurpose Internet Mail Extensions (MIME) encoding should be checked for Windows and Mac users with recent versions of Netscape, Internet Explorer, or AOL. BinHex is best for recipients with old Macintosh mailers and early versions of Eudora. Way back in 1982, when e-mail standards were first set, very few people had any idea that we'd be sending anything but text to each other. To overcome this shortcoming, MIME was developed as a way to package these image files, and any file that is not plain old text, for e-mailing. Since most of us are, hopefully, using updated versions of our e-mail software, stick with MIME and you'll be fine.

Remember that digital photos take up a lot of space and if you are going to be sending images of more than 100 k or so in size, make sure that the person on the other end wants to receive them in the first place. There is nothing more frustrating than opening up an e-mail that holds an attachment that locks up your PC for an hour while it downloads. In the body of your e-mail, warn the recipient that there are digital photos attached.

Online providers

"You've got pictures!" In mid-1998, Eastman Kodak company signed a deal with America Online to create an on-line photographic database for Kodak and AOL customers. Kodak, who had been working on the concept for a few years, had linked a large number of photo labs to a digital network where customer photographs were digitized and sent to the network, waiting to be viewed from the customer's home computer. America Online, boasting the largest number of connected users in the world (15 million at the time of this writing), leveraged its huge client base and large digital network to bring photographs to the desktop of all 15 million.

This heralds a huge change in the way we view and share pictures. Simply by writing "PhotoNet" (the name of Kodak's image network) on the processing envelope of a participating retailer, a digital copy of all your photographs is created and sent to the network, free for the first month. For a few dollars a month, a number of images are held on-line so that not only can you access them but anybody you give the access code to can access them as well. This is where imaging and photography in general is heading. Within a few years, certainly by the time this book is tattered and dog-eared, every single photograph that you take into your photo retailer will be digitized at time of development and those images will be stored away for later retrieval.

There are advantages to this beyond simply storing and sharing pictures. You can download the images and store them on your hard drive. You can give others access to your digital photo album so that they can download and store them. You can have them printed out on your home inkjet printer or printed out on the high-quality digital photo printer at the lab simply by clicking a button in your web browser (the software you use to access the Internet). The next time you go to your lab your photos are sitting there waiting for you. Not only that, anyone that you give access to your account can have digital prints made at their local photo lab or at home too.

This solves a lot of problems. It eliminates a need for a scanner in your home or business because the images are digitized at the photo lab. It allows you to use your existing camera, you are still using film, and you are still getting back regular prints but you also have access to a digital file. It keeps you from having to buy and maintain supplies for the digital printer in your home or office.

And you can use the high-speed and high-quality photographic printers at the lab because the images are on-line and always available. It also eliminates the need for finding the negative of a picture taken long ago that you suddenly need a copy of. Not that we suggest you do away with your negatives once they are processed, but you won't have to search through the back of the closet to find the negative you are looking for. It will already be digitized and waiting to be printed.

For folks far away, this service is an incredible benefit. Now Grandma in Florida can have her own copies of the baby's first steps instead of bugging you over and over because you keep forgetting. She simply goes to her local retailer, accesses your account there (Don't worry, they will help her), and orders her own copies, allowing her to claim bragging rights at the next senior get-together around the swimming pool.

For commercial users, particularly small businesses, on-line photo repositories mean always having access to your photos and not waiting for the company's computer jockey to free up time to help you make copies of last week's project. You can access them yourself from your desk or the local photo retailer as well. In addition, these networked photo sites will have copies of the software necessary to work with your images and helpful hints for you as well. While Kodak and AOL are the first companies to offer the service to a widespread clientele others are on the way. Already Sony and Fuji have announced or currently have similar capabilities.

The Internet

The Internet, known simply as "The Web" (as in World Wide Web) to the technically hip, is spreading around the world faster than a cold through a kindergarten class. In discussing it, we use "Internet" and "Web" interchangeably, even though the Web is technically just a subset of the Internet. One count of on-line hosts, or individual machines connected to the Internet, taken in the Summer of 1998 found 36,739,000 such hosts. In the January 1998 survey, taken only six months before, 29,670,000 individual hosts were found. The January 1997 survey taken the year before counted 19,540,000. The thing doubled in size in one year! Now that's growth. If you are reading this book and 1998 seems like a while ago, you can be sure that this many sites will seem like a mere drop in the bucket.

So what does this mean to you?

On-line photo services such as the Kodak and AOL partnership offer access to their networks through the web because they know that it is the cheapest and easiest way to reach any number of customers, at any time, anywhere.

The Internet offers the same capabilities to you as well. Anyone can put up a web page or two that can be seen by anyone with a connection to the Internet. Usually, the access fee you pay to your Internet service provider will include enough disk space on their web server to put up a few web pages of your own to create a personal website. This is true of Internet providers such as AOL, as well. If you currently have a provider, call them to find out the details for putting up a few pages.

Having your own website, while trendy, also allows you to share your pictures with friends and family miles away. Putting together a website isn't all that hard but you will have to do a little studying to understand some of the ins and outs. Luckily, web page design tools are becoming available that allow you to put together professional looking sites relatively easily. Your Internet service provider can also help you get started with pointers and information on how to structure things so that they can be served up from their equipment with minimum headaches.

Modem-to-modem

File Transfer Protocol (FTP) is the method websites use to transfer files from one site to another or from a site to your PC. It is also a method for transferring files from one PC to another over standard phone lines. The software that comes with your modem usually includes an FTP application that will allow you to connect to another PC via phone lines to transfer files from one site to another. FTP also comes in handy if you want to set up a website that will allow people to download higher resolution pictures than are displayed on the monitor. Check with your service provider for more details.

Specialized carriers

We won't begin to try to describe all of the mutations of digital image delivery services. Professionals and large companies that send a lot of image files around should definitely look into a specialized carrier. Companies such as Wham!Net, DAX, even UPS, have private networks that you can rent space and time on to transfer your files between sites. These service only make sense if you are doing professional digital photography and send something in the neighborhood of 20 or more megabytes of images per day.

- Sneakernet is an inexpensive way to send lots of digital images from here to there. Make sure the disk you send is compatible with the recipient's system.
- Sending images via E-mail as attachments is the simplest way to send them electronically. Be judicious in how big a file you send to someone.
- Start your own photo website. Your Internet service provider can help you get started.
- FTP will help you transfer files from one point to another via phone lines at the speed of the slowest modem on either end.
- Specialized carriers are available if you send lots of images every day.

Storage and transfer, the overlooked digital aspect

Storage and transfer involves saving your pictures forever, finding them when you want, and sending them to friends. While not the most glamorous aspect of digital photography, perhaps it is the most important. Because digital photographs force us to think differently about pictures in general, we need to keep in mind how the digital world affects how we store our pictures, organize them, weed through them, and send copies to friends, family, and associates. Taking great digital photographs is only half of the battle. You also need to be able to find them when you want them and get them to people.

Chapter 7
OUTPUT

Printing today is digital-based. The majority of printing technologies will use:
- Ink
- Toner
- Inkjet

Digital printing can be either:

Monochrome		Color			
Electro-photography	Inkjet	Electro-photography	Inkjet	Thermal Wax	Dye Sub

The defining devices of paper-based replication are:
- Printer
- Copier
- Press

A printer uses inkjet or toner technology to make marks on paper from data, resulting in the production of first-generation originals where every one can be different, thus allowing the production of a collated document.

A copier uses inkjet or toner technology to make marks on paper from an original, resulting in the production of a second-generation copy, which, when copying multiple originals in an automatic document handler, can also produce a collated document.

A press is a mechanical device that uses an image carrier to replicate the same image on paper, resulting in a large quantity of the same images. A press may also handle larger sheets, resulting in multiple pages on one large sheet of paper, used in a binding operation.

It was reported that the number of pages printed on printers in 1995 for the first time exceeded pages printed on all models of copying machines. This led H-P to coin a new buzzword: "mopier," a multiple original printer. If you make multiple original prints from an original-producing printer instead of an original-copying copier, it is a mopier. Since copiers are evolving to digital approaches, they become scanners on the top and printers on the bottom.

Printers at the high-end, like the Xerox Docutech, are challenging offset duplication at the low end of the black-and-white printing world. Low-end printers are absorbing some of the work of both offset duplicators and mid-level copiers. The copier is pretty much a dead duck over the next decade. As scanners become cheaper and wind up on virtually every desktop, we can easily scan hard copy and print. The last nail in the copier coffin is the fact that most files that would have been printed out and then copied are now just printed out in the required quantity. So over time we arrive at:

- Printer
- Printer-press
- Scanner-printer (copier)
- Press
- Press-printer

A printer is easy to fathom. A printer-press is the way we presently describe a high-end color printer. It may be that instead of re-imaging the image carrier for each copy, we image it once for some number of copies or even for all copies. It becomes a high-speed, high-capability printer. A scanner-printer is a printer with a scanner somewhere in the system. A press is just what it is now with plates and ink. A press-printer is a printing press with automated on-press image carrier generation and some level of variable printing integrated into the process.

The objective of replication technology over the next decade will be to build into the printing press the kind of automation that is now built into copiers and printers. By de-skilling the process and automating it at a high level, the cost of paper-based communication comes down. Its cycle time is reduced, which leads to all the current buzzwords: short run, on-demand, just-in-time, distributed printing, and more. Maintenance of graphic arts quality levels is assumed.

The reproduction of information on paper falls into two categories:
- Static printing
- Dynamic printing

Static printing refers to traditional ink-on-paper approaches, offset being the most common, where each and every sheet is reproduced from the same image carrier, which is fixed with the same image. The copies look exactly the same. Toner-based printers, conversely, use an image carrier that is imaged each time a sheet comes in contact with it, re-imaging for each copy. The copies look the same, but each is generated individually. Dynamic printing means that the printer must re-generate the image for every page; thus, every page can be different—variable data printing.

Process differences

	Static *Offset printing*	*Dynamic* *Digital Printing*
Image Carrier	Fixed	Variable
Material	Ink	Toner, Inkjet
Quality	High	Medium+
Variability	None	High
Quantities	Moderate to high >2000	Low to moderate <2000
Paper selection	Wide-ranging	Limited
Sheet size	Small to large	Small*
Documents	Moderate to long runs	Short runs

*except for 20-inch Xeikon engines

The advantage to static printing is the cost effectiveness of long runs. The advantage of dynamic printing is that the re-imaging for each sheet lets you do two things you cannot do with a printing press:

- Personalize each sheet to a person or company
- Produce one multi-page document at a time

There are some other advantages, but, newer printing presses with built-in automation compete in the areas of:

- Very short runs
- Very fast turnaround
- Distributed printing

Digital printing

Digital printing is any reproduction technology that receives electronic files and uses spots (or dots) for replication. Ink, toner, inkjet or any other dye- or pigment-based transfer system may be used. This covers almost every present system for outputting graphic information to film, plate, or paper.

Pretty much everything involving output today is "computer-to-this" or "direct-to-that" as the printing industry finds new links from programs that create formatted information to devices that output that information in some manner.

The first photographic typesetting machines had a keyboard attached to them. Later, the keyboard became an off-line input device, but in both cases the operator made the hyphenation decisions. By the 1970s computers were used to drive phototypesetters, either via tape of some kind or on-line, and operators no longer had to make end-of-line decisions. "Computer-to" technology was born.

Imagesetters became the first complete page "computer-to" printout systems and computer-to-film grew to dominate printing prepress. This eliminated all of the other analog film steps and brought us to one piece of film (or more, if color) with everything included. The "imposetter" is a filmsetter that imposes pages on large sheets of film and the result reduces stripping to a minor operation.

Computer-to-paper applies to digital printers and presses that use toner or inkjet to create variable data page information. In this category there are desktop printers, production printers, wide-format printers, and digital color presses. They all put marks on paper without traditional film and plates.

Computer-to-cake uses a desktop inkjet printer with tasteless food coloring replacing the inks and rollers modified to print a thin sheet of icing on a piece of wax paper. The image is 360 or even 720 dpi and is then carefully mounted on a cake or even cookies. So help me, I am not making this up. The result is personalized pastry.

Computer-to-cloth results from inkjetting directly to a T-shirt or some other cloth, bypassing screen printing. The indirect method uses sheets of transfer material which are then heated to transfer the image.

Computer-to-mylar are plotters that use a small knife to cut adhesive-backed mylar that is mounted on a carrier sheet. The logos or letters that are cut are then peeled off and affixed to glass or metal or whatever for signage.

Computer-to-stitching drives a sewing machine that stitches words or logos onto caps, jackets, shirts, or whatever. Multiple-colored threads can be used to create rather complex images.

Computer-to-bandsaw uses the computer to drive a saw that cuts shapes out of wood or even metal.

In other words, the world of printout is all about spots and dots.

Although you can make the case that making plates and film with spots and dots is digital printing; as we use the term in this book, digital printing refers to the use of a re-imageable image carrier or no image carrier for the transfer of toner or inkjet ink to paper. Digital printing often uses pixels—spots with gray levels. Inkjet is a direct-to-paper technology with no intermediate image carrier. Toner-based reproduction requires a drum or belt to create the toned image and then transfer it to paper. In essence it is an image carrier, like any printing plate. The difference is that the plate is fixed in that the image does not change during reproduction. The toner-based image carrier must create a new image for every reproduction and is thus re-imageable.

This means that toner-based systems are inherently slower than fixed-plate ink-based systems, since re-imaging in zero time is not really a possibility. The downside to re-imageability becomes the upside in the ability to produce variable printing. Totally electronic printing devices are printers, not presses or copiers.

Variable printing

Variable printing means that customized and personalized printing can be produced for target marketing purposes. Customized means that documents particular to selected audiences can be assembled. Personalized means that each unit is particular to a specific person or other entity. Inkjet systems capable of competing with today's toner-based electrophotographic color printers are not expected to be introduced until 1999-2000 and thus will not impact the printing industry until 2002-2003. Projections for inkjet in terms of pages handled for 2006 are modest.

On-demand printing

"On-demand printing" is another way of saying short run, distributed, just-in-time printing, no matter how it is produced, but many consider it as totally electronic printing. The term is so fraught with misunderstanding that it will hang on for a long time because it can mean anything for anyone who wants to exploit its ambiguity. Just remember that printers and prepress services have always produced work on demand—the customer demands, we deliver.

Distributed printing

This aspect of printing is often lost in the on-demand rush. It essentially says that the print-and-distribute model is not always valid. With distribute-and-print we can send digital files anywhere and print the quantity required proximate to the point of distribution. As large printing companies acquire medium-sized printers in different geographic regions, they are establishing networks for distributed printing. Loose affiliations between other printers is on the same track. But keep in mind that not all printing can or will be distributed. The economics for centralized reproduction are still strong for many types of printing.

For each run-length area, a particular reproduction technology or technologies are applicable. For 1998, we estimate the percentage of that area covered by each reproduction technology in this table:

Run length vs. Reproduction Approach

	Digital Printing	Direct Imaging	Offset Litho	Flexo	Gravure
Ultra Short Run					
(1) (12% of all volume)	100%	—	—	—	—
Very Short Run					
(2-500) (15% of all volume)	85%	10%	5%	—	—
Short Run					
(501-2,000) (14% of all volume)	19%	35%	43%	2%	1%
Moderate-Short Run					
(2,001-5,000) (13% of all volume)	2%	39%	55%	2%	2%
Moderate Run					
(5001-10,000) (10% of all volume)	—	23%	65%	9%	3%
Average Run					
(10,001-50,000) (9% of all volume)	—	15%	70%	11%	4%
Moderate-Long Run					
(50,001-250,000) (11% of volume)	—	2%	80%	12%	6%
Long Run					
(250,001-750,000) (7% of all volume)	—	—	76%	14%	10%
Very-Long Run					
(>750,001) (9% of all volume)	—	—	50%	15%	35%

(Does not total 100%)

Source: GAMA

Non-impact printing

With a non-impact printer there is, of course, no contact between the printer and substrate, except for drums and/or belts that carry the computer-generated image and transfer it to the substrate. Most non-impact printers use toner that is attracted to the substrate by an electric charge rather than an impact mechanism that contains every character that the printer can create. Non-impact printers developed as a result of users wanting faster printout than the original impact typewriters that were attached to early computers. They wanted all points addressability. Impact printers that housed characters on belts and wheels were too slow, broke down often, and could not produce high enough resolution. There are basically six categories of non-impact printers:

- Inkjet
- Thermal (and thermal transfer)
- Electrophotographic
- Ion Deposition
- Magnetographic

The push to develop non-impact printers began in 1978 with the introduction of Xerox's 9700 Electronic Printing System, a fully capable typesetter, plateless printing press, and automatic printer. The 9700 worked like one of Xerox's copier/duplicators, but without the need for an original because it was created by the Xerox Integrated Composition System (XICS) software. This was also one of the very first on-demand printers. On-demand printers have the capability to produce documents in almost any quantity desired, and on short notice because the original can be stored in memory and brought back when the time is needed. Xerox tried to expand and improve on the 9700 by developing the 8700, a lesser version, the 5700, designed for the network market, and the 2700, a much smaller version.

There were many competitors joining the market when Xerox introduced the 9700. There was the IBM 3800, Xerox's biggest competitor, the Agfa P400 together with scanner, and an ion deposition printer from Delphax. Sales of this new technology rose dramatically in the years following the first introduction.

Today the impact printer market has all but disappeared, with users preferring the ease, speed, and quality found in non-impact printers, mainly laser printers. Xerox's Docutech has wiped out much of the offset duplicator business, and electronic printers like the Xeikon and Indigo are making inroads to the color on-demand printing market. Many critics have predicted that this advancing technology will soon do away with traditional printing, like offset and gravure, but that prediction is still far too early to worry about.

Electrophotography

The first attempts at developing the process of electrophotography were explained in a patent in 1922. These attempts were directed toward the utilization of photocurrents to activate electrosensitive papers, which were sandwiched between a photoconductive layer and a conductive plate. A Belgian engineer came closer to Chester Carlson's discovery with his patent in 1932. This invention involved the use of a selenium plate and a Leyden jar to form an image as a powder pattern on another plate placed close to the selenium surface. This never developed into a practical process. However, pursuit of these experiments may have led to Carlson's inventions. The active history of electrophotography, most commonly known and referred to as xerography, begins with Carlson's invention in 1938.

Carlson's first electrostatic image was produced on a photoconductive surface, developed with powder, and transferred to a piece of paper. The sensitive plate consisted of a layer of sulphur on a metal plate. The plate was then charged by rubbing the surface with a cloth, and the electrostatic image was produced by contact exposure to a hand-prepared transparency. His historical patent was filed on April 4, 1939 and was first issued on Oct. 6, 1942 as number 2,297,691.

No further experiments were performed until autumn, 1944, when the Battelle Memorial Institute in Columbus, Ohio, began its laboratory investigations. Between 1944 and 1948, the experimental effort at the Institute produced many important discoveries, improvements, inventions, and developments that made Carlson's invention feasible, and eventually made xerography a commercial success.

Major discoveries included E. N. Wise's cascade development and the two-component triboelectric developer; J. J. Rheinfrank and L. E. Walk's contributions to corona charging; C.D. Oghton's introduction of vacuum evaporation as a means of making xerographic plates; R. M. Schaffert's introduction of electrostatic transfer; and W. E. Bixby's discovery of amorphous selenium electrophotographic plates.

An important event occurred in 1947 when the Battelle Memorial Institute began to receive additional funding for research and development from The Haloid Company, now known as the Xerox Corporation, of Rochester, NY. At this time, the lab work became oriented in the direction of photocopy applications—the prime interest of The Haloid Company. In 1948, The Haloid Company won the interest of the U.S. Army Signal Corps and in mid-1948, the Signal Corps began sponsoring a project on continuous-tone electrostatic electrophotography.

Beginning in 1950 with the Xerox Corporation's debut of the first commercial xerographic copier, new products began to come on the market frequently. Xerox's first copier consisted of units for charging xerographic plates, a camera for exposing the plate, a device for developing with powder, and a unit for heat fixing the image. In 1954, Young and Grieg of the Radio Corporation of America (RCA) announced a modified form of xerography, known as Electrofax. In 1958, the 3M Company introduced an electrophotographic process utilizing persistent conductivity (a concept first reported by H.P. Kallman of the Signal Corps) in combination with electrolytic development. The process was first used in a microfilm reader-printer.

In 1960 Xerox introduced its 914 copier. Its successors, the 720 and 1000, are similar but faster. Then, in 1963, Xerox introduced its 813 copier, a smaller desktop copier. Just one year later, Xerox introduced the 2400, a fast copier-duplicator. This was followed by the 3600, which operated at a speed of 60 copies per minute, and the 4000, which was capable of copying on both sides of a piece of paper. In 1970, IBM came on the scene with its Copier I, which used an organic photoconductor. Two years later, IBM came out with the Copier II. Companies have continued to come out with new and improved products; however, the basic technology of xerography has remained the same. In the late 1960s and early 1970s, the first color copiers, such as 3M's Color in Color, entered the market. 3M's release was followed by competitive products that established the use of color within the formerly black-and-white market. Xerox introduced its color copier, the 6500, in 1973, and Canon announced its Canon T machine in 1978. All these approaches had two things in common. The mentioned color copiers were based on a three-color concept and, therefore, used three toners. Furthermore, they used a system of lenses, filters, and light to reproduce the original image. As late as 1988, when Kodak released its ColorEdge copier, manufacturers used three toners and a light/lens system. Color copier technology, however, changed dramatically in the same year with Canon's introduction of the CLC-1. The CLC-1, which was further developed to the CLC 500, used four toners (including black), and used laser imaging technology.

Because copiers as well as laser printers employ related technologies, it is not surprising that the historical development of laser printing technology shows some parallels with copiers. Xerox was the first to enter the market with its 300 dpi laser printer in 1978. Xerox adjusted and modified its copier concept and released this laser printer under the number 9700; it was based on the electrophotographic process. Although every manufacturer added some unique features to their product or changed the print engine to enhance the performance, the concept remained the same throughout further developments.

The landmark year in the history of laser printers was 1983. In 1983, Canon introduced the LBP-CX, which was an affordable and reliable desktop 300 dpi laser printer. Canon's inventions were adopted by Hewlett-Packard and sold in its HP laser printers. With Apple's 1985 introduction of its Laserwriter, another important step in the history of output devices was made. Apple did not make any significant changes to the printing process but Apple's Laserwriter was the first

PostScript printer. During the ensuing years, a large number of manufacturers have entered the market, such as Apple, Canon, Lexmark, Xerox, and Texas Instruments.

Some results of the competitive atmosphere are cheaper prices, improvements in performance, and speed. While PostScript established itself as a de facto standard since the mid-1980s, manufacturers accomplished significant improvements in terms of output addressability. Within 10 years the standard output addressability of 300 dpi doubled to 600 dpi. Lexmark's Optra series, however, released in 1995, offers an output addressability of 1200 dpi. As far as the number of copies is concerned, Xerox's Docutech set the benchmark. Released in 1990 with an output speed of 135 pages per minute, Xerox's Docutech was up to 10 times faster than previous output devices.

The achievements in electrophotography not only have improved the performance of laser printers, but also have added color. Due to technological advances, laser printers were able to provide the user with the four process colors cyan, magenta, yellow, and black. While Apple's Laserwriter or Hewlett-Packard's Laserjet are black-and-white output devices, Indigo's E-Print 1000, Agfa's Chromapress, and Xeikon's DCP 1 are able to print the four process colors. Because they utilize the four process colors, these output devices are referred to as digital printing devices.

Both Indigo's E-Print and Xeikon's DCP-1 were announced in 1993. Whereas the Indigo provides the operator with an addressability of 800 dpi and liquid toner, the DCP-1 (now the DCP-32D) is 600 dpi and uses dry toner. It should be noted that the Indigo is a combination of electrophotographic and traditional printing technology because of its use of an offsetting blanket. The high demand for color output put pressure on the competing manufacturer. Canon reacted to the market needs with its CLC 900 and CLC 1000. In the meantime, Xerox had entered the arena with products based on alliances with Fuji and Scitex.

Recent products indicate that the trend is to merge copier and printer technologies. This trend is supported by the close relation of the technologies and it was the answer to the demands of the market for affordable, flexible, yet high-quality color output.

Technology

Copiers and laser printers use a similar technology to reproduce images. Because of the close relation and the number of similarities, it becomes more and more difficult to differentiate properly. However, there are distinct differences and some limitations that might apply to one, but not to the other technology. A copier will reproduce an original (whether or not it is a halftone) to the best of its capabilities. A laser printer, on the contrary, must rasterize the image. Consequently, the source for a laser printer is a digital file. Although both technologies are combined into copier/printer in recent products such as Canon's CLC 800, this discussion divides the toner-based output devices strictly into four categories:

- Laser printer, black-and-white
- Laser printer, color
- Copier, black-and-white
- Copier, color

Laser printer, black-and-white

Toner-based laser printers use electrophotography, often referred to as xerography. The core of this process is a revolving drum or belt that is coated with a photoconductive material such as selenium. This photoconductor drum is uniformly charged prior to its exposure by a laser or light-emitting diodes. During the exposure, the laser eliminates the charge on the drum in the non-image areas. In other words, the laser transfers the image information onto the photoconductor drum. For this purpose, the laser beam needs the appropriate commands to decide which part must be exposed and which part must not. The required information for controlling the laser is provided by a print controller, such as a Raster Image Processor, that can interpret image information stored in PostScript format and send it to the printer. After exposure, an electrical charge remains in the image area and attracts the applied toner, which has the opposite charge. At this point the drum carries a copy of the image. Finally the image is fused onto the paper with heat and pressure. At the end of the transfer process, the drum is cleaned and recharged.

A typical imaging workflow would involve scanning the original artwork, processing the scanned image with image manipulation software, and outputting to a laser printer. Like any traditional printing process, a laser printer has only two possibilities, either it applies toner to the paper or it does not. Therefore, originals have to be converted into halftones prior to their reproduction with a laser printer. The quality of the printed result depends on the number of gray levels that should be reproduced, the chosen screen frequency, and the output addressability of the laser printer.

The higher the screen frequency, the fewer levels of gray one will get with a given output addressability. Consequently, the two possibilities to work around this obstacle are to either increase the output addressability or decrease the screen frequency. Recalling the fact that the number of gray levels is determined by the number of dots in a halftone cell, one can see the relation between screen frequency and levels of gray. The finer the screen ruling, the fewer number of dots reside in each halftone cell. Resulting from this ratio, fewer levels of gray can be rendered.

By applying the above equation, the limitations of an output device can be calculated. If a laser printer with an addressability of 600 dpi has to handle 256 levels of gray, the screen ruling is limited to 38 lines per inch (lpi). One might be surprised by the low screen ruling, but the key is that 256 levels of gray are not always necessary. Often fewer levels of gray are enough to render an image.

Even more important is a limitation given by PostScript. PostScript can only create 256 levels of gray and ignores everything that exceeds this number. Even with an output addressability of 2400 dpi, a PostScript device will only render 256 levels of gray. The same is valid in terms of screen frequency. If the screen frequency is reduced to a coarse pattern, the number of gray levels that can be achieved is limited to 256. Two unwanted effects tend to appear if not enough levels of gray can be reproduced. They are known as posterization and banding. Both occur if the output device cannot render sufficient levels of gray to ensure a smooth transition from one gray level to another. Banding, however, might also be caused by the deficiencies of the motor that operates the print engine.

Focusing on output quality, one will be confronted with the term "resolution." Resolution is the ability of an output device to render detail. Although resolution mainly depends upon the sampling rate of the used scanner and the chosen reproduction size, the laser printer becomes involved if it comes down to output. The gain of a high-resolution scan might be lost because the amount of information exceeds the rendering capabilities of the laser printer. At this point the screen frequency plays an important role. If one makes a high-resolution scan to enlarge an original but still wants to keep a high screen frequency, the laser writer will render the image to the best of its capabilities. In other words, a high-resolution scan might result in a large file that slows down the output process but does not necessarily enhance the image quality.

Output addressability has an important impact on how good or bad images can be rendered. The output addressability, which is a measure of how many marks an output device can make within a linear inch, is determined by the spot size the laser beam can create and the size of the toner particle.

After receiving the necessary commands from the control unit, the laser exposes the photoconductor drum. If the laser spot has a large diameter, the addressability will decrease. If the laser spot's diameter is small, the addressability increases. A 20-micron spot, for example, equals a two-percent dot at a screen ruling of 200 lpi or a one-percent dot at a screen ruling of 150 lpi. Conversely, a three-percent dot at 200 lpi has a size of 25 microns and at 150 lpi, 33 microns. However, the smallest laser spot size is not always the better choice. To create a solid black, the neighboring spots need to overlap. For that purpose a specific size is required.

But the appropriate spot size has to be chosen carefully. If the spot size is too small, one will not achieve solid blacks; however, if the spot size is too large, the resulting overlap might cause a loss of gray values. Unfortunately, there are no rules for the "right" spot size, and each manufacturer has his own philosophy about the optimum spot size. Some recommend the inverse of the addressability, others tend to a value between two times the inverse of the addressability and the square root of two times the inverse of the addressability.

Nevertheless, the most important part is still the mark on the paper, which is caused by the toner. It is basically the size of the toner and the control over the toner spread that determines how many marks within a linear inch a laser printer can create. To achieve an output addressability of 1200 dpi, Lexmark decreased the particle size of the used toner to 8 microns. These 8 microns are a fraction of the size of previous toner. Assuming that a 600 dpi laser printer has a toner particle size of 16–24 microns, one can see that the particle size limits the output addressability as well. Moreover, at higher screen frequencies, single toner particles might account for variations in tone value.

Closely related to the size of the toner particle is the control of the toner transfer. In order to achieve good halftones, the toner spread has to be kept in narrow tolerances, and the thickness of the toner layer should be stable. The finer the toner particles are, the more difficult it is to control their spread. As a result of uncontrolled toner spread, the image might look brittle.

Recalling the electrophotographic process, one could see that toner is applied to the exposed photoconductor drum, utilizing the fact that opposite charges attract each other. In addition to the problems already mentioned, charge voltage decay can affect the output. Due to the time delay between charging and exposing the photoconductor drum as well as between exposure and toning, the electrical charge might not be consistent. These inconsistencies in the electrical charge might lead to drop-outs, which affect the image quality. Some electrophotographic devices have difficulty with large areas of solids or with tints and gradations.

Laser printer, color

Color laser printers face the same problems as their little black-and-white brothers. Even worse, with the addition of color, the reproduction of halftones becomes more difficult. A decrease in output speed is based on the fact that for each process color, one revolution of the photoconductor drum is necessary. Consequently, a four-color image requires four revolutions, whereas a black-and-white reproduction is printed in a single pass. The imaging process is the same as for black-and-white laser printers. However, each color is "painted" on the photoconductor drum separately. In the next process step, the appropriate toner is applied and transferred. The photoconductor drum is cleaned, recharged, and exposed to the next color of this particular image.

As far as the transfer process of the toner is concerned, two concepts are available. Either the single colors are sampled on an intermediate drum or belt and transferred to the paper all together, or each color is transferred directly to the paper, which remains in a fixed position until the imaging process is completed.

The additional problems that occur within the imaging process are similar to those of the lithographic printing process. In addition to the issues of addressability and screen ruling, the imaging process requires the highest accuracy in terms of registration and screen angles. If a proper registration cannot be maintained or if the screen angles of the process colors are not correct, the printed image will feature obvious misregistrations and an unwanted moiré pattern.

Furthermore, the toner used will have a major influence on the image quality. The toner particle size affects the graininess of the image. In addition, the toner and its distribution determine the color gamut that can be covered. Color toners are translucent and act as filters. Often, those translucent color toners are based on polyester particles that are mixed with iron-bearing carrier particles. The iron-bearing carrier particles are necessary to maintain the toner quality of being electrically charged. Colored toner particles vary in size, but an average size is approximately 12 microns. High-quality images require small particle size to increase the resolution and to decrease the graininess. Small particles, however, are difficult to control. If the amount of toner cannot be kept stable, varying toner film thicknesses will occur, which results in changing color reproduction from one print to the next. Moreover, light-scattering effects that are caused by the particles as well as surface modifications due to the fusing process make the color output difficult to predict. One approach to minimizing the problems of colored toner particles is the use of liquid toners. The drawback of this technology is the handling of the liquid carrier component, which has to be recovered somehow.

To avoid misregistration or an uneven distribution of toner, all mechanical components should be adjusted with high precision.

Copier, black-and-white

Today's copiers are both copier and printer. Therefore, most copiers utilize electrophotography. As a result, copiers have to struggle with the same restrictions as laser printers. Earlier models, however, did not rely on a laser but a light/lens system to expose and discharge the photoconductor drum. An original was placed on a glass plate and exposed to light. The reflecting light was projected on the photoconductor drum by a system of lenses. Similar to the laser printer concept, the toner was applied to the photoconductor drum and the image finally fused onto the paper.

Some manufacturers used a technology known as electrostatic technology, which is based on charging the paper stock directly. To ensure a secure imaging process, specially coated paper is necessary. Both concepts have unique drawbacks that add to those already described. Using light and optical means to copy an original, one depends completely upon the quality of the optical unit. If the lens system is not able to resolve sufficient image detail, the copy of the original will lack important image information. In addition, the original's substrate causes light absorbency, which leads to darker copies. Copies of continuous tone originals, which are captured by the optical unit but not rasterized result in poor output because the copier either applies toner or does not apply toner.

As far as the electrostatic process is concerned, one should be aware of the fact that certain areas of the stock may not accept the charge properly, which might cause drop-outs and less-than-solid fills in, in some parts of the image.

Copier, color

Because today's color copiers have the same considerations as discussed for color laser printers, this section provides an overview of the earlier color copier technology. Most of the early color copiers were three-color toner devices. By incorporating appropriate color filters into the light/lens system, the manufacturer achieved the separation of the original's color into the process colors cyan, magenta, and yellow. Three successive exposures through the filters exposed three images—one for each color—onto the photoconductor drum. Prior to the transfer of the image from the drum to the paper, the right toner was applied. The transfer of the image to the paper took place either directly or by using an intermediate belt or drum.

It was the missing fourth color that accounted for the major disadvantage of this approach. Black areas of the original were reproduced as muddy brown, and shadow lines tended to lose their sharpness. Although modern color copier technology compensates for those deficiencies and gives better color accuracy, the new color copiers face the same problems as color laser printers.

Toner-based printing

The first forms of toners were used in 1938 when Chester Carlson and Otto Kornei performed their first experiments with electrophotography. These experiments used a "powder" to transform printed images to a paper sheet. These experiments were conducted from 1944 until 1948. In 1948, E. N. Wise, at the Battelle Memorial Institute, Columbus, Ohio, discovered cascade development and a two-component triboelectric developer, and forever changed the way quick copies and reproductions would be made.

In 1948, the Battelle Memorial Institute teamed up with US Army Signal Corps Laboratories and The Xerox Corporation (which was then known as the The Haloid Company) to research electrophotography. In 1950, Xerox released the product of these experiments, the first xerographic reproduction equipment, to the public. The equipment consisted of units to charge xerographic plates, a camera to expose them, a unit for heat-fixing the image, and a device for developing with powder. Since the introduction of this equipment, toner has become one of the most widely used reproduction vehicles. A toner consists of the reaction product of resin particles containing hydroxyl or acid groups and an alkylene-glycidyl methacrylate polymer; pigment particles; and a wax component. The toner has stable triboelectrical characteristics for extended time periods and there is an improved dispersion of the resin and wax. There are three major groups of toners: dual component, mono component, and liquid. Dual component is the most common type of toner used today.

Dual-component toner

Dual-component toners are made up of two distinctive parts, toner and carrier beads. There are three major ways of developing dual-component toners, the most common of these is cascade development. It is based on "triboelectrification," which is the process of exciting toner particles by causing an electrical charge through the use of friction. The triboelectrification process causes excited toner particles to cling to a beaded carrier. Toner is 3 to 30 µm in size, depending on the desired resolution of the printed image.

The higher the resolution, the smaller the toner particles needed. Carrier beads are about 70 to 400 µm in diameter and usually are a metallic or magnetic compound. Carrier beads consist of a blend of organically treated inorganic fine powder that acts as a developer and lubricant, while providing releasability. Because the toner particles are insulative, toner images on the photoreceptor are easily transferred electrostatically to plain paper. These particles are small, charged, pigment particles, usually "powders," which triboelectrically attached themselves to much larger carrier beads. A single carrier bead can hold multiple toner particles. The name "carrier bead" comes from the idea of "carrying" the fine toner particles to the latent electrostatic image where the toner is stripped from the carrier, thereby developing the image. Carrier beads are designed to be large enough to prevent the developer (toner and carrier) from contaminating the air and producing dirt, yet they are small enough to provide excellent flow characteristics and high-resolution images. In most cases, the carrier beads are magnetic materials, which are specially coated with a polymeric film to provide the proper triboelectric properties for attracting toner. The magnetic material can then be transported from one location to another through the use of magnetic fields. The following methods are used to adhere dual-component toner particles to a charged material, until it is torn away from that material, primarily by the competing electrostatic force exerted by the electrostatic latent image.

Cascade development

Cascade development is the method most widely used for document copying. Commonly called cascade developer, because in use the mixture is poured or "cascaded" over the inclined surface bearing an electrostatic latent image.

Magnetic brush development

In the case of the magnetic brush developer, the carrier is approximately the same size as the toner, rather than being much larger. High-quality line-art images can be produced by this development method.

Continuous tone development

In the case of continuous tone development, the charged density within the electrostatic image varies from point to point. The density of the developed image is a result of the amount of charge at each point on the surface to be printed. The material most commonly used for this process is ball-milled charcoal (carbon black). Ball-milled charcoal cannot be fixed by heat or by solvents. Such toners are described as powder-cloud toners and they are generally charged by turbulent impact of the particles with some conducting wall or nozzle, through which the powder-cloud is blown on its way to the development zone and fixed by pressure in some cases.

Dual-component toner is used in over 90 percent of the current xerographic copiers and digital printers. Printers such as the Xeikon and Xerox Docutech use dual-component toners.

Mono-component toner

Mono-component toners differ from dual-component toners in that they do not require the use of carrier beads for development. There are several ways to charge mono-component toners: induction, contacting, corona charging, ion beam, and traveling electric fields. The easiest and most commonly used of these is induction charging. Through induction charging, a conducting particle sitting on a negative surface becomes negatively charged.

Because the opposite charges repel each other, the negatively-charged particle is repelled by the negative plate and drawn to the positive plate. Through this process, particles lose their negative charges and become positively charged. Once toner particles become charged, they can be transferred to the substrate. This change in charge causes toner to move in a direction opposite to a magnetic roller, forming a conductive path. It is then attracted to the latent image and adhered to the substrate by a photoreceptor and Coulomb force. Fusing then bonds it to the substrate.

Liquid toner

Liquid toners are comprised of toner and solvent. The use of solvent instead of developer caused them to be liquid instead of solid. Liquid toner solvents are non-conductive and primarily made up of thermoplastic resin particles, which are suspended in a saturated hydrocarbon. In many respects liquid development is related to or considered with powder-cloud development. In both cases, freely moving charged toner moves under the action of the electrostatic field of the image. Currently Indigo is the only major user of liquid toners. Their printing devices account for over 90 percent of the liquid toner currently being used. Indigo's liquid toner consists of 1 to 2 μm toner particles suspended in a highly refined kerosene known as isopar. The isopar acts as the controlling agent of the solution by carrying the charge placed on it.

Toner charge

The magnitude and polarity of toner charge is critical. The charge on the toner must have the correct polarity or no development will occur. The magnitude of the charge is also critical because the development force is directly proportional to toner charge. Development will occur only when the electrostatic development force exceeds the adhesive force. In many cases, the carrier beads are coated with a polymer that transfers the amount of charge to the toner. Carrier coatings and toner materials can be selected from a tribo series, which is a listing of polymers in order of charging polarity. The tribo series lists polymers according to charge. Polymers appearing higher on the list will charge positively with respect to any polymer lower on the list. The total amount of charge exchange between the toner and the carrier is a function of the total number of toner particles contained on each carrier bead.

Toner concentration

The image density is highly dependent on the concentration of toner within a given area. Image density is not completely determined by charge because the developability of a given developer is dependent on environmental conditions such as humidity, and temperature. Toner concentration may vary from .5 percent to approximately 2 percent by weight, depending upon a number of chemical and reproduction variables. Toner concentration is under the control of the operator, and is usually run at the highest level of tolerance the machines specifications will allow. The toner transfer efficiency of printers and copiers is 85 percent. The 15 percent scraped off the photoreceptor is waste. In the USA, around 21 million lbs of waste toner is disposed of annually. It is non-toxic and inert, so it is put into landfills. It resists ultraviolet light, and, being black, is unsightly. Economic incentive to recycle toner is minimal; due to this, under one percent of US waste toner is recycled. Because of low volume and unreliability, recycling options are local and limited.

Xerographic toner

The toners normally used for xerography contain fusible organic polymers, which resist aqueous metal-etching solutions. Xerographic toner images can be transferred from the selenium plate to a thin metal layer laminated to a thick insulating base. The exposed metal can be etched away chemically, leaving a pattern of metal under the toner, which can then be removed. The xerographic toner can be transferred from a selenium plate, where the energy in the latent image is used directly to produce the final print. The initial toner deposit can be used as a sticking or an anti-sticking agent to transfer more toner. A toner with catalytic properties may be used to cause a color-forming reaction, or the toner may be used as a chemical resist, to permit the selective etching of metals.

Dye sublimation, dye diffusion

The U.S. Army Map Service was the first to implement photo-mechanical off-press proofing during WWII. The overlay system, known as "Watercote," was developed by Direct Reproduction Corporation for map makers who needed to check color and linework but did not have the time to prepare plates and printed samples. Due to Watercote's success, more experiments were done, which resulted in a system, which was not widely accepted, called the "Potter-Cushing-Pitman method of quick color proofing before etching." A more successful off-press proofing system was the OSACHROME overlay which was introduced by Ozalid Corporation (GAF). Dyes, which were very unstable at that time, were carried on three diazo-coated films mounted in register over a black print on paper. In 1960 a more stable system known as Color-Key, in which the dyes were substituted with pigments, was introduced by the 3M Company.

In 1971 Dupont introduced the Cromalin system as an integral or composite proof in which color layers were laminated together to form a single sheet. In the analog market of the 1990s, Cromalin's competitors include the 3M Matchprint, Enco Pressmatch, Fuji Color Art, Agfa AgfaProof, DuPont WaterProof, Kodak Signature, and others. These competitors were also the first dominant producers of digital color proofing devices. The dye sublimation process was originally used for applying color print patterns onto fabrics ranging from custom t-shirts to industrial bolts.

In the traditional prepress environment, analog proofs were made from the films produced by an imagesetter. As the industry moves to the digital prepress environment, a problem arises. If the department uses a computer-to-plate system or other filmless printing technologies such as digital presses, analog proofing is not an option. Therefore, Direct Digital Color Proofing (DDCP) systems are being implemented where film is being eliminated.

The first aim of the direct digital color proofing devices was to produce halftone structure such as the screen ruling, dot shape, and rosette pattern similar to the analog proofing systems. In 1987, DuPont teamed up with Xerox to announce the DX System. But, after two years, the companies decided that there would not be a demand for the product with such a high selling price.

DuPont, however, in 1991 introduced the Digital Matchprint. The following year, Kodak released their Approval System. All had considerably high price tags that opened the market for other less expensive technologies such as continuous tone inkjet and dye sublimation devices.

As with all technology, there is a compromise between quality and price. How much is good enough? On the design and composition side, less expensive devices can be used to produce rough proofs in the early stages of design. For photographic-quality output, inkjet and thermal transfer printers are not the best choice. Laser devices tend to produce saturated colors that cannot be reproduced on press. Dye-sublimation and continuous tone inkjet printers are becoming the DDCP systems of choice.

Inkjet and dye-sublimation devices are available in a wide range of price and capability. The moderate- to high-priced proofers are suitable for advertising agencies and design firms, service bureaus/ trade shops, small-to-medium sized commercial printers, and publication printers. The 3M (now Imation) Rainbow was one of the first low-cost dye sublimation digital color printers. It was targeted at companies with prepress applications; therefore 3M refers to the

Rainbow as a digital color proofer instead of a digital color printer. Since the Rainbow's introduction, several other manufacturers have introduced dye-sublimation proofers.

The competitors in the digital color proofer market are similar to the analog color proofer market—DuPont and Screen, as well as Tektronix and Seiko. As of 1996, there are at least 40 different digital color proofers available. The Kodak Approval and the Polaroid PolaProof are the only ones that can make halftone proofs using the same screening algorithms as those used later to make the film. All other systems make continuous-tone proofs. The Imation Rainbow is one of the first desktop digital proofers on the market to become the industry benchmark for continuous-tone digital color proofing. Although it cannot make halftones, it can simulate the look of the printed product.

Large advertising agencies and design firms were one of the first markets to adopt the dye sublimation technology. The rich, vibrant, photo-realistic color images were well suited for scatter proofs and comps as well as layouts that were subject to multiple revisions. The acceptance of digital color proofing relies on the color characterization and calibration of the output device. If the device is not calibrated to the printing process, it is impossible to simulate the actual printed product. The better DDCP systems can be adjusted to meet the printing process in use and increase in the reliability of the devices, the better DDCP will be accepted for contract proofs in the printing industry.

If kept in control, dye sublimation printers are ideal for the printing and publishing industry as well as for the home, business, or education user with needs such as presentation graphics. Photographers, desktop publishers, and designers were among the first to incorporate the digital color printer into their workflow. Dye-sublimation prints are unusually bright, brilliant, and vibrant, and are well suited for exhibition or fine art prints. Dye-sublimation printers have been designed for publishers and photographers as well as the scientific fields. Dye sublimation does a superb job of bringing out the details in an information-dense image for complex engineering and scientific analysis. Large-format printers have become useful for satellite data and other bitmapped or scanned images. The lower quality dye-sub printers may have a tendency to "band," producing pronounced delineations between color and shading gradations, and not a smooth continuous tone. To ease the burden of expensive dye-sublimation consumables, some manufacturers are producing digital printing devices that are capable of both dye-sublimation and wax thermal prints. Wax thermal consumables are much cheaper than dye-sublimation consumables; therefore, inexpensive proofs can be made for positions and content checking. For higher quality desktop output, the device can produce dye-sublimation proofs.

Dye sublimation

A web of ribbon the width of the page carries blocks of the special set of dyes coated on a plastic film. The ribbon is sometimes referred to as the color donor ribbon because it contains the coloring agents. The coloring agents, which are coated onto the plastic film, are consecutive panels of cyan, magenta, yellow, and (sometimes) black dyes. A three-color ribbon containing only cyan, magenta, and yellow produces a black by overlaying all three coloring agents; this saves time and money although the black areas of the image may appear brownish. The transfer roll passes across the print heads. This is a multipass process in which each block of CMYK on the ribbon passes beneath the same print heads.

The linear thermal head contains many resistors—an electronic component that resists the flow of current. The resistors act like heaters when the current passes through them. The resistors get hotter as the current increases. The resister array in the dye-sublimation printer instantly heats up to transfer a variable spot of dye from the ribbon to a receiver substrate. The spot size is based on the pixel value for that spot. The print heads are warmed to a varying intensity to heat the dyes on the carrier ribbon. Once the dyes are hot enough to vaporize, they diffuse onto the paper's surface. The process in which the dye goes from a solid form to a gas form without going through an intervening liquid phase is known as sublimation.

The heat source is constructed of rigid elements but because a gas is formed, a continuous tone image results. The 2400 heating elements are a tightly focused heat source and are capable of precise temperature variations. The dyes from one heating element diffuse through the gap to the paper, blending with neighboring dots to eliminate the distinctly visible dots that plague other printing technologies. The dyes blend to create pure colors devoid of dot patterns. Each heating element in the thermal head produces 256 different temperatures, and the hotter the temperature, the more dye is transferred from the transfer roll to the paper.

The transfer process requires high heat—as much as 400 degrees Celsius. The different color hues are formed according to the amount of heat applied to the dye. The diffusion processes make it easy to control the process of transferring any specified amount of dye (from none up to virtually the entire amount on the ribbon). The process has low contrast at low densities, allowing precise control at low densities where the eye is sensitive.

The resolution of most dye-sublimation printers is 300 dpi, which one would expect is relatively coarse. Because of the diffusion process, the quality is close to photographic. Increased resolutions do have an effect in text and in line art areas.

The paper is a coated thermal-dye-receptive paper capable of absorbing the vapor dyes, which diffuse onto the surface on contact. The paper is similar to photographic paper in thickness; transparent material is also available. The coating on the paper is a polyester resin coating. The receiver has the same paper base as Kodak's photographic paper, except that a plastic receiver emulsion is placed on the base instead of a silver halide emulsion.

Dye-sublimation color photographic images appear quite sharp due to the diffusion process. Line art and text are often soft or fuzzy on some proofers; therefore dye sublimation proofers are not usually used for contract proofs. The advantages of dye sublimation printers include convenience and flexibility. The consumables are very expensive but it is cost-effective for photo proofing. The dyes used are capable of a color gamut that exceeds that of photography.

The disadvantages include cost, output speed, and the need for special photo-like coated paper. The cost per print is unaffected by the amount of color on a page because the process uses a full block of transfer ribbon for each page printed. The media and the equipment are both very expensive. Producing text in small point sizes with good character shapes and smooth edges is a problem. Fine-line detail like hairlines printed perpendicular to the paper path have inherent problems because it is difficult to quickly heat and cool individual pixels to produce fine levels of detail under certain circumstances.

Improvements on the horizon include better lightfastness and better quality, although the devices will probably remain at the 300 dpi level. Higher resolution is not particularly important for continuous-tone rendering. Machines to serve new markets include the dual-technology devices that can produce thermal-wax transfer and dye-sublimation output. Venders are introducing large format printers as well. Dye sublimation printer units range in price from $5,000 to $25,000.

New digital color systems

Agfa announced Chromapress in September, 1993. It is actually the Xeikon DC-1 which became the DCP-32D. It is an integrated computer-to-paper system for on-demand, affordable, high-quality color printing. Chromapress is said to be a complete solution, incorporating prepress through reprographic technologies to support the production of timely, cost-effective color documents. This "systems" philosophy extends from the creative concept to PostScript files and on into printed and finished documents, and it embraces the critical ownership issues of training, service, and long-term support.

The Chromapress system is a "turn-key solution," which means that Agfa sells a package including front end, support, and consumables. It is one of the systems, if not the only system, which is based on

Macintosh-based software. The Chromapress software is designed in a workflow metaphor with divisions for job tickets, job scheduling, input queuing, color management, imposition, multiprocessor RIPping, and automatic duplexed printing.

Chromapress's core technologies are evolutionary. The print output engine, for example, is an extension of the electrophotographic concept—xerography, to some. Some team members worked on Agfa's first laser printer, the P400, which at its introduction was 400 dpi and the fastest PostScript printer available. Chromapress also incorporates color management, automatic imposition, job tracking, multi-tasking RIP technology, and other components critical to productivity.

Chromapress consists of four major components: system and server software, RIP ("raster image processor"), and the output print engine. Each element is specifically designed to support the system, and the integrated solution is said to be easily assimilated within existing prepress systems. Input is accepted as PostScript files, providing compatibility with a broad range of front-end systems. Job files may be entered on-line with direct connections through standard network interfaces, or off-line via a variety of storage media, as with all digital printers.

Input jobs are passed to a press server. This unit uses specialized software and off-the-shelf Sun hardware to integrate prepress and communications functions, providing complete, centralized system control. Jobs flow from interconnected systems and networks into the server's print queue, where they can be tracked, reordered, or canceled.

Both the print server operator and/or the original job creator are provided with easy-to-use job production controls to specify variables such as color management, paper type, single- vs. double-sided printing, page order for multi-page documents, and web cut-off length. The press server uses this information to process jobs into RIP-ready imposed files. Software automatically notifies the user of any production errors before the high-speed print engine receives the job. The press server software also supports the industry-standard OPI "Open Prepress Interface" file server specification. This allows high-resolution image data to remain in a single location, dramatically reducing network traffic, improving front-end system throughput, and assuring data is readily available to the high-speed RIP.

Jobs from the print server are routed to the RIP over a high-speed SCSI interface. This Server/RIP interface, combined with centralized file storage, assures that adequate data volumes are delivered to the print unit. This is said to minimize the communications bottleneck normally encountered in short-run printing systems that work with high-resolution color images.

The PostScript-compatible RIP was specifically designed as a high-speed, multi-processor, multitasking architecture that supports simultaneous job processing. The RIP also incorporates custom "halftone" screening technology developed for the print engine's variable density imaging technology. Each pixel can have 64 gray levels by varying the amount of toner deposited on the paper. This increases the available output color range while maintaining image sharpness.

Rapid RGB to CMYK color conversions are supported within the RIP as well, eliminating the requirement for pre-separated color files. Color management is also integrated. Remote diagnostics are built into the RIP, allowing rapid hardware and software analysis from technical support as well as "instant" software upgrades.

Complete, processed jobs flow from the RIP to the print unit over a dedicated, high-speed video interface. Dual job, full-page buffers within the Print Unit use high-speed RAM to maximize page transfer rates from the RIP. The print unit includes a high-speed, four-color, perfecting digital web press. This uses a 600 dpi, variable dot density (64 gray levels) electrophotographic output engine. Throughput is 17.5 duplex oversized A3 pages per minute, 12.6 x 17.9 or 35 A4 duplexed pages per minute, 8.9 x 12.6. This is equivalent to 1,050 and 2,100 pages per hour, respectively. A note about speeds: most laser printers report their speeds in 8.5 x 11 inch sheets per minute, single sided. Since the Chromapress prints both sides at the same time you could say that it is printing 70 A4 (close to 8.5 x 11) pages per minute.

Roll-fed paper

The print engine uses eight individual color units to simultaneously image both sides of the paper web for perfecting or duplex printing. Each set consists of an imaging cylinder and a tone area. After the cylinder has been charged, it transfers the charged image to the paper, which immediately picks up toner. This provides high throughput speeds that are unaffected by the number of colors applied or by duplex printing.

Web "roll fed" paper used within Chromapress means long print runs—up to four hours with lighter paper weights—about 4,200 duplexed 8.5 x 11 sheets. Agfa emphasizes that there is no sheet feeding mechanism to jam, adjust, or maintain. Further, the system automatically compensates for different paper weight, colors, and finishes without manual adjustments. Fifty-four to 135 pound paper can be handled; paper rolls cannot be changed on the fly. Maximum roll width is 12.6 inches.

Web rolled paper is slightly less expensive than sheeted paper. Many paper grades, including coated stock, are available. As the paper leaves the roll and enters the imaging cabinet, it is charged in order to better accept the image and the toner. If the machine is stopped, the paper in the machine loses its charge and thus the first ten or so pages of every run are blank.

The print engine images the web of paper by means of organic photoconductor (OPC) drums using arrays of light-emitting diodes (LEDs) whose average life expectancy exceeds five years. The core LED technology is installed in thousands of Agfa black-and-white laser printers. Chromapress incorporates sophisticated monitoring and feedback mechanisms, insuring consistent light output and, consequently, color—across the page, from page to page, and day to day. The stationary LEDs and continuous-paper web are said to ensure excellent inter-color and inter-page registration. LEDs do not emit coherent light as typical lasers do. They are thus harder to focus. Rather than using a scanning laser beam, Xeikon has placed an array of 7,400 LEDs, evenly spaced at 600 dpi, close to the paper and each LED is responsible for one dot of imaged output.

Agfa developed the specialized toners and discrete LED intensities used in Chromapress to deliver variable printed densities inside each printed pixel, which allows it to achieve a claimed 2,400 dpi and 150 lpi equivalent image quality, which is said to maximize the available color range and image acuity. Dry toners are instantly fused using a non-contact, oil-free process. If the paper web stops, the fuser is immediately pulled out of the way.

The paper web is automatically cut to size with an on-line, automatic sheeter, delivering output to a stacker for use as-is, or for subsequent finishing operations. Every sheet could be cut to a different width. Chromapress includes advanced temperature and humidity control systems. Paper is conditioned prior to and following printing, ensuring dimensional stability and process consistency. It is charged prior to LED exposure. The entire print engine is housed in a sealed cabinet about six feet high, six feet wide, and two feet deep.

The print unit operates in office surroundings. Toner is replenished using sealed, dust free, recyclable containers and the non-toxic OPC imaging drums are recyclable as well. All serviceable areas are readily accessible. Chromapress is self-contained and emits no odors, maintaining a clean working environment. Routine maintenance is performed by minimally skilled personnel. About 30 minutes per day of routine maintenance is required, usually cleaning corotron wires.

One of the most important Chromapress advances is the way workflow impact is addressed. Any high-speed, color, demand printing system requires some new skill sets and generally necessitates broader responsibilities for the document producer and/or new skills for machine operators. There is the ability to change a limited area of each page on the fly. This personalization can only be done to an area of about five square inches and can contain text or graphics in full-color. We see this as a major application for digital printing, but there is a lot to be done in rasterizing, bandwidth, and other technology issues in implementing it in the printing industry. The target application is in the 1 to 5,000 range.

This discussion of the Chromapress was presented to describe the first introduction of the Xeikon engine. Agfa developed a complete system to support their digital printer, linking Macintosh workstations at the creative level as well. The Chromapress was introduced at the same time as the Indigo engine.

Indigo

Indigo was founded in 1977 by Benzion "Benny" Landa, the chairman and CEO. In 1992, Indigo went public. According to *Israel Business Today* (July 23, 1993), the event that triggered the stock offering was international financier George Soros (Soros Venture Capital) buying $50 million in stock (15 percent control). After that, Indigo Graphic Systems was founded in 1992 with funding from First Boston Corporation, Toppan Printing, as well as other financial backers. The balance is held by Landa and his family.

Landa is involved in all aspects of Indigo, with special emphasis on strategic development and marketing. He holds over 100 patents, including those for ElectroInk, Indigo's unique ink technology.

Until the E-Print was introduced, Indigo was better known in the office copier market than the professional graphic arts market. It has more then 200 U.S. patents and hundreds more worldwide patents in copying technology. According to Indigo, it is hard to find a copier that doesn't include at least one Indigo patent. Just as a number of senior staff at Xeikon came from Agfa, a number of senior staff at Indigo came from Scitex.

Indigo began developing its digital press in 1983 and is reported to have invested more than 2,000 person-years and more than $150 million to bring it to market. The technology in the Indigo was under final development for at least three years before it was first introduced on June 22, 1993. The E-Print 1000 is a sheetfed digital offset press that prints four to six colors on most of the popular paper stocks at 800 dpi, 11 x 17 inches in size (A3), at 4,000 sheets per hour, at one color on one side, 67 per minute. Thus, for black-and-white work it is just about the same speed as a Xerox Docutech (135 8.5 x 11 inch pages per minute).

It stands 6'3" long at its longest point by 4' at its deepest point, taking up only 20 square feet. Compared to a traditional press, the operation is nearly soundless. Although originally marketed as a press that could accept paper stock from almost any source, the erasabilty issue, discussed below, required a pretreatment that limited the paper sources.

Paper can be coated or uncoated, varying in thickness from very light to card stocks. It can print one color on 4,000 (11 x 17) pages per hour, or 67 per minute. Up to 3,000 sheets can be loaded in the feeder, though single sheets are handled separately.

In some ways, Indigo uses the same principles as traditional offset printing, with plates, blankets, and impression cylinders and ink. The image on the plate cylinder is transferred to the blanket surface and then is "offset" to the paper held on the impression cylinder. However, in other ways the Indigo works like a copy machine, charging a cylinder and using a laser beam to create an electrophotographic image.

As a sheet is finished, it moves to the booklet maker, where booklets are automatically gathered and folded, stapled, and stacked. From the job setup, the booklet maker knows how many sheets to grab to make the booklet, whether to staple, etc. Thus, the E-Print's final product is the finished piece itself.

At the input station, the operator manipulates each individual print job by adjusting color brightness and saturation, color correction curves, and the document composition (moving individual elements of a page, adjusting imposition, or finishing).

The storage options include additional hard disks, optical disks, and Exabyte tapes. In addition the E-Print can also be on-line to a local area network so you can connect any storage system you want.

ElectroInk. Besides being able to expose and image on the fly, the machine is designed such that each revolution can create a completely different image. This is enabled by the reusable plates and by the inks (which are actually liquid toners). The 100 percent ink transfer and reusable plates allow each image to be different. In color printing, it could be the next color separation in database printing, it could be personalization of each page. In four-color printing it is the Ink Color Switcher that changes the ink color. Indigo has systems that can go from four to seven colors.

The ability to transfer 100 percent of the ink is unusual in traditional printing. This is made possible because of Indigo's patented liquid ElectroInk. The ElectroInk uses pigments similar to regular offset inks, but has two dramatic differences. First, it acts electrostatically, meaning it can be charged, and, second, it dries very quickly.

Contained in the inks is a dispersion of pigmented polymer particles ranging in size from one to two microns in size. (In contrast, the dry toners used in copy machines have an average size of eight to 15 microns.) When transferred to the blanket and heated, these polymers turn into a tacky polymeric "film."

When the ink film polymer comes in contact with the paper, it hardens instantly and peels away from the blanket. There are two interesting contrasts with traditional printing. First, with E-Print the ink does not bind with the paper as in traditional printing but laminates or coats the paper. Second, with the E-Print, 100 percent of the ink is removed with each revolution, while in conventional offset printing half of the ink is transferred to the paper and the balance stays on the blanket, to be re-inked on the next revolution.

There are several advantages to the ElectroInk technology. It allows for individualization or personalization of each page. The small particle size results in a printed product that "feels" more like offset then the raised image from copying technologies. And Indigo claims that this process results in sharper images.

According to Indigo, print from the E-Print has better edge definition or "acutance." The acutance is higher because there is no wicking or bleeding of the ink as it hits the paper, which occurs in a wet ink transfer. The dots show no feathered edges, and there is no dot gain because the ink doesn't flow onto the paper; it bonds to it.

Indigo claims that show-through to the other side of the paper is minimal for the same reason. Yet, at the same time, the ink film is so thin that it doesn't appear plastic, as with thermal proofers. Indigo explains that the ink film is thin enough to replicate the texture of the paper fibers because the ink particles are so small. The disadvantage of the ElectroInk technology is the erasability issue. In conventional printing, the ink dries by absorption, evaporation, or heat, while with the xerographic printing process the toners dry by heat or pressure fusing them into the paper. The drying process for ElectroInk is different. Figuratively speaking, the ink is "laminated" into an ink-plastic film, and then both ink and film are peeled off the blanket and applied to the paper with the help of the transfer oil. This occurs for each of the four colors.

In conventional printing, the ink binds with the paper. With ElectroInk, the ink is dried to a film for removal from the blanket before it reaches the paper. The ElectroInk does not sink into the paper, and thus it has a lower degree of adherence.

Although Indigo originally dismissed the erasability issue, saying that none of its customers, or prospects, had withdrawn from contracts on that basis, it has recognized the problem and developed a "work around" solution that increases the adherence of the ink. The solution, called "saffire," is a pretreatment of the paper with a chemical. According to company officials, this process is not unlike running the paper through a press with the water dampening on. This process may work by allowing the paper fibers to rise off the paper so the ElectroInk in the ink film stage adheres to the fibers.

Another issue in the operation of the Indigo is ink supplies. Currently only Indigo makes the ElectroInk in Japan (with Toyo Ink), North America, and Europe. The issue, of course, is that competition drives prices down. The inks can approximate SWOP (a printing standard for color reproduction) and other process color standards. The inks are made in a light mineral oil base and come in sealed cartridges many users refer to as "spray cans."

Another technology that makes the Indigo printing possible is very tight press registration. The paper is held in place on the impression cylinder throughout the imaging process for each side of the paper. Since the page remains on the cylinder as additional colors are applied, it prints one-color pages faster than two, two-color faster than three, etc.

Once all of the colors have been printed on the first side of the page, the sheet is transferred from the cylinder into the duplex buffer. Next, the trailing edge of the paper is picked up and pulled back to the impression cylinder such that the other side is presented to and retained on the impression cylinder. At this point the colors can be applied to this side of the sheet.

It is difficult to compare E-Print speeds to conventional press speeds. Conventional presses print one, two, three, or four colors at the same speed (on a multi-color press). The maximum speed of 133 A4 black-and-white pages per minute. is interestingly about the same speed as a Xerox DocuTech, which prints at 135 A4 pages per minute. But the Docutech resolution is 600 dpi and the E-Print's is 800 dpi and has the ability to print full color.

To calculate four-color pages, we need to divide the 4,000-impression rate for 11 x 17 (A3) pages by four (for four-colors), which results in 1,000 impressions per hour. For duplex four-color printing, the speed is cut in half, to 500 impressions per hour. The Mobius will be faster. Using the electronic collation and the booklet maker option enables completion of booklets without manual intervention. The imposition and the job setup specifications are input on the Sun workstation. The collation is handled in the controller during the print process.

At the end of the press the finished pieces come off either as sheets or as folded and stitched books containing a maximum 100 pages each. This is quite different from conventional sheetfed or web press-es, which print the same image over and over in succession. In the conventional press workflow, collation is performed in the bindery process, with a mechanical folder.

One of the unique issues for the Indigo press is data storage. Since all the pages for a single piece are printed together, in succession, all the information must be stored. Maintaining and utilizing all the infor-mation over and over requires a significant amount of memory and fast processing.

There is a 640 megabyte RAM buffer to store this information. If a particular job does not take up the entire 640 Mb RAM buffer, addi-tional jobs can be queued while printing proceeds on the first job. Using the booklet maker, however, requires that the entire job be stored in memory throughout the print run. An additional advantage of the RAM buffer is that it is useful in the process of personalization or customization. The elements on the page that are repeated from page to page are stored in the RAM buffer in a rasterized form. In this workflow, only the variable data has to be identified and loaded from the database in a rasterized form.

Indigo compares itself to conventional wet ink printing as well as powdered toner printing. On the wet ink side, they claim several advantages: show-through is minimized since there is no water, dot gain is virtually non-existent, and the ElectroInk is very thin and bonds to the paper. Each color is translucent. Paper shrinkage, curl, or other artifacts of wet ink printing are not a factor. Against powdered toner technology they claim a quality advantage: the 800 dpi provides excellent typographic quality. To duplex print, the sheet is released by the impression cylinder after it is printed into a duplex buffer. The trailing edge of the paper is clamped back onto the impression cylinder and the second side is printed. Each side can be printed with as many or as few colors as desired.

The printed sheet is then ejected. An optional booklet maker retains the printed sheets (up to 100 pages) and then releases them to an online folder/stapler. There is no trimming. Once again, speed is difficult to completely measure. Once rasterized, pages are sent to the Sun workstation in the printer, and about 100 pages with some photos on each can be buffered. At that point the printer operates at its full speed, printing a combination of full-color and black-and-white pages as well as some with spot color.

The list price is $400,000 for a fully-configured system (the E-Print 1000+), but with the six inks and the booklet maker it would be closer to $450,000. The automatic booklet maker is a finishing option that enables the E-Print to produce fully finished booklets of up to 100 pages. Printing, collating, folding, and stitching are carried out in a single step without intervention.

Indigo adds new digital presses

At IPEX '93, Indigo's launch of the world's first digital offset color press, the E-Print 1000, heralded the dawn of the digital printing era. At IPEX '98, with the introduction of the E-Print Pro, the UltraStream, and lower cost-per-page show that Indigo continues to innovate. Indigo launched two new digital presses, one at lower price point and the other at faster print speeds. The new E-Print Pro is priced at $249,000 and is the lowest-cost digital color press on the market, according to Indigo. The new UltraStream is purported to be the fastest digital color press available, although Xeikon disagrees. It is the fastest sheet-fed four-color digital printer.

The E-Print Pro is also purported to be the world's lowest cost digital color press, if you do not consider Canon CLC-1000 or Xerox DocuColor. Simultaneously, the company unveiled the Indigo UltraStream, which they claim is the world's fastest digital color press, if you do not consider Xeikon or its ilk. In addition to the presses, Indigo also announced new consumables plans offering the industry's lowest cost per page; however, no numbers were provided to support this claim.

The four-color E-Print Pro enables newcomers to digital color printing to enter the market with a modest capital investment and achieve profitability from relatively low volumes of short run jobs. As their businesses grow in volume or migrate to higher value digital printing work, E-Print Pro customers can trade up to the fully-featured TurboStream, making a seamless transition to the highest margin markets. E-Print Pro uses TurboStream digital front-end technology, but will not support options such as auto-duplexing, electronic collation, high definition imaging (HDI), 5th and 6th colors, personalization, and extended 36 Gb page memory. This may be a strategic error in that personalization, at least, is one of the driving forces behind digital printing.

Because it is a simplex device, the E-Print Pro will compete as an alternative to short-run color offset printing, especially the Heidelberg Quickmaster DI. Indigo's entry-level price point can now compete with the Canon CLC-1000 and the Xerox DocuColor 40. The lack of auto-duplexing and electronic collation could be a limitation. The E-Print Pro is really aimed at the Quickmaster DI.

Indigo TurboStream customers can trade up to the new UltraStream. Engineered for high-volume users, with its seven-color capability and 240 feet-per-minute process speed, the UltraStream is the most powerful, highest productivity digital press in the Indigo product family. TurboStream (the upgraded E-Print 1000) is the fastest of its kind for simplex printing and second only to the Xeikon DCP/50D for duplex printing. (The DCP/50D is capable of printing 100 8.5 x 11 duplex color impressions per minute.) In addition, at these speeds the UltraStream is unique in its seven-color printing capability, which opens new quality levels for matching colors. Estimate pricing at $550,000 for a 4-color base machine but over $600,000 with all the bells and whistles. The sheet-fed UltraStream is designed for high-volume production. It can print with up to seven-colors and is double the speed of the E-Print 1000 via a new double-size impression cylinder.

Xerox DocuColor 100 Digital Color Press

The DocuColor 100 Digital Color Press has an 18.7 inch-wide image area that can print two letter-sized images side by side—generating 100 impressions per minute (ipm) in two-sided mode. DocuColor 100 is as much as 50 percent more productive than the Xerox DocuColor 70 Digital Color Press. The DocuColor 100 is expected to accelerate the migration from offset to digital printing among commercial and in-plant printers because it delivers greater productivity and offers capabilities that enable creation of individually customized materials—enhancing the effectiveness of documents ranging from marketing brochures to catalogs. The new model has running costs of less than 20 cents per impression, two to five times less than offset run lengths of less than 500 impressions. The new DocuColor 100 is based upon the DCP/50D engine from Xeikon N.V. and uses the same proven, high-quality imaging technology as the highly successful Xerox DocuColor 70. It features Xerox-exclusive digital front-end (DFE) controllers from Scitex Corp. and Electronics for Imaging (EFI). Pricing for the base configuration begins at $550,000.

DocuColor 40 advances

Xerox Corporation has expanded its DocuColor 40 color copier/printer line, solidifying its leadership in the fast-growing market for color digital copying and printing in offices and the production environment with:

- The DocuColor 40 CP, a new model that delivers high-speed, networked copying, and printing to lower-volume production environments at a much lower cost.
- The rechristened flagship, the DocuColor 40 PRO, offers enhanced digital controllers for network connectivity.

Both models operate at up to 40 prints per minute (ppm) and include a new feature that can produce acetate transparencies at 15 ppm. The DocuColor 40 CP is a network-connected color copier/printer equipped with a newly designed digital controller manufactured to Xerox specifications by Electronics For Imaging (EFI). It is designed to provide digital walk-up copying as well as network printing for lower-volume production environments such as entry-level centralized reprographics departments, color-intensive offices, and price-sensitive print-for-pay businesses that produce an average monthly page volume of up to 30,000 prints. It is priced 20-30 percent less than the previous generation of network-connected DocuColor 40 models.

The Xerox DocuColor 40 PRO improves the price/performance of the color copier/printer system with a variety of newly updated digital controllers designed for sophisticated color document production environments where speed, color quality, and workflow are paramount and print volumes range to 100,000 pages per month. The Xerox DocuColor 40 CP with controller carries a manufacturer's suggested U.S. list price of $135,000. The stand-alone Xerox DocuColor 40 PRO copier carries a manufacturer's suggested list price of $117,000. Controllers for the PRO, which enable network print capabilities, are available from Scitex, EFI, and Splash, and range in price from $42,500 to $52,000.

Canon pioneers mid high-speed color segment

Canon U.S.A., Inc. continues its 10-year history of innovation in the color copier market with the introduction of the 24 page-per-minute CLC 2400 Color Laser Copier/Printer. The CLC 2400 features a full-color copy speed of 24 pages per minute, exceptional 400 x 400 dots-per-inch image quality with 256 gradations, a proven four-drum engine, the ability to run 110 lb index stock through the bypass, automatic duplexing, plus plug-and-play connectivity with the addition of an optional ColorPASS controller. A 5,250 sheet paper supply, first copy time of 16 seconds, and the capability to produce 11 x 17 full bleed further enhances performance. The 5,250 sheet standard paper supply includes two front-loading, user-adjustable paper drawers that accommodate paper sizes ranging from statement through ledger. Each drawer holds 500 sheets, and there is a 250-sheet stack bypass for copying onto paper stocks ranging from 20 lb bond to 110 lb index for covers, labels, and transparencies, as well as letterhead. The standard 4,000 sheet paper deck for letter size media increases on-line paper capacity to 5,250 sheets.

IBM launches new Infoprint products

IBM has several new products in its InfoPrint line that offer more printing options, including the ability to deliver output to devices anywhere in an enterprise. The products include the IBM InfoPrint Manager 3.1, InfoPrint Color 100 (based on the wider Xeikon engine), InfoPrint Color Off-Line RIP, and the InfoPrint 4000 high-resolution IR3/IR4.

Building on the InfoColor 70, IBM is adding the InfoPrint Color 100, capable of outputting up to 105 full-color pages per minute (50 duplex pages). The printable area is 18.7 inches on a 20-inch web. Personalization is supported by a range of variable-content offerings, including IBM's MergeDoc and Content Adder, Barco's VIPDesigner, and customized solutions from FAIR Information Services. Bitstream's PageFlex, which is designed for the InfoColor 70, will also run on the InfoPrint Color 100. Increased RIP speeds (a 40 percent increase, to be exact) are achieved through the use of a dual 400-MHz Pentium II processor. Standard features include a 64 Gb collator, which provides a high-speed variable-data system that can handle the most complex requirements. Considered the fastest book printing solution in the industry, the InfoPrint 4000 high-resolution Printing System, model IR3/IR4, is nearly 50 percent faster than the existing high-resolution model and enables statement-size document printing at a higher quality. The system outputs documents at speeds up to 708 pages per minute at 480–600 dpi selectable resolutions.

Almost all the digital color press and printer suppliers are developing lower-cost-per-page approaches. Xeikon, for instance, states that the cost per page is a quarter of what it was in 1993. As we count them, here are the worldwide digital color printing units shipped through the end of 1998:

Digital color shipments

By year	1993	1994	1995	1996	1997	1998
Units shipped	31	295	674	1782	6187	9602

High-level digital color printers

	Res.	4C	Base	Avg. RIP	Street price
Agfa					
Chromapress 70	600	35/70			$420,000
Chromapress 100	600	50/100			$550,000
Canon					
CLC 2400	400	24/10	$ 40,000	$20,000	$ 60,000
CLC 1000	400	31/11	$ 75,000	$30,000	$105,000
IBM					
InfoColor 70	600	35/70			$420,000
InfoColor 100	600	50/100			$550,000
Xerox					
DocuColor 40 CP	400	40/15			$135,000
DocuColor 40 PRO	400	40/15	$117,000	$40,000	$167,000
DocuColor 70	600	35/70			$420,000
DocuColor 100	600	50/100			$550,000
Indigo					
E-Print 1000+	800	70/35			$380,000
TurboStream	800	70/35			$420,000
E-Print Pro	800	70/35			$249,000
UltraStream	800	80/40			$550,000
Xeikon					
DCP 32/D	600	35/70			$420,000
DCP 50/D	600	50/100			$550,000

Ion deposition

As the 1980s approached, impact printers were causing data processing logjams at mainframe sites everywhere. The situation inspired imaging companies to research and develop faster, more reliable, and higher-quality printing technologies. Three corporations responded with products offering non-impact technologies—Xerox Corporation with laser electrophotography, Bull Printing Systems with magnetography, and Delphax Systems with ion deposition.

In 1980, the Dennison Corporation and the Canadian Development Corporation formed Delphax (initially to explore methods of improving photocopier performance) to further develop the budding ion deposition technology. Three years later, Dennison created Presidax, a service bureau that used ion deposition technology for printing in the tag and label manufacturing business. With a slight modification to the original technology, Presidax successfully established itself as a printer of bar-coded tags and labels. In 1984, the Canadian Development Corp., having made a significant return on its investment, sold its interest in Delphax to Xerox. In 1987, Delphax began marketing a press-integrated, ion deposition print station—but only for sale outside of North America, so as to not compete with its successful service bureau operation. When Avery merged with Dennison, the imaging systems division of Dennison was sold to Delphax. Finally, in 1990, Olympus Optical became a third partner in Delphax. And in 1997 Xerox acquired the rest of Delphax.

Ion deposition principles

There are four basic steps in ion deposition printing: imaging, developing, transferring, and cleaning. A stream of electrons is projected from a print cartridge containing a matrix of holes. Under computer control, the stream of electrons is selectively projected onto the rotating imaging cylinder, called a dielectric cylinder. A dielectric cylinder has a special coating allowing it to become selectively charged. (This surface is also extremely durable, having a print life of over two million feet.) The electrostatic image projected onto the cylinder is still a latent image—it is not yet visible to the naked eye.

As the dielectric cylinder continues to rotate, the latent image comes into close proximity with a supply of single-component toner held in place by a rotating magnetic toner brush called a developer roll. (According to proponents of the technology, it is the use of the single-component toner that gives ion deposition printing the ability to better cover large areas of a substrate.) In a manner similar to development in electrophotographic systems, an electrical field created by a voltage differential between the cylinder and the developer roll causes the toner to move to the image areas of the cylinder.

The newly-toned image on the dielectric cylinder continues to rotate to a point where the substrate and toner pass through a nip created by the dielectric cylinder and a pressure roller underneath. The toner is then actually squeezed onto the passing substrate. This method of transferring and fusing of toner in one operation is known as transfixing. Studies of this method of toner transfer give it an efficiency rating of 98 percent.

Last is the erasing process. The toner is scraped off the cylinder with a scraper blade and any residual latent image is neutralized by an electrically-charged "erase head." After the erasing process is complete, the imaging process is set to begin again.

The process involves three electrodes called, respectively, the drive electrode, control electrode, and screen electrode. These units, isolated from each other, consist of thin metal layers that resemble printed circuit board elements. In operation, bursts of high-frequency electric current, applied to the drive and control electrodes, generate a stream of charged-air molecules—the ions. The control electrode imposes the image signal on the ion stream, allowing ions to pass when an image element is to be created.

To develop a high-pixel resolution, the print head is arranged for multiplexing, a technique of geometrically arranging multiple arrays of electrode strips and actuating them in synch with the cylinder rotation so that several rows of ion-emitting sources form pixels as the cylinder elements pass underneath the print head. The screen electrode focuses the ion stream and prevents reverse ion flow in the multiplexed arrangement.

Since ionography does not use any effect of light in creating the latent image on the intermediate image carrier, neither selenium nor any other photoconductor is used. Like such a photoconductor, however, the ionographic cylinder must accept and hold a charge without leakage to surrounding areas. A hard aluminum surface is usually used. A controlled cylinder and print head surface temperature of about 180°F keep airborne chemical effects of ionization from affecting the critical cylinder surface property.

Resolution of ion deposition printing is rated at 240 pixels per inch; however, this is misleading because the actual dots per inch resolvable is higher than the number would indicate. Essentially, real resolution may be gauged at 300 dpi. In terms of speed, ion deposition web printing devices can reach 400 feet per minute.

For today's use, an inherent advantage of ion deposition technology is that it can be readily integrated into a web press. Most other non-impact printing technologies are off-line. Because of its 300 dpi print resolution, ion deposition is capable of printing a variety of densities. Also, since this system fuses toner by transfixing, heat is of no concern—allowing for printing on a wide variety of substrates. Because of this, ion deposition is commonly found integrated into flexographic systems.

With its modular design, substrate flexibility, print quality, and speed, ion deposition has transcended its original intention of supplementing the photocopier and "data processing" industries. In fact, ion deposition has found quite a niche market with the tag and label industry. Ion deposition is especially suited for high-quality, short runs on jobs that require variable data on each page. Examples of this are customer statements and bills from banks, utilities, and service companies.

Continuous inkjet printing

Inkjet printing is a form of non-impact printing in which droplets of ink are expelled from a small orifice toward the printing substrate. According to R.H. Van Brimer, the principles of inkjet printing have been known for hundreds of years, and inkjet devices have been constructed for more than 100 years. However, the technology has only been applied commercially since 1970. Since then, date-coding requirements and the move toward a databased society have driven development in this area.

Inkjet printing is a form of non-impact printing. The first inkjets were created in the 1970s by Dr. C. Hellmuth Hertz, a physics researcher at the Lund Institute in Sweden. Inkjet printers have become increasingly essential in the wake of desktop publishing because of the great demand by high-quality printers for character and color printing. There are two kinds of inkjet printing: drop-on-demand (DOD) and continuous. Continuous inkjet printers have a marked advantage over DOD because of their ability to produce high-quality images that closely resemble those of a photograph.

The fact that it is a non-impact technology makes inkjet excellent for printing on surfaces that are difficult or uneven, etc. In addition, inkjet printers are controlled by microprocessors that can vary their output, meaning that each time something is printed, it can be numbers, words, logos, bar codes, or any combination of these. And lastly, inkjet printers are capable of matching speeds to the manufacturing line-in automated factories, allowing printing as a step in the total process.

Inkjet printers have a wide range of applications in the printing and packaging industries. Inkjet printers can be used for marking products with dates, such as "best before," as well as coding information like prices and product tracking. There are hundreds of different products that can be coded through the use of inkjet printers: food and beverage containers, cosmetics, pharmaceuticals, electronic components, cable and wiring, PVC and P. E. pipes, glass and PET bottles, and industrial components. Ticket numbering and high-speed addressing for magazines and mail are just some of the applications in the printing industry.

There are several steps in the process of continuous inkjet printing. According to the Hertz technology:

- The formation and electronic control of micron-sized droplets starts when a highly viscous ink is forced through small nozzles at high pressure, producing a stream of ink that is invisible to the naked eye.
- Surface tension causes the stream to break up into small, relatively uniform droplets about 8–10 microns in diameter.
- By applying voltage to an electrode surrounding the nozzle orifice, it is possible to mark and place a charge on the droplets.
- The flight path of these charged droplets can thereby be controlled as they pass through an electrical field.
- This technique applies charges to the droplets if they are not to be used to form an image.
- When they are charged, they are deflected downward by a strong electric field created by a deflection electrode.
- The deflected droplets are caught in a gutter structure and siphoned away.
- Uncharged droplets, unaffected by the strong electric field in the control structure, pass through and are deposited on the paper.
- Approximately one million droplets per second are produced by a single nozzle.
- A single "off" pulse permits some droplets to remain uncharged and to reach the paper, which is mounted on a rotating drum.
- The resulting tiny dot will be one of millions required to produce a full-color, high-resolution image.
- The high rate of droplet formation permits very high rates of information transfer and correspondingly fast print times, even for large formats.
- Printing speed is approximately 45 square inches per minute.

The Hertz technology that created inkjet printing is known for the high-quality images it can create. The main reason that the quality is so high is because the inkjet can produce true halftones, such as different gray levels, or color tones, which can be generated with every single pixel. This true halftone printing is achieved by varying the number of drops in each pixel. The number of drops can vary from zero to about 30 for each color, which means you can get a number of different density levels for each pixel and color. It is possible to increase the number of density levels per pixel from zero to 200 for each color.

Another point to keep in mind when discussing continuous inkjet printers is that they use a system of recirculated ink in which evaporation can cause changes in ink composition. The physical properties of ink, such as viscosity, conductivity, and density, depend on its composition. Serious printing problems can be caused by changes in these physical properties. Changes in stream velocity, drop charge, and drop mass can lead to the problem of drop misplacement or a variation in character size, while levels of solvent in ink can alter its drying time. Ink control systems must be added to the recirculation of the ink in order to compensate for any evaporation loss that occurs over time.

Since the introduction of the continuous inkjet printer, there have been several modifications and improvements to the system. The two main concerns of the early inkjet printers—nozzle clogging and uncontrolled ink mist—have been addressed by the creation of the IRIS continuous inkjet printer and others.

After each cycle is complete and the nozzle has stopped firing, the nozzle tips are vacuumed to remove any residue ink. Then, an automatic nozzle maintenance cycle is built into each system. When the printer is not in the print mode, the system powers up on timed cycles and fires ink through the nozzles for a few seconds, shuts down, and vacuums the tips again.

Uncontrolled ink mist is a result of the reaction between the dropping ink and the printing surface. Ink droplets are forced out of the nozzle at about 650 pounds per square inch of pressure. This means that the droplets travel at about 30 millimeters from the nozzle tip to the print surface at a speed of 20 meters per second, or 50 miles per hour. The mist develops from the millions of drops that are hitting the paper every minute. A mist shield was created to control these random ink spots. The mist shield consists of an absorbent material positioned near the printing surface that catches the ink as it bounces back toward the ink nozzle. This allows for a clean print surface with fewer random background spots, as well as clean internal surfaces.

In the IRIS system, there is a print resolution of 240 x 240 dpi with lateral printing speeds of about one or two inches per minute. The IRIS IRIS 2044 System is a large format system, and images covering the 34 x 44 inch maximum size can be created in about 30 minutes. There is also an IRIS 2024, a medium format, that can produce images covering a maximum of 24 x 24 inches in a printing time of 15 minutes. The substrate is manually sheetfed so that the printing sequence can always be varied. The quality of the color image produced on an IRIS system, in terms of the resolution and the color shades that are possible, depends on the number of separate color dots per square inch that compose the final page. This technology uses more than 230,000 dots per square inch to compose a full-color image at 240 dpi per color.

Continuous inkjet printers are used for a variety of useful applications, which include bar coding, pharmaceutical and food packaging, etc. They have a wide range of specifications that make them very flexible for printing on various substrates of all shapes and sizes. Bar coding seems to be one of the most popular applications of the continuous inkjet printers. They can produce medium-density codes and they are able to print up to 17 mm high, which means that the bar codes produced can only be read in what is called a "closed system."

Closed systems are controlled systems where reading or scanning devices are necessary, such as the scanners you find in grocery stores. Bar-coded products can be scanned by these systems. If alphanumerics are going to be printed under a bar code, you have the option of using an inkjet with two printheads: one to print the bar code and one to print the alphanumerics. In general, inkjet printing is used to print on the product directly. The unique construction of the jet valve allows for printing on non-absorbent materials such as PVC tubing, shrink films, or ceramic tiles.

Two type of inkjet printing

In contrast to continuous, in which the droplet stream is continuously expelled from the nozzle (with the unwanted drops caught and recycled back into the ink source), drop-on-demand forms and expels droplets only at the moment of need. Drop-on-demand printers provide a larger letter size, the ability to use more than one printhead, and a less critical viscosity requirement for the ink. Most use multiple nozzles.

Each system has limitations because of the inter-relationship between image height, image quality, and print speed, determined by the size of ink drops and the rate of production. There are three subtypes of drop-on-demand: piezoelectric liquid, bubble jet/thermal liquid, and solid ink. In piezoelectric crystal inkjet printing, stress on the piezoelectric crystal produces an electric charge, which causes the droplet to be expelled. The advantages of this method include reliability and the potential for high speed. Its disadvantage is the relatively high cost of manufacturing. These systems are sometimes supplemented with a jet of air to impel the ink drop.

In 1984, Diablo Systems produced the series C color inkjet printer with four nozzles per color, capable of printing about 14,000 drops per square inch. Manufacturers of piezoelectric crystal liquid ink printers today include Sharp (Model JX 735), Tektronix (ColorQuick), and Epson. Siemens, a pioneer in the piezoelectric crystal inkjet technology, had abandoned the market by 1993.

The bubble jet printer is a development of Hewlett-Packard and Canon. The first commercially available bubble jet printer was the Hewlett-Packard Paint Jet, a letter-size, monochrome printer with 180 dots per inch (dpi) resolution. It was capable of printing on coated paper and transparency film. In 1991, HP introduced the DeskJet 300C, the first 300 dpi color printer. A three-color printer, the DeskJet 300 could not print a true black. This deficit was remedied in 1992 with the four-color HP 550. Canon entered the market in 1992 with its line of Bubblejet printers. Today, most bubble jet printers, including those made by HP, Apple, Star, and Lexmark, use the Canon engine. The Epson Stylus line of color printers offers resolutions of up to 1440 dpi.

In bubble jet/thermal liquid inkjet printing, an electric charge is applied to a tiny resistor, which causes a minute quantity of ink to boil and form a bubble. As the bubble expands, a drop is forced out of the inkjet nozzle.

- Current applied to the resistive heating element causes bubbles to form.
- Small bubbles consolidate, and the pressure begins to expel the drop.
- Bubble continues to expand and push out drop.
- As drop is expelled, heating element cools, and pressure of the bubble is countered by pressure of the ink.
- Bubble is expelled and system returns to wait state for next bubble.

Advantages of the bubble jet/thermal liquid ink method include low cost, excellent print quality, and low noise. However, liquid ink, for both piezoelectric and bubble jet, generally requires special coated paper, which is expensive, and limits the applications of these printing methods.

The third type of inkjet printer uses a solid ink (also called "hot-melt"). A wax-based solid ink, similar to a crayon, is quickly melted, then jetted to the paper. The ink solidifies on contact, preventing smudging. The advantages of hot-melt include ability to print on a variety of substrates, excellent print quality, and the potential for high speed. Experts cite advantages of hot melt as low cost, high reliability, flexibility, media independence, user safety, and environmental friendliness. Color and image quality are independent of substrate properties, and the prints are water-resistant and lightfast.

One main disadvantage of hot-melt is clogging of the nozzle by dried ink. Hot-melt inks perform poorly on transparency film, because they scatter light too much. This can be controlled by precise temperature control within the printer, on a platen. Also, because the wax ink sits above the printing substrate, it has reduced resistance to abrasion, cracking, and peeling. Different manufacturers use different methods to compensate for this. Brother uses a "Transparentizer," an extension to the paper path. Tektronix offers an optional laminator, and Data Products offers an optional post-processing transparency enhancer.

The first solid ink printer was the Phaser III PXi tabloid printer, costing roughly $10,000. Introduced in 1991, it could print with a resolution of 300 dpi on a page up to 12 x 18. It featured a 24 Mhz reduced instruction set computer controller and used Adobe PostScript Level 2 page description language. It could print full-color pages in 40 to 60 seconds, and monochrome pages in just 20 seconds. Dataproducts, owner of several key patents in the solid ink area, offered its Jolt printer in 1991. Brother is also a player in this field, with its HS 1PS.

Technological developments and considerations

Continuous inkjet was the first form of inkjet printing, and still predominated as of 1994. It boasts higher resolution and higher speed than drop-on-demand. However, over the past nine years, developments in drop-on-demand technology have given rise to new applications in a wide range of industries. By 1993, the advantages of drop-on-demand included low cost, compact size, quiet operation (only the ink strikes the paper), excellent print quality, the ability to produce excellent color, and the potential for high speed.

It is essential to consider the drop-on-demand printer as part of a larger system of printer, ink, and substrate. To that end, considerable research into the physics and chemistry of drop-on-demand printing has been conducted. The frequency response and print quality of a drop-on-demand inkjet system are determined principally by the time taken to replenish lost ink after ejection of a drop. Mathematical analysis was extended to multijet, systems connected to a common reservoir, and it was found that if all jets are fired simultaneously, refill is slow and drops are large, due to the inertia of ink and over-filled tubes. Sequential firing provides quicker refill due to uniform ink flow rate and minimum inertia.

Much attention has been given to the development of ink. Considerations include temperature dependence of ink properties, aging, evaporation loss, acid-base resistance, corrosion, and ink mixing. Also important are viscosity, pH, surface tension, dielectric properties, optical density, and environmental impact.

Aqueous inks were the first to be used, but their limitations (mentioned above) led scientists to research both improvements and alternatives. Clogging has been another sticky problem. In drop-on-demand thermal inkjet printers, non-volatile fluids are mixed with the primarily water-based inks, in order to minimize precipitation in the nozzles, which can result from evaporation of the water. This problem has been addressed by the use of highly water-soluble, low-molecular-weight additives, which are claimed to be 3-5 times more efficient than glycols in reducing water evaporation, and useful for prevention of nozzle failure in DOD printers. It is believed that the additives form a readily ruptured membrane at the surface of the nozzle during the dormancy period of the jets.

Questions of droplet air drag and the effect of electrical charge on the ink have also been studied. For most liquid ink printing, the substrate is still more critical than it is for hot-melt. The transparent inks appear to better advantage if they are not absorbed into the substrate. Accuracy of reproduction depends on constant diameter, regular contour, maximum intensity, and instantaneous drying. In 1985, the

French firm of Aussedat-Rey produced its "Impulsion" paper, which was claimed to be of the correct absorbency for accurately timed drying. Many printer manufacturers sell their own line of coated stocks. Paper manufacturers also have their own lines of inkjet papers. Some printers now claim high resolution on plain paper. It is the paper that gives the color output the look and feel of a photographic paper.

The most frequently cited uses for drop-on-demand printing have been low-end office printers and case/carton marking. Other applications include direct mail personalization, labeling, ticketing, barcoding, dating, and marking.

In about ten years, drop-on-demand inkjet technology has become a versatile method of printing, capable of working where nothing else can, or of replacing expensive, wasteful technology with cleaner, quieter, waste-free methods. As of 1992, wide-width industrial printing is performed by continuous inkjet, piezoelectric DOD (drop-on-demand) inkjet, valve DOD inkjet, and other technologies. It is used for carton and product coding and marking, web, mailing, and bindery overprinting, and large area printing, such as carpets and signs.

Desktop inkjet gets down to business

Inkjet printers spray a wet ink onto paper which soaks into the paper, or press a melted ink onto the paper. Printers are categorized as hot or cold. "Hot" ink printers (Canon BubbleJet and HP Deskjet families, for instance) use a fuser to heat the ink and paper. The boiling of the ink causes the ink to be squirted out of the nozzle and the heated paper expands, allowing the paper weave to soak in the ink more precisely. "Cold" ink printers (Epson Stylus II family) allow ink to soak in without the heating process.

Other ink technologies have resulted in a huge leap in image quality. The Epson printers use a new method of squirting ink from a nozzle. Instead of boiling the ink and letting it expand out of the nozzle, the new Epson printers electrically charge the ink. When the charge is turned off, excess ink is pulled back into the nozzle rather than spilled onto the page. This allows precise placement of ink dots for higher resolutions.

Alps developed a proprietary "dry ink" technology that fuses ink directly to the paper. Instead of a cartridge filled with liquid ink, Alps has printer ribbons (much like typewriter ribbons) in different colors. This allows very precise ink placement and eliminates any smearing that would occur with wet inks. This advance allows for wild variations including metallic inks and a special "finishing" ribbon which adds a glossy look to plain paper.

Print quality, performance, ink consumption, paper handling, and size are all important factors that interrelate in complicated ways. You won't get top-quality color output from three-color printers. Three-color printers combine cyan, magenta, and yellow inks (CMY) to create black (K) in color documents. The composite black is often brownish, reddish, or greenish. When you print text-only documents, you can swap in a black cartridge for better results.

Get a printer that holds both color and black ink cartridges at the same time—a four-color (CMYK) or a six-color (photo ink) printer. They cost only a few dollars more, and your blacks will be sharp and, well, black. Despite the hype about photo ink, photo ink printers may not necessarily deliver the best results: plain-paper output from some is better than some photo ink printers with special paper. The Epson Stylus Photo 700 does a great job at printing high-quality graphics on coated paper.

Consider resolution. Some low-end printers can't print color at a resolution higher than 300 x 300 dpi and others go up to 1440 x 720 dpi or 1200 x 1200 dpi. Higher resolution tends to mean sharper text, the capability to use smaller fonts, and better-looking graphics. But you can't judge an inkjet by its dpi, so always ask for print samples. Despite the low prices of these printers, their ink cartridges can be expensive, running about $20 to $75 for one set of black and color. Obviously, if the cartridges have a short life span, you'll soon find yourself spending more on ink than you did on the printer. One voracious printer uses $1.30+ worth of ink to print one full-page graphic; the most economical uses 20 cents worth.

Paper must be considered. Though inkjet printers can function with plain old copier paper, inkjet output generally looks better on coated stock, which costs 10 to 15 cents per sheet, compared to plain paper, which runs around half a cent per sheet. Coated paper is usually essential for printing decent-looking photographic images. Several vendors sell two kinds of coated paper, one for 300 to 360 dpi, and a slightly more expensive, high-resolution stock for 600 dpi and up. Be sure to buy the high-resolution paper for critical color output. Although you can economize with generic inkjet paper, most vendors recommend using their own brand. Most printers can also produce color transparencies.

Check an inkjet's dimensions carefully before you buy. Although many of these products are quite small, most use L-shaped paper paths, where the paper is loaded vertically and ejected horizontally. Such designs demand as much as half a foot of airspace above the printer and up to a foot of space in front. If you want to put the printer on a shelf, or if you have a cluttered desk, you need to consider the space requirements beyond the physical size of the printer.

Inkjet performance used to be characterized as extremely slow, but new printers prove that speed is increasing geometrically. Text printing speeds average two pages per minute, and graphics can take five minutes or longer per page. You can speed up performance by switching to a lower resolution or draft mode, if your printer supports that mode of operation.

Here are some of the popular desktop inkjet printers. The quality range is from text-only to full-color documents and we take responsibility for the quality opinion expressed:

	Street. price	Quality rating	Text ppm	Colors	Max. resolution
Canon BJC-4400	$179	poor–fair	2	4	720 x 360
Canon BJC-5000	$249	fair–good	2	7	1440 x 720
Canon BJC-7004 Photo	$299	good–poor	1.7	7	1200 x 600
Epson Stylus Color 440	$149	fair–excellent	1.6	4	720 x 720
Epson Stylus Color 640	$199	fair–excellent	1.8	4	1440 x 720
Epson Stylus Color 850	$349	fair–good	3.5	4	1440 x 720
Epson Stylus Photo 700	$249	fair–excellent	1.1	6	1440 x 720
HP DeskJet 1120Cse	$499	poor–good	3.7	4	600 x 600.
Lexmark 1100 ColorJet	$119	poor–fair	.4	3	600 x 600
Lexmark 3200 ColorJet	$179	excellent	1.8	4–6	1200 x 1200
Lexmark 5700 ColorJet	$249	good–good	2.3	4	1200 x 1200
NEC SuperScript 650C	$169	poor–fair	1.4	5	1200 x 600
Okidata Okijet 2020	$149	poor–fair	0.8	4	600 x 600
Okidata Okijet 2500	$199	poor–fair	1	4	600 x 1200
Xerox DocuPrint XJ6C	$150	poor–fair	1	3	1200 x 600
Xerox DocuPrint XJ8C	$250	good–excellent	2.3	4	1200 x 1200

Digital photography and digital printing were made for each other. Whether you use a desktop inkjet printer for outputting the equivalent of photographic prints or a high-end toner-based printer for document reproduction, digital photography lets you include images easier than ever before.

Chapter 8

WIDE-FORMAT PRINTING

Wide-format printing, sometimes referred to as large-format printing, can be defined as the production and reproduction of documents that are 36" wide or wider. What is produced are large, color images that would most generally be considered impractical or even impossible to produce by conventional printing methods, be it offset, digital offset, or even screen printing.

The wide-format printer and its end product can range from very simple to very complex. There are plotters that produce simple engineering and architectural type drawings. At the high-end, photo-printers are producing incredibly accurate continuous tone images.

Wide-format printing is being used for many applications. Users are graphic design studios, advertising agencies, prepress operations, corporate in-house art departments, architects, and engineering firms. Each user usually has a unique use for their printer. Creations include posters, banners, signage/art for construction areas, window displays, fine art reproduction, and engineering and architectural blueprints and drawings. And with these already established users and markets, new users and markets are being created and developed every day.

Wide-format printers can print on a wide range of substrates—from paper to canvas to vinyl—just about anything you can get through the printer. The printers offer a variety of resolutions, and handle colors ranging from the standard four-color gamut to eight-color gamuts.

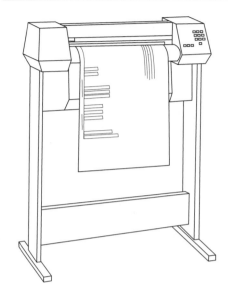

Wide-format printers, like the one illustrated at left, rely on two primary technologies to produce printed images—electrostatic and inkjet, with inkjet being the most common of the two. However, electrostatics is still an important topic, because it is still a choice.

Electrostatics

Electrostatics became a popular term with Chester F. Carlson's invention of xerography. Electrostatics is the foundation of the concept of xerography, which we know as the process of toner being electrically attracted and then fixed to a piece of paper.

Originally, electrostatics was used in creating decorative metal tiles, where electrostatic forces attracted powder to the tile, and then the powder was burnt into the surface when the tiles were furnace fired.

Electrostatics in printing is actually a function in the process of electrography, or electrographic transfer printing. This process involves the conversion of electronic signals to a latent image charge pattern onto a reusable dielectric material. The information is held to the dielectric material by electrostatics. Toner is attracted to the electrostatic charge and then transferred to the paper and fixed. The dielectric material is then made ready to repeat the cycle by cleaning the remaining residual toner and discharging the surface.

In the digital printing process, the use of electrostatics is a little bit different. The difference is that in digital printing, the transfer step is removed. This means that there is no transfer from the dielectric material to the paper. Instead, the toner is applied directly to the charged paper. Another form of electrostatic printing is known as Corona Powdered Electrostatic Transfer. This process takes place when paper is placed in contact with a photoreceptor and the back of the paper is flooded with ions carrying a charge opposite that of the toner. The opposite charge attracts the toner to the image areas on the paper. As the paper is pulled away from the photoreceptor, the toner will adhere to the surface with the strongest attraction. Where the toner sticks to the paper is the image area.

Inkjet

Inkjet is the more popular of the technologies used in wide-format printers. Although an acceptable definition of inkjet printing would be the process of an ink being sprayed onto a piece of paper, the technology of how that ink is moved through the cartridge to the jet nozzle and then to the paper is a much more involved process. There are four predominant inkjet technologies used for wide format: electrostatic, piezo drop-on-demand, thermal, and phase-change.

Electrostatic principles return to inkjet technology in the process of deflected inkjet. The same basic principle applies here as in electrography. However, instead of a converted latent image being placed on a dielectric cylinder, the latent image is now placed into a stream of ink droplets. The droplets then pass through a electrostatic field, causing a deflection of the droplets. This deflection directs the droplets to their proper location on the substrate. Unchanged droplets pass through the deflection field to a return path for reuse.

Piezo drop-on-demand inkjet

Piezo drop-on-demand inkjet technology works on the principle of an electrical reaction creating a mechanical reaction. Piezo is also known as PZT, for its chemical composition of lead zirconate titanate. In the drop-on-demand process, this electrical-to-mechanical conversion takes place at the PZT, usually a crystal.

When an electric charge is applied to a crystal, it undergoes minute dimensional changes, as either a contraction or expansion. The amount of contraction or expansion is determined by the polarity of the electrical charge applied to the crystal. This contraction/expansion creates a change in pressure in the ink inside the chamber. The ink's reaction to the volume/pressure change in the chamber determines how the ink is forced out of the chamber opening. Within a few milliseconds, the crystal shrinks and creates a vacuum that draws new ink into the chamber. The advantage to using piezo technology is that it produces a smaller, more uniformly shaped dot. These factors provide a more accurate and higher quality print. Many of the high-end inkjet systems being introduced are piezo. Eastman Kodak and CalComp Technology jointly developed a piezo inkjet technology. The agreement is intended to leverage CalComp's Crystal Jet-based technology and Kodak's imaging science and color management technology.

Thermal inkjet

Thermal inkjet printing (also known as bubblejet) is mechanically very similar to piezo inkjet. An electrical pulse creates a reaction, and that reaction causes the ink in the chamber to be forced out of the chamber. In thermal inkjet, the reaction created by the electrical pulse is heat in a resistor. Heat causes the resistor to form a bubble, which separates the ink from the resistor. When the ink cools down, the bubble breaks, resulting in a pressure that forces a droplet out of the nozzle. Although this process may seem like it is taking a long time, keep in mind that it is all happening in milliseconds.

Phase change

Phase change (also known as hot melt) is another form of inkjet printing. Phase change, like thermal inkjet technology, is made functional by heat. However, rather than using liquid inks, phase change uses solid waxy pigment. A heated resistor heats and melts the wax and the melted wax is jetted through the chamber's opening onto the substrate.

Each technology, electrostatic and inkjet, has its advantages and disadvantages. Electrostatic technology has an advantage in fade resistance and printing speeds. However, one of the most important factors to consider is price. Initially, electrostatic systems were much more expensive to purchase than an inkjet system. Even though electrostatic supplies were less expensive than inkjet, the initial cost was often a major determinant in which system users would purchase, regardless of quality and printing speeds.

Over time, however, advanced technology has made electrostatic printers more cost-effective than inkjets for a wide range of wide-format printing applications. A lower-cost writing head, a single toner channel, and modifications in the writing technique enhance price and performance, reducing the initial cost to about one-third that of similar techniques of the past. Also, eliminating liquid toners and liquid disposal, reducing hydrocarbon emissions, and purifying and reconstituting ink concentrate improve ease of use, reduce environmental hazards, and cut supply costs.

Inkjet ink for wide-format printers

Ink selection plays an important role in wide-format printing. Each ink contains a vehicle and a colorant. The proper choice of each component will affect droplet formation and image quality. The colorant of an ink can be either a pigment or a dye. Pigments tend to provide better contrast, have better light and water fastness, and adhere better to the substrate. This would make pigmented inks more suitable for outdoor use. Dyes tend to be more stable in suspension, and are less apt to clog in the tiny orifices of ink cartridges.

Carriers are aqueous and non-aqueous. Aqueous inks are preferred in systems like electrostatic deflection because they assist in the formation and deflection of drops, which tend to have high viscosity, high surface tension, and moderate to high conductivity. Two more important characteristics of inkjet ink are viscosity and surface tension. These properties work hand in hand, but each also has its specific function in drop formation. Viscosity determines the way the tail of the droplet breaks away from the orifice of the cartridge. Surface tension determines characteristics such as drop formation, drop size, and drop shape.

Inkjet ink and substrates

As with inkjettability, viscosity, and surface tension play a major role in ink-to-paper reactions. Factors controlled by these determinants are initial contact angle, wetting and wicking, smearing, and bleeding. These are all factors to take into consideration when combining inks with substrates. The substrate/ink interactions for inkjets are very different from those of conventional printing. Drops hit the paper at a very fast rate and at high velocities, covering a moving substrate. Also, there is no pressure to assist in impregnation of the substrate and and drying by absorption. Sometimes, inks and substrate don't work perfectly or as anticipated. The following is a list of various problems that can occur when inks and substates are improperly matched.

Fluorescing: Colors look brighter than they should. Could result from pH imbalance between the substrate coating and ink. Color shifts from original color expectations.

Mottle: Non-uniform media coating causes ink to be absorbed at different rates. Unevenness in color-fill areas.

Bleed: One ink color runs into another due to excessive dot gain and slow ink absorption. Poorly defined edges and lines and unwanted color mixes at junctions.

Pooling: Ink is unevenly absorbed by coating and swims on top of coating, almost like a puddle of water. Puddle defects occur in heavy ink coverage areas.

Feathering: Ink travels through coating and follows substrate fibers. Can be color-specific, unlike color-to-color bleed, causing loss of edge definition. The image has thin spikes protruding past printed edge.

Strike-through: Ink travels deep into the substrate coating and is visible on backside of media. Image may lose color gamut value and media may cockle (wrinkle).

Repelling: Usually seen when inks are not compatible with one another. When dot attempts to lie on top of another dot, it is repelled and falls to the edge. Color shifts from the original; image appears grainy.

Banding: An image appears to have lines or pinstripes in the direction of the print. Usually found in gradients and color blends.

Choosing your substrate

Choosing the proper substrate for your job can make you the hero or the goat. A popular solution is to follow a procession of steps that ask the same questions each time through. The following is a typical example of these basic steps.

Step 1. Determine the image type and complexity of the image to be printed. Most images can be divided into three categories:

- Simple: Images that are made up primarily of lines and text: there may be a limited amount of small area fill. The key characteristic is the lack of large areas where the ink coverage is more than 100 percent. Typical examples include signs, CAD drawings, charts, and simple graphs.
- Complex: These contain detailed graphics, clipart and/or other image elements that contain large area fills and require reasonably accurate color matching. The key elements are significant areas with 100 percent or more ink coverage and/or the need to match colors. Examples are images with company logos, in-house posters /announcements, maps and advertising signs.
- Pictorial: Any image containing a photographic element or a very complex graphic. The key characteristic is that the image covers a large area and requires well over 100 percent ink coverage to print well. Examples are photo posters, back walls or signage, art reproductions, murals, point-of-purchase displays, and trade show stands.

Step 2. Determine the primary use of the printed images. Use can be divided into five primary categories, which are, in turn, divided into three "image quality" levels.

- Indoor use: use for one week or less, or for over one week.
- Outdoor use: use for one week or less, or for over one week.
- Presentation, point-of-purchase, trade show: typically mounted on a substrate.
- Banners: Free-standing banners, normally grommeted and hung; can be used indoors or out.
- Backlit: Translucent images illuminated from the rear.

The image quality levels include:

- Cheap and cheerful: The least expensive medium that will provide an acceptable image quality.
- Wow: Image quality and color that will "wow" most audiences and give an outstanding result.
- Stupendous: When only the best image quality will do.

Step 3. Choose the best media type for the project. Although the types of media being offered seem to be increasing each year, there are certain categories that remain constant. Here is an overview of some of those, by type, characteristics, uses, and limitations. Various manufacturers/suppliers label their specific products differently.

- CAD color bond: A bright, white paper good for lines and text; inexpensive. It will not, however, take heavy ink coverage; cockle and blend can occur. Uses: CAD, simple signs.
- Presentation bond: A bright, white opaque bond, weighted from 24 to 60 lb; will take moderate area fill. This medium is slow to dry when it has heavy ink coverage, and it can cockle under pictorial images. Uses: presentations, signs, low-cost graphics.
- Photobase: A totally opaque media available in matte, satin, and glossy finishes; 5 to 7 mil calipers are common. Provides a quality image no matter how much ink. Can be difficult to laminate if not completely dry, and can be torn. Uses: pictorial images.
- Glossy bond: Bond paper with a glossy top coating and a barrier coat underneath; it will take much more ink that other bonds. Lighter than photobase media. Uses: Graphics, large area fill, some pictorials.
- Glossy film: A very bright, white, totally opaque polyester film, 3-5 mil caliper. Physically tough, this medium provides a superior image. It will, however, show finger marks, so it's best laminated for handling purposes. Uses: Whenever highest image quality is required.
- Clear film: Optically clear film, 3-5 mil caliper, that provides excellent image quality. This should be used only where transparency is needed. Uses: Overlays, window displays, backlit (with laminate).

- Adhesive film: Both glossy and clear films with adhesive backing, available in pressure-sensitive and cling types. Needs care in mounting, and cling effect will not work on all surfaces. Uses: As for other films, but adhesive enables easy mounting.
- Backlit film: 4-10 mil translucent film, with the translucency set so that the image is visible with both backlight and reflected light; image quality is excellent. Note, however, that any flaw in the image will stand out; needs care in mounting in a light box. Uses: Backlit displays for trade shows, malls, airports, etc.
- CAD vellum: Semitransparent cotton paper that can be used for low-cost backlit applications. Images, though, must not have areas of high ink coverage. Image is not as good as film. Uses: simple, in-house backlits. window displays.
- Canvas: A heavyweight medium available in matte and satin finishes, this provides excellent image quality and is designed for pictorial images. Cutting is difficult, however, and care must be taken when printing due to weight and thickness. Uses: Artistic look for any application; banners and hanging displays.
- Art paper: A companion product to canvas, this medium gives the look and feel of paper used for watercolor painting. Best mounted or framed; take care in cutting. Uses: Artistic look for photorealistic images.
- Vinyls: Available in various weights and finishes, available with peel-off adhesive backing. Designed for pictorial images, but image quality can vary; extra care is needed in lamination. Uses: Banners, hanging displays; use for physical strength.
- Foils: A thin base material with "glittery" surface that provides dramatic effects. Note that the colors in the image must be chosen carefully; also, laminating can be difficult. Uses: Special effects for signage, point-of-purchase applications.

Step 4. The final step involves entering all of the properties of a project into a chart that can outline the specific information described above. Other important factors to consider are lamination, media quality, availability, and price.

Wide-format printers are usually fairly similar in appearance. However, each has certain characteristics and limitations. Widths range from 36" on up. Most models use both a cut sheet and roll media format. However, wide-format printers cannot print full bleeds because a portion of the paper needs to be grabbed by a paper-handling mechanism. This margin ranges from a fraction of an inch to two inches.

Wide-format printers run at speeds measured in square feet per hour rather than in pages per minute. This is one factor to take into consideration when determining how much attention the printer needs when producing a job in order to make the printer cost effective. Ink capacity is another determinant. Capacity ranges from 20 ml to a full liter. Some printers also come with the capability to self-feed rolls of paper.

As with any other printing process, resolution is an issue in wide-format printing. Resolution is usually dictated by the intended use of the printed piece. Wide format output is usually viewed from a distance, so the resolution of wide-format prints can be much lower that that of letter or tabloid size pages without a noticeable loss of clarity. If you use your wide-format printer for color proofing, high-resolution models are available and will most likely serve your needs much better.

Quality and speed developments

It does not seem likely that over the next few years there will be very dramatic increases in the speed of inkjet technology, due to the basic printhead design. The trend will most likely be to double up nozzle counts to increase quality.

Many wide-format printers are designed for high-volume production, working in server and network configurations. More expensive models have the RIP built into the printer. Other models can be used with a variety of software or hardware RIPs. The RIP usually determines how much RAM is available. RAM amounts range from 8 to 256 megabytes.

As with other printing operations, wide-format printing is becoming more of a cross-platform environment, with the ability to be compatible with Windows or Macintosh. The most common network interfaces are serial and parallel. Most printers also feature Ethernet or EtherTalk connections, but a few offer SCSI or LocalTalk ports. Networking options, PostScript support, and additional RAM are often bundled with the RIP, available through either the printer manufacturer or a third-party vendor.

Slowly but surely, the applications for the tools and end products of wide-format printing have been expanded. Large posters and other related applications, including commercial and fine art and the continued applications of billboards and mass transit, have developed as part of the continually growing wide-format picture. The market is discovering that wide-format has few limitations.

An interesting consideration is that this growth of the wide-format market has not been planned, especially by the industry's manufacturers and suppliers. Instead, to a large degree, it has been the people who use wide-format technology who have started the fires and developed the new applications.

One of the primary drivers of the wide-format market is advertising. US retailers are looking for quick responses to their products and they're only stocking products targeted to the needs of their customer base. Retailers are trying to react faster to customer buying habits by changing their signage and point-of-purchase displays more often. Digital printing, especially wide-format, is an answer to their needs.

Superwide

For the superwide inkjet (40" and up), the market is highly specialized and, so far, small in the U.S. Growth tends to be in international markets. Nevertheless, there is a developing market for superwide systems in the U.S. based on a new and poorly understood market related to the events industry, such as trade shows, seminars, and conferences.

Wide-format printing is an emerging technology. In the era of digital printing, wide-format is another option. Many markets can be served with wide-format printing. The printing industry itself sees wide-format as an attractive means to creating new business opportunities. As with any other technology, decisions on what to buy or implement, or what needs improvement, need to be informed decisions.

Having an understanding of the technology, and then applying that knowledge to the wide array of specific product information available rather than knowing the buzzwords, is the best way to make those informed decisions. It has been predicted that wide-format printing will be the most revenue-generating segment of digital printing. In any case, the fact is that wide format is an exciting development, especially to those with creative intentions.

Chapter 9

COLOR MANAGEMENT

What is color management? Color management is the idea of making sure that the colors you see, the colors you capture with your digital camera, the colors displayed on your monitor, and the colors that print out on the printer or printing press all match. This is no easy feat, primarily because in many cases this is impossible to do! Our eyes, brains, the pigments in inks and toners, phosphors in monitors, and the CCDs in digital cameras and scanners all "see" or display color a little differently, hence the purple in the grape you see may appear violet to the camera and print out as more of a lilac.

Home users are fairly limited in their ability to control color. If you're just getting into digital photography or digital printing, aside from a few adjustments in the print driver, you are more or less at the mercy of your system, for now. One of the biggest headaches digital printing for the home market is facing right now is how to make sure the color Mom sees on her monitor is pretty darn close to the color she gets out of her inkjet printer. The pros have some old tricks up their sleeve to help them a bit; Mom is out there on her own.

Since every aspect of the imaging chain has an effect on color, everyone in the consumer industry is trying to improve or simplify their product and achieve predictable color. Inkjet paper makers are working on their coatings, printer manufacturers are improving their inks and color algorithms, digital camera and scanner manufacturers are improving their sensors, at a willy-nilly pace. The problem is that when one thing changes, it affects everything else. They say that enough monkeys beating enough typewriters can write *War and Peace*. By agreeing a bit with each other and establishing a few standards to rally around, the makers of digital products probably can get us close to "automatic color" probably sooner than you think. In the meantime, home users, follow along; serious amateurs, semi-pros, and pros, pay attention.

The serious color part

Before we talk about controlling color, let's first talk about what color is. For most of us color is one of those things you think you know but really can't explain very well, like how a caterpillar becomes a butterfly or how the engine in your new car works. It just does. Unfortunately it isn't as simple as that, so knowing the basics helps understand the problem.

What is color?

Color is kind of this esoteric thing that exists partly on a theoretical level. First a Zen-type theoretical question reminiscent of sophomore philosophy class. If a banana falls in the forest on a moonless, inky black night, what color is it? Yellow?

Wrong! It is absolutely no color whatsoever.

Okay what if it is the middle of the day, in bright sunlight, and the banana falls but there is nobody there to see it. What color is it then? Same answer. No color whatsoever.

"Huh?"

This is not a trick question. The reason that the banana has no color is that in order for a color to exist we need three very important things:

    1. a light source
    2. an object
    3. an observer

The light source

Without light, your eyes can't see color. It is the light reflected from an object that brings us the wavelengths that mean "yellow" or "blue" or, perish the image, "mauve" to us.

Most of what we know about light comes from that great big light in the sky—the sun. The sun sends all kinds of energy at the Earth. This energy travels in waves, some very short like cosmic rays and X-rays and some very long, like radar and radio waves. Somewhere in the middle of all of those are light rays. These light rays make up what we call the visible spectrum and they are what we see when we see color. At one end, down by the short waves, are the violets and blues and at the other end, by the long waves, are the oranges and the reds. In the middle are the greens. At the blue end, just past where we can normally see are the ultraviolet (UV) waves and at the red end, just past where we can normally see, are the infrared waves (IR). Everything in between makes up all the colors we can see. Various parts of that make up all the colors we can capture, display, and print.

White light is what we see when all of the colors in the visible spectrum hit us at once. White paper is all the colors in the spectrum being reflected to our eye. If that light hits an object—a tree, a car, an apple, or ink on the white paper—we see whatever parts of the visible spectrum the object reflects.

To make things a little more confusing, light itself has a color associated with it. This is known as the color's temperature and is measured in degrees above absolute zero called Kelvin. Red is around 2400 Kelvin while Blue is around 9300 Kelvin.

Have you noticed that at sunrise or sunset the color of the light is warm, almost yellow/orange? The Earth's atmosphere acts like a filter that filters out the blue and green light, leaving light at the red end of the spectrum for us to see. Incandescent lights give off a warm, yellow light. Daylight tends towards cool or blue. Electronic flashes are made to mimic daylight and have the same color. Fluorescent lights give off a greenish cast. You've seen this in pictures you have taken because most film is balanced for daylight/flash. Pictures taken in the house without a flash look very warm and yellow. Pictures taken in the office without a flash look a little greenish.

Color Temperature (in degrees Kelvin)

100 watt lightbulb (tungsten)	2,800 K
Photographic Standard	5,000 K
Printing Standard (Europe)	5,500 K
Electronic Flash	5,700 K
Cool White Fluorescent	6,000 K
Printing Standard (US)	6,500 K
NTSC Standard (Television)	6,500 K
Daylight (at noon)	6,500 K

Color is a psychological sensation that is caused by light energy entering the human eye. Color is a human experience. To experience color you must have three basic things:
- A sighted human being, who is not "color-deficient."
- An object or "scene."
- Light. (You might think about this and say that you don't need #2 if you are looking directly at a light source, like a computer. However, most "light sources" that we can think of are also objects.)

Light is defined as the part of the whole spectrum of radiation that is visible to humans. An incredible range of radiant energies exists in nature. It is called the "electromagnetic spectrum." The relatively tiny portion of this vast energy spectrum that we can "see" is called "light." It is essentially the rainbow colors.

Back in 1666 Sir Isaac Newton used a triangular glass prism to recreate these rainbow colors in his laboratory, from a ray of sunlight entering his window. This experiment was an important beginning to color science. Color art and color perception, of course, were already quite well established at that time. If you look closely, the rainbow consists of three major bands of color that we've called red, green, and blue.

Because light has color itself, in that it can contain more or less of some parts in the visible spectrum, the kind of light you look at or capture something under is important. Because of this variability, professionals, when viewing prints or photographs to judge color correctness, view them under special controlled lighting that approximates daylight. There are two standards that are used for viewing. The photographic world looks at things under light that measures 5000 Kelvin, known as D50. The print world prefers light that is a little bluer, measuring 6500 Kelvin, known as D65. Go figure.

The object

We obviously need to have an object first in order to know what color it is. In nature, the physical properties of the object modify the light that hits them absorbing some wavelengths and reflecting others. It is this action of absorption and reflectance that allows us to perceive an object's color. Our banana reflects yellow light and absorbs most everything else. Roses (most of them) reflect red and absorb everything else.

Man-made objects reflect light according to the pigments, dyes, and inks we put on them. Red paint contains pigments that reflect red light. And by changing the types and amounts of pigment, we can make a can of paint that will reflect almost any color we want. In printing, we mix various concentrations of inks—usually cyan, magenta, yellow, and black—to reflect the color light we want although sometimes it is easier said than done.

Objects can also reflect wavelengths of light that we can't see with our eyes, either at the high-end, or UV part, of the spectrum or at the low end, or IR, part of the spectrum. This is called fluorescence. Brighteners used in laundry detergents and paper manufacturing, for example, fluoresce a little in the UV end of the spectrum to give the illusion of brightness. This is what you see when someone walks under a blacklight. Fluorescent paint works in the same way, which is why that fluorescent painting on black velvet used to glow like that in college. It wasn't just the beer.

The observer

This is where a lot of variability can come into the whole color picture. As light bounces off an object and particular wavelengths are reflected, they strike our eye or a piece of film or the sensor in our digital camera. Each of those perceives the color a little differently. In humans, the reflected wavelengths hit our retina, which sends a message to the brain which thinks "ahh, yellow." So no observer, no eye, no brain, and no color.

To prove the point, try this: Close your eyes and have someone hand you an apple that you have never seen before. What color is it? Could be red, could be green, could be yellow. You can't tell them what color it is. You have an object, and you have light but, because your eyes are closed, you have no observer.

For people, the observer is a function of the eye/brain combination. The brain is an important variable because it filters the information coming from the eye based on past experiences. That's why you don't often realize that light comes in different colors—your brain is trained to figure that all light is white. In fact, until the light shifts radically towards one color, you usually don't even notice the difference. Some colors are "memory colors," like green grass and blue sky. We have a sense of what they should be and are sensitive to color shifts that affect those "memories."

The film/camera/processing observer works a little differently. Because that combination is a carefully controlled (usually) system, it sees light only in one way. In most cases, this way considers everything in terms of daylight. In a well-controlled photographic process, if the color of the light is anything different, we see it as a color cast and use terms like "warm" or "cool" to describe it. In print making, because there is an intermediary step in which filters can be added, we can correct for most color casts, but the film sees what it sees.

The digital camera observer works similarly to the traditional camera. Because there is an intermediate step between capturing and viewing, we can filter out color casts as well.

3 in 1

Because you need all three aspects—light, object, and observer—to have color, change in any of those will more than likely mean a different color. That is why objects viewed under daylight look a little different (particularly to the camera) than they do inside on the dining room table. It is also why a print printed on one device with its set of inks may look different from the same print made on a different device.

- Color is a combination of three things: light, an object, and an observer. Take away any one and there is no color.
- Visible light is just a small part of all the energy the sun sends toward Earth. It is the part that our eyes can detect.
- White light is actually a combination of all colors of light from blue to red.
- Objects reflect some parts of light and absorb others. The ones they reflect give them their color.
- An observer captures and processes the light reflected from an object. It can be a camera, a scanner, or a person.

The headaches of digital color

No doubt you have looked at something on your monitor and been befuddled when it came out of your printer looking entirely different. Blues look purple, grass looks a dull greenish brown, and Aunt Tilly's hair is blue when we all know that Aunt Tilly has been dying her hair a distinct shade of platinum for years. Whether you are a real estate broker who wants the grass on your flyers to actually be the color of grass, an administrative assistant who is responsible for printing out the Powerpoint presentation for the shareholder's meeting, or just the person in charge of printing the invitations for Aunt

Tilly's retirement party, you are faced with the same challenges as professional color experts who get paid lots and lots of money and have years of training. Except that you have to make it work without the benefit of either.

For the most part we will discuss digital color printers, such as inkjet, electrophotographic, and thermal devices, that the majority of people have access to and print on every day. The same theory and practice applies to the world of commercial printing for the most part, and the concepts you learn here will have you well on the way to understanding the terminology of color and printing well enough to avoid having a blank stare when talking to those high-paid, highly skilled printing professionals.

Much of what we will discuss focuses on capabilities found in higher-end image manipulation tools such as Adobe Photoshop. It applies to any imaging application in one way or another. The reasoning is that most people who need to work with images need the features found in these applications. Programs such as Photoshop give us the features we need to have some control over the way images are created and reproduced.

From whence we came

One of the biggest buzzwords in the printing and publishing industry in the past year or two is "color management," and with good reason. Until recently, the creation and production of color output was the exclusive domain of specially trained professionals, utilizing million dollar high-end electronic publishing systems. Today the face of digital color creation is changing because of the technological advances in the publishing world. At every step of the production process, prices have fallen, quality has risen, and ease of use has increased.

A parallel force has shifted the industry as well, as these changes prompt a flood of new color users who now have the ability to work and play in an arena once the exclusive domain of skilled operators and business owners with millions of dollars to spend. The result is a host of color users who have the will to produce high-quality color output, but neither the know-how or, in many cases, the inclination to do so.

An interesting side effect of the above is the increased pressure on existing color houses to produce work faster and cheaper than ever before, yet sustain the level of quality they have traditionally been known for. Enter color management, the purported savior of the masses, that can solve all of your color woes and produce high-quality, predictable color at the touch of a button. Or so we are led to believe.

In the past and even today, color publishing was done by companies through the implementation of high-end publishing systems such as those from Scitex and Crosfield. These companies are known as color separators and predictable, accurate color was, and still is, the product of this combination of equipment and experience. Often the files created through the use of scanners and page layout programs are intended for output on known imagesetters whose parameters are closely matched to a particular press or set of conditions. These are closed loop systems, where the characteristics of most, if not all of the devices in the loop are known. One or two scanners, a few PCs, and a few film imagesetters are the most you have to worry about. This makes color conversion a fairly straightforward, though not always easy and efficient, process.

These color separators work closely with the printers they supply and, through a process of trial and error, together they arrive at the recommended settings at both ends of the process that allow them to produce CMYK output that closely matches the original. As a measure of insurance, the resulting color separations are printed or proofed on an analog system such as an Imation MatchPrint or Fuji Color Art to serve as a visual contract from client through separator to press that, for all intents and purposes, becomes the original. Analog proofs are created from the same films that are used to make the printing plates that are used to print the job. It is this that clients sign off on as meeting their expectations for output. Very few print buyers would commit to printing without a "contract proof."

The films and proof then are supplied to the printer, who burns printing plates, mounts them on a press, and begins printing the job. During the printing process, ink amounts are adjusted to encourage the combination of ink and paper to closely match the contract proof. The result is a significant investment in both time and money on the part of all involved parties and often is a faithful reproduction.

We say a faithful reproduction because they are many variables that can conspire to lead us astray and the above-described procedures are not without their stumbling blocks. Color separators and pre-press houses who scan in original artwork and transparencies traditionally allow (if they have a choice at all) the drum scanner to handle the conversion from RGB to CMYK. Often this conversion is done to a particular specification such as SWOP (Specifications for Web Offset Printing), which acts like a kind of recipe.

The printing company that will create printing plates from the film separations will also run to SWOP or some other predetermined group of settings to help insure that color stays the same throughout the process. Because of the link between color separations and the final press output, and in order to ensure a quality result, the relationship between separator and printer is important.

With the emergence of fast, inexpensive PCs and color-enabled design, manipulation, and layout software, the work of the color separator could be done faster, easier, cheaper, and with fewer people. Fueled by advances in desktop scanners, high-capacity storage devices, and the doubling of processing horsepower every 18 months, it wasn't long before anyone could be their own separator. This has caused all kinds of hubbub in the printing industry.

Today, we often don't know the characteristics of the devices we are working with. Scans come to us from who-knows-where and under what conditions. We may or may not know the characteristics of our digital camera(s) or even the printer we will be printing on.

This throws a monkey wrench into the works of getting predictable color as we quickly lose control over the various devices in an ever-expanding loop. Where in the past we had to control a handful, today we are faced with a wide open loop, where things scanned or captured who knows where are brought together and printed who-knows-where, yet we still want to have accurate color. It is a little like shooting in the dark.

A little color power can be dangerous

We are at an important milestone in color publishing, a time in which the ability to produce color publications is open to anyone with the inclination to do so. Drum scanners have shrunk in size and in cost. Their interface has been replaced with software drivers that can be accessed from the desktop and built-in intelligence allows even the most uninitiated user to achieve professional quality results. More experienced users can achieve levels of quality and throughput that far surpass those of units in existence only a few years ago. Desktop flatbed scanners, whose benefits include ease of use and far simpler mounting procedures than their drum-based cousins, have risen in quality and fallen in price as well.

Today a desktop flatbed scanner whose level of output quality meets the needs of all but the most exacting user can be had for under $5,000. An excellent desktop for the average business user or ama-teur digital photographer can be had for well under $1,000. Contrast this to the $250,000 dollars asked for a scanner but ten years ago—a superior unit, yes, but at nearly 100 times the cost? Is anyone but the art director going to really notice? The day of the $250,000 scanner is over. The power to image can be had by anyone.

Graphics publishing systems have entered the mainstream. The trend begun in 1984 with the introduction of the Apple Macintosh has exploded with possibilities. Today a "high-end" publishing workstation can be had for $8,000 to $10,000, depending on the software and hardware configuration. This rather modest investment affords the user the same relative capabilities as the color separator of only seven years ago with his or her one-half-million-dollar Scitex workstation. In fact, a stroll to your local computer store can have you coming home with a digital printing system for under $2,000! A desktop computer and inkjet printer do a digital printing system make, and many a small or home office uses a system such as this to produce magazine, quality flyers, brochures, and even business cards.

Advances in output devices have made the production of high-quality output accessible to designers, photographers, and printers. While ten years ago the only choice for four-color output was the printing press, today professionals can choose from a whole host of digital devices, from laser copiers through full-scale digital printing presses. These digital devices are not only available to the mainstream user, their short-run nature has put increased pressure on traditional printers to produce their products faster and for less money. The same file you print on your inkjet printer can be output on a high-end digital printing press as well, giving anyone the ability to create and output color pieces.

All of this creates a host of users with the ingredients to produce quality color, yet often with few tools or a generic recipe for it. Not to mention none of the years of experience professional color separators have in the intricacies associated with color reproduction. In the past, these users relied on professional color separators and production people, who made these concerns transparent to their clients. Now everyone is on their own.

It's like the Old West of color reproduction out there and sometimes it ain't pretty. This has proven to be a headache not only for users of color but for the printers and prepress operators they interact with. Which all goes to show that a little power can be a dangerous thing. Just because you can do something does not mean you should, or more accurately that it will come out as you expect. This is one of the challenges that color management attempts to meet.

Color management explained (in a nutshell)

Color management is the idea of making an image or a page look the same no matter what it is printed or displayed on. Now this seems like a simple enough task. After all, this is a digital process isn't it? Scan in a picture, look at it on your monitor (calibrated of course), and send it to the printer. What you see is what you get (WYSIWYG) … right? No. While much of the digital imaging chain is indeed digital, the ins and outs of the system rely on the forces of nature to do what they do. Chemistry, physics, aeronautics, fluid dynamics … even static cling, all work together (and occasionally against each other) to create, display, and output color.

From a simple point of view there are, for all intents and purposes, two color spaces that you need to be aware of and understand, RGB and CMYK. These represent the sum total of the colors that can be seen and reproduced. RGB is an additive color space. It starts from black and as light is added, the colors get brighter, or more saturated. CMYK is a subtractive color space. It starts as white (the paper) and increases to black as more colorant is applied. Objects themselves have no color per se. What we perceive as the color of an object is merely the wavelengths of light it reflects. A rose reflects red light and absorbs blue and green light. A picture of a rose absorbs cyan light and reflects magenta and yellow. The eye (a wonderful imaging device) perceives a red rose, but the red of the actual rose and that of the picture is different.

The above is important to know because, while RGB and CMYK in theory seem like rather easy concepts to get a grasp on, in practice, they are not as straightforward. RGB and CMYK are device-dependent color spaces. In other words, the particular flavor of RGB or CMYK a device produces is very dependent on the characteristics of that device. These characteristics are a little different, and sometimes very different, from one device to another—even between two models of the same device.

- RGB is an additive color space. We start with black and add color until we get to white.
- Scanners, film, digital cameras, and the human eye are all RGB devices.
- CMYK is a subtractive color space. We start with white and add color until we get to black.
- Each device sees or displays color a little differently.

Why yellow isn't yellow isn't yellow

Consider for a moment a lemon cake baked by two different chefs. Each chef has the same basic ingredients to choose from, but can select the particular brand of those ingredients herself. One chef, who is a graduate of the Culinary Institute, only chooses hand-picked lemons from the shores of the Mediterranean while another, working from a recipe in *Lemon Cakes for Dummies*, uses Lemenz reconstituted juice for her cake. Both bake a lemon cake, both use lemon juice, but the cakes are markedly different from each other. It is a lemon-dependent cake. Get the idea? Color is the same way—it is device dependent. That is, depending on the device, a particular color may be a little (and sometimes a lot) different on one device versus another. An easier, and perhaps more relevant, way to prove this concept to yourself is to stand in front of the wall of televisions at your local Sears store. Each TV is emitting RGB values, yet no two sets match each other. This is device-dependent color. Some of the difference relies on the calibration of each television but even considering the differences in adjustments, no two TVs look alike.

This helps to explain why a natural scene, a photograph of that scene, the image the scanner gives you, and the image that is displayed on your monitor all rarely match each other. Each device in the chain—your eye, the film, the photo paper, the scanner, and the monitor—all work in RGB, but each sees or displays a different flavor of RGB. Calibrating each of these devices helps, but only brings them to a certain state of evenness or middle ground where the device is best "tuned." Once the devices are calibrated, we are still faced with the natural differences between each device. Printers and presses have the same problem (but in CMYK) and offer even greater challenges as not only do the mechanical differences between various devices cause them to create different flavors of CMYK, the many combinations of ink and toner and substrate that can be combined to produce an image throw an entirely new set of variables into the mix. More on this later.

The range of colors a device can reproduce is called its "gamut." A gamut is akin to the number of crayons in a device's crayon box. Some devices have a bigger box of crayons that others. Some colors can be made by one crayon alone and some must be made of a number of crayons mixed together. Some colors can't be made at all. A color that cannot be made by a device is known as "out of gamut." The size of the gamut differs from device to device, and to a larger extent between color spaces. If the gamut of a color laser printer is a box of 32 crayons, a monitor is a box of 64, a scanner is a box of 82, then your eye has enough crayons to fill a file drawer.

As we discussed, every device sees, displays, and outputs color a little differently and the same holds true for the human eye. But we have to start somewhere, so in 1931 the Commission International de Eclairage (CIE)—which is a fancy French name for the International Commission on Illumination—ran a group of people through a battery of standardized tests to determine what the gamut of the human eye was. This has formed a basis for the way color is measured, seen, and created.

From the work of the CIE, we have found ways to relate the gamut of the eye to that of other color devices. By showing the gamut of one device or color space versus another and as compared to the limits of human vision, we can describe how colors on one device will appear on another. More importantly, we can determine how colors on one device can be reproduced on another. What do we do if all the colors in the crayon box of Device "A" simply can't be made with the crayons in Device "B"? The ability to reproduce color from one device to another is called gamut mapping.

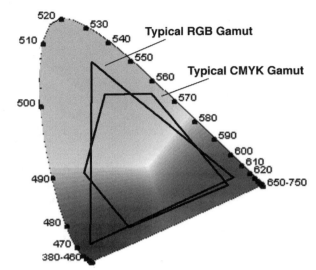

The CIE color diagram is a model for measuring color.

The diagram above gives a simple example of the differences among the gamuts of an RGB monitor, a CMYK printer, and the eye. Immediately you can see that colors in the extreme corners of the RGB gamut are outside the CMYK gamut. This is why the brilliant blue you select for the background of your Powerpoint presentation prints as a dull bluish-purple. As well, there are colors in the CMYK gamut that are not available in the RGB gamut, but this tends to offer less of a problem. By far the biggest challenge is when it comes time to convert the image you have captured, scanned, or created in RGB to the CMYK of your printer.

So, what can we do to make sure what we see is what we get? It all comes down to compromises. For artificial images, those created in a paint or drawing program, you should pick colors that you are reasonably certain are reproducible on the device you are going to print to. The easiest way to do this is to buy a color patch chart that has sample CMYK patches and their CMYK percentages. Swatchbooks from Trumatch and Pantone (make sure you get the process color version) can help you select colors that you can be relatively confident will reproduce well on your printer. Build your images using these colors only and you will find fewer surprises when you go to print. Another way to get predictable color is to create these images in CMYK to begin with. Most drawing and painting programs allow you to choose the color space you are working in. This avoids the RGB to CMYK conversion all together.

The above only goes for images that you create from scratch, when you have a choice of what color space to work in. A much greater challenge is the need to convert images from the RGB of a monitor, scanner, or digital camera to CMYK so that they can be printed. A simple and particularly crude way to do this is to simply let your desktop printer do the conversion. Send it an RGB file and the printer converts the RGB to CMYK and prints the image out. Of course, you get what you get and don't have much control over the final results. This form of color conversion is like buying a one-size-fits-all jacket. Sure it works, but rarely does it fit well.

A more intelligent approach is to give the system more detailed information about the gamuts of the devices you are using. For every color or gamut conversion, there must be a source and a destination. In other words, "Where are you coming from?" and "What are you going to?" By telling the system some things about these two parameters, you help it make a more accurate conversion between the two. Adobe Photoshop, for example, allows us to enter values that relate to our monitor and to the characteristics of the device we are printing to. It uses this information to more elegantly convert our RGB image to the CMYK of the printer.

"CMYK of the printer" is somewhat of a misnomer, however. We are actually converting to the CMYK of some generic version of our printer, which is close to the number of crayons we have in our box, but may leave a few out. This is an off-the-rack jacket that is in our size but still needs a few alterations to be a perfect fit.

Can we ever get a perfect fit? Yes and no. As we said before, there are some colors that just can't be reproduced from one device to another, particularly if we are going from RGB to CMYK. But we can do everything in our power to make this transition as elegant and predictable as possible. Enter color management. While the process can be involved initially, color management systems do offer us the most accurate way to, as closely as possible, match what we see to what we print. They are custom-tailored jackets.

- The gamut of a device is the range of colors it can see or make.
- The RGB gamut and the CMYK gamut are different; some colors exist in one but not the other.
- Even devices within the same color space have different gamuts.

What is color management anyway?

The theory behind color management is that if you know where you are coming from and where you are going to, you can achieve accurate color reproduction. Color management systems gather information on the way a device sees, displays, or creates color and use this information to convert images from the color space of one device to that of another. With the trend to open loop systems, where images can come from any source and be output to any destination, the ability to describe these color spaces and convert between them is a necessity. For color reproduction novices, the functionality color management systems offer is the only way to get predictable and consistent color output.

In digital color systems, good color is all about algorithms, digital recipes that tell the system how to change from one color to another, create a halftone of an image, or break it into color separations. Color management systems make extensive use of algorithms and the better they are, the better the results. Things are always improving and everyone is trying to make a better digital mousetrap.

Color management, though often described as a "push button" process, takes work and diligence is the key. A color management system consists of a color matching module (CMM), the "engine" of the system that actually handles the conversions, and profiling applications that describe the characteristics of various devices through color measurement devices and software.

Each device in the imaging chain must be characterized or profiled. This profile describes to the color management system the color gamut and reproduction characteristics of the device. For scanners, a profile is created by scanning a target of known color patches and comparing the values to what the scanner thinks they are. For monitors, a series of color patches is displayed and read by a color measurement device, held against the screen, which goes through the same process. A similar approach is used to profile a printer.

A target file is printed and the values read by a color measurement device and software that goes through the same steps. This information is then used by the color management system to convert from the color space of one device to another. Profiling is an ongoing process. Each change to the system causes a change in the reproduction characteristics. For monitors, phosphors change over time and these devices must be characterized on a regular basis. Scanner light sources and CCD arrays also change over time. Output devices are even more unstable, as any change in the unit is likely to knock the system a little out of whack, causing a shift in imaging characteristics. New toner, different paper stock, even changes in humidity will cause a shift. For each change in the chain a new profile must be created.

Once the profiles are created they can be used by the color management system to convert between color spaces. The CMM reads in information from one profile (the source) combines it with information from another profile (the destination) to convert colors from one to the other. Macintosh users have the easiest access to color management systems as every Macintosh made over the past few years has a color engine, or CMM, built into the operating system.

Called ColorSync, this engine allows Macintosh users the ability to apply color management to their workflow right away. For Windows users, there is light at the end of the tunnel. Microsoft has an improved version of its color engine in the works and it should appear in subsequent releases of Microsoft Windows.

Proprietary systems are available for both platforms that can profile devices and convert between gamuts, they even have their own CMMs. They are, however, expensive and daunting to say the least.

- Color management is the art and science of reproducing the colors in one gamut with another, or at least trying to.
- Profiles describe the gamut of a particular device.
- The Color Matching Module (CMM) converts from one gamut to another through the use of profiles.

Budget color management

You can employ color management today, for free, if you fall into both of the following categories:

1. You use an Apple Macintosh.
2. You use Adobe Photoshop.

Apple offers free plug-ins for Adobe Photoshop that will allow you to transform images from one color space and/or gamut to another through ColorSync, Apple's built-in CMM. Windows users take heart, built-in color management is coming. Don't get too worried if we are talking about a system that you don't work on; the theory and the practice are the same and can be applied to other color management tools.

Apple offers a fairly simple and painless path for implementing color management on a small scale, so we will describe the process in terms of the Mac. But word from deep within the catacombs of Microsoft is that a color management engine will appear on Windows 2000. Proprietary color management systems exist in many flavors and can cost from $1,000 to ten times that amount or more. Costs in terms of time spent can easily double that amount. But for those of us interested in getting closer than we are, there are some low-cost approaches we can use to try out the various aspects of color management without breaking the bank.

Using ColorSync and pairing it with plug-ins for Adobe Photoshop, available for free from Apple's website (www.ColorSync.apple.com), we can apply the theory of color management to real world situations. In fact the ColorSync site is a great reference for anyone at all serious about using digital color, regardless of platform.

It is important to note that the following examples work only for PostScript printers, those for which we can directly control the information that goes to the printing heads of the device. This leaves out desktop inkjet printers. Due to the way desktop inkjet printers lay down ink, RGB to CMYK conversions take place deep within the bowels of the printer and we have no control over the process. This too should change as time goes on. For those of us printing to office color laser printers or digital copiers, dye diffusion printers or digital presses, the following steps will bring you close to matching what you see on the monitor to what comes out of your printer. Either way, the theory is the same.

If you want the most accurate colors you can obtain from your devices, it will take a little bit of work and a fair amount of time. There exists a range of professional color management systems that use various tools and techniques to convert between gamuts and color spaces, most of which are pretty unwieldy. You need to be serious about using them because professional-level color management is a continual process.

Step 1. Calibrate and characterize your monitor

Most profiling applications for the monitor include calibration capabilities. If you do not have access to this equipment, the Gamma Control Panel by Thomas Knoll is a reasonable low-tech approach that works pretty well. Find it on the web and give it a try. Characterizing, or profiling your monitor, generally involves hardware and software tools that can cost $500 or more. One approach, offered by Pantone, claims to offer results through software similar to one of the most sensitive color measurement devices known, the human eye, for $30. For most uses, however, the monitor profiles that ship with Apple system software are pretty accurate and can be used with good results.

For our purposes we will consider the monitor to be our source. Unless we scan images ourselves and have the necessary software to create a profile of our scanner, it is nearly impossible to know the characteristics of the devices our images have come from. Clip art, stock photos, Photo CD, these are where a great many of our images come from and who knows how they were scanned or how the scanner itself sees color. To make life easier on ourselves, we will consider the monitor to be our source, since it is what we are looking at and trying to match anyway.

Step 2. Profile the printer

If the printer comes with a calibration routine, run through it. A stable, calibrated printer is easier to profile and the resulting profile, more reliable. Printer profiling software can be had for as little as $400 but the majority of the expense in profiling a printer is in the color measurement device. Most color management systems utilize a spectrophotometer and even low-end versions of this highly accurate color measurement tool cost in the neighborhood of $1,000. But for anyone serious about accurate color for reproduction, this is a worthwhile investment.

Generic printer profiles tend to be less accurate than generic monitor profiles due to the greater number of variables involved. This is one area where it behooves you to bite the bullet and invest in a profiling application and spectrophotometer. However, if this is unlikely, try the profiles that come with your printer or those you can find on the web to see what you get.

Step 3. Convert from RGB to CMYK

In ColorSync, while still in RGB mode, select File/Export/Tiff with ColorSync Profile. The dialog box will give you the ability to match the image seen on the monitor to a selected output device, as closely as possible.

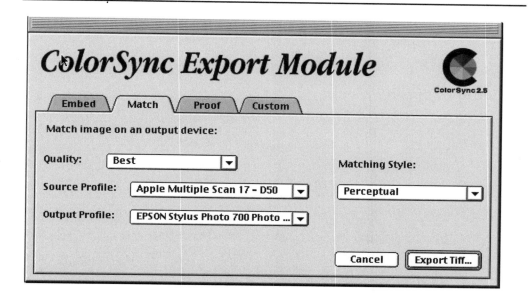

The ColorSync CMM takes the profile information from the source (in this case the monitor), compares it to that of the destination (in this case an Epson Stylus Photo Printer) and maps the gamut from one to the other. In the case where colors on the monitor cannot be reproduced on the printer, the CMM compresses the gamut of the printer to fit within that of the monitor. This will change the appearance of some colors depending on the selected settings but nonetheless is a more accurate way to handle RGB-to-CMYK color conversion issues.

The result is a CMYK file tuned expressly for your printer. When printed, the image should match your monitor fairly closely. By following the approaches listed above, your chances of getting what you see are increased immensely. By intelligently selecting colors when creating images or presentations you can avoid unrealistic expectations from your output device. A combination of these two disciplines will insure that the things that come out of that printer in the corner of your office print as you expect them to. Aunt Tilly does not have to have blue hair.

Where to from here?

Getting the color you expect from your printer isn't rocket science or to a large extent even color science, at least not entirely. With a basic understanding of how color is seen, perceived, captured, displayed and output, anyone can get more accurate, predictable results from their desktop system.

There is a desperate need for standards so that devices can all sing from the same color songbook. The ever-controversial sRGB color space looks like it has found favor with the imaging powerhouses. It describes a color space that is within the gamuts of a broad section of monitors, capture devices, and printers, supposedly eliminating device-dependent color. Backed by early promoters Microsoft and Hewlett-Packard, embraced by Adobe as the default color space in Photoshop 5.0, sRGB just may be a standard we have been looking for, but probably not the standard. It was made the default, but this can be changed.

Its somewhat constricted gamut makes it unattractive to color professionals who want to squeeze every crayon out of their crayon boxes. As home devices become more and more robust, they will have to print a wider range of color, not less. But as a standard, sRGB is a target we can shoot for to try and have a common language between all color devices.

The future looks only bright. Software applications will become more automated and intelligent in their use of profiles to convert between color spaces. Color measurement devices will slowly drop in price and innovative companies will find creative ways to achieve color management between devices. Look to Microsoft to bring color management to the masses. Depending on the path they take, this will also improve cross-platform integration, solving most of the color management problems Windows users, and those that must prepare files for Windows, are faced with. In addition, color management capabilities are being built directly into page layout applications, printer drivers, and RIPs that will allow all of this to take place behind the scenes, where it should be anyway.

It will still take an informed user to make it all happen. The good news is that it isn't as complicated as it seems to be.

Chapter 10

WORKFLOWS FOR PRINT

Digital workflow for digital printing with digital photos often comes down to two basic approaches: raster and vector. There are almost 20 different raster-based file formats available in the Macintosh version of Photoshop alone—many with configurable subsets—plus vector formats. All of these formats come together in a container of sorts, which holds all page elements and combines them. The container application may vary throughout the workflow, which results in two distinct types of job control—component files, which are created by the designer or creative professional in the initial preparation, and consolidated files.

Component files

Component files for high-end printing are assembled using Quark-XPress or PageMaker or Illustrator or FreeHand (the latter two for packaging) and FrameMaker or Corel Ventura Publisher for object-oriented, text-intensive documents. The components are raster and vector files.

Consolidated files

Consolidated files are used to bring all of the component files, both raster and vector, into a single format—a container—that is accepted by an output processing system, a RIP or CEPS system. CEPS stands for Color Electronic Prepress System and refers to the early color systems with proprietary image fomats. The consolidated format has been PostScript, but PDF is now an alternative. PDF and PostScript come from the same roots. Font handling, color handling, resolution, target output device, and compression must be set up in advance in order to achieve an acceptable consolidated file. In PostScript, altering the consolidated file after creation requires re-creation from the original component files. PDF started the same way, but now there are many tools for editing PDFs. When PDF lacked these tools, CT and LW formats, either in CEPS native formats, or as TIFF/IT files, found a reason to remain in production. These formats stayed in use because of the requirements of specific output devices. However, raster files are uneditable and voluminous and this can affect network performance.

CEPS raster-based CT and LW files have a limited set of editing tools, usually based on proprietary systems. TIFF/IT has no editing tools. PostScript never really lent itself to interactive editing, although there were some attempts on the part of third-party developers. PDF is moving rapidly via plug-ins to provide high levels of editability.

Embedded elements

Vector files are usually saved in EPS; raster files have loads of options, with production efficiencies such as image replacement, data compression, and color management. It is almost impossible to control the file formats from clients; it is useful to try to control those used in internal operations. Now that we are moving to digital photography and scanning very early in the process, we must re-think the way in which we capture and apply our files. We repeat that it is almost impossible to control the file formats from clients; it would be useful, at least, to try to control them in our internal operations. If technology helps us work faster, better, and more efficiently, why is it that it doesn't always work, particularly in graphic arts?

We have too many variables. In the printing industry there are many variables that affect the production process. Although is important to note the amazing technological developments that are helping printers and service bureaus serve their clients better and faster, it is also very important to point out that this is a developing industry, lacking a great deal of standardization. Fortunately, digital photography, because of its consumer orientation, has imposed standards which will eventually affect digital workflow systems.

Automated systems

The ultimate and ideal workflow is a totally digital workflow. Unfortunately in this industry, in only a few instances is this the case. Traditional print publishing is plagued by incompatible equipment and disconnected islands of automation that electronic publishing and digital printing have created, unintentionally, as entirely new forms of digital bottlenecks.

This last sentence contains two key terms, "islands of automation" and "bottleneck." Starting with the first one, islands of automation refers to those highly automated processes inside the workflow that do not have continuity with the other steps or processes that follow in the workflow. It is like having computer-to-plate technologies and not having reliable digital proofing. The benefits of having a filmless and time-effective platemaking process are diminished by the fact that some customers require a film-based proof. The second definition is bottleneck. A bottleneck is any process or workstation with capacity less than the demands placed on it. Capacity is the measure of the system output. For example, on a digital printer, it is the number of impressions that it can produce in a time frame, measured by the minute or the hour.

Every process is composed of many steps. Every step or production operation has a certain capacity. The capacity of each of these operations is not the same. Some stations work faster than others, meaning that at some point some workstations will be idle while others will be overloaded. In the case of islands of automation, we may have very fast, highly automated processes linked with slower processes that will constitute system bottlenecks. The problem with bottlenecks is that they determine the capacity of the entire system. If in my system I have very fast workstations linked to others that are not so fast, so the capacity of my system equals the capacity of the slowest workstation, not the fastest. To be effective, workflows should be entirely automated. We talk about automation, digital file transfers, etc., but the full benefits of the technology will not be seen if a fully digital workflow is not in place.

Why workflow automation?

Automation permits the combination of complex and simple tasks that do not need manual intervention to achieve lower costs and faster deliveries. However, in graphic arts, there are probably as many exceptions as rules. Exceptions are those jobs that do not run easily through the workflow. Managing exceptions is more difficult and more expensive than managing regular standardized processes because exceptions require operator expertise and intervention. This concept applies not only for the production process alone, but also for customers, since they now have to archive, retrieve, manipulate, and reuse digital information. They must also deal with exceptions and lack of standardization.

Workflow design

We can have as many workflow models as we wish. The bottom line is that when designing a workflow, it is necessary to analyze the different steps that are encountered most frequently, then identify the individual processes to produce the desired results, and finally design a workflow, or a group of workflows, that can handle those steps in an efficient manner. The idea of workflow design is not to streamline each task in order to save time in each step of the process, but rather to automate the entire process. The whole is the sum of its parts. Each piece of a system, from the workstations, to the servers, to the output devices and all the software in between must be optimized. The following section details the many steps involved in workflow for printing and publishing production of documents incorporating digital photography.

Image manipulation

In traditional workflows, images are scanned. In digital photography, images are manipulated. The most popular program for this is Adobe's Photoshop. The digital camera and the image manipulation process replace the traditional camera, film, processing, scanning, and probably some manipulation as well. Many professional photographers are now imaging experts as they have moved from the darkroom to the computer program. Image manipulation is still a labor-intensive process.

Preflighting

Preflighting (from the airline industry's "preflight checkout") a job is nothing more than checking if the digital file has all the elements necessary to perform well in the production workflow. Many software programs are designed for this task. Among other items, these programs check if the fonts are embedded, if all images are present and with the right format (RGB or CMYK), etc. The idea of preflight checking is to avoid mistakes before the job reaches the first output production steps. Preflight checking attempts to avoid problems by fixing them up front.

Color management

Color management has been an area of controversy. It has became more popular recently as digital printing and digital proofing become more popular. As it is used in this book, color management is the effort to match color as it is captured by various devices, displayed by various monitors, and output from various different output devices for a given job. It is important to maintain the consistency of quality of the same image across different media and output devices. Today, color management is based on profiles for encoding color as it relates to a specific image to and from specific devices.

PostScript file creation

Most jobs are created in some sort of page layout application like QuarkXPress or PageMaker. Most RIPs (Raster Image Processors) do not understand applications, they "speak" another language—PostScript. Therefore, at some point, it will be necessary to transform those application files into PostScript code. When you click *Print,* the application program builds a PostScript file from your screen image, the underlying data, and some information from the operating system. In the graphic arts, when you print, you are sending PostScript code.

PDF file creation

PDF is an excellent file format for file exchange. As we will discuss later in this chapter, it is one of the most versatile file formats due to its portability and cross-platform characteristics.

Trapping

When you have adjoining elements of different colors, registration is critical. The problem is that press registration is not one hundred percent perfect; therefore it is necessary to overlap these colors to compensate for misregistration, and we call this image trapping. Today trapping is accomplished using different software packages. Some are more sophisticated than others, but the question is when in the workflow is trapping done. Some do trapping before RIPping, some do it while RIPping, and others after. Approaches depend on the configuration of the workflow, but for the most part, it will depend on the kind of applications and products service providers provide.

Imposition

Imposition is the arrangement of individual pages on a press sheet, so that when it is folded and trimmed, the pages are in correct orientation and order. To impose is a responsibility that should not be taken lightly. As in the case of trapping, there are advanced imposition software packages that do this automatically. However, this task can be done manually in the application software, depending on the type of operation.

RIP

The RIP (Raster Image Processor) takes in high-level page description files and outputs low-level data streams that can be fed directly to a digital printer, imagesetter, or platesetter for image rendering, or to a video display to be viewed. The RIP has three main internal functions: interpretation, creation of the display list, and rasterization.

- Interpretation: In this stage, the RIP interprets the PostScript code. It decodes PostScript and prepares the information for the following step, the display list.
- Creation of the display list: In this stage, the RIP builds an intermediate list of objects and instructions before rasterizing. It is a list of objects in a page description file that have a determined order. The order the page elements have in this display list is the same order in which they will be displayed or imaged.

- Rasterization: In this stage, the RIP converts graphic elements into bitmaps for rendering on a monitor, digital printer, or imagesetter. In other words, the RIP takes the display list and converts it into pixels. This stage is necessary because every output device needs to generate spots, dots, or pixels.

Proofing

A proof is an output of the job before it gets printed. There are different kinds of proofs available that range from conventional proofs, which are film-based, to soft proofs, which use a calibrated monitor, to digital proofs, from a digital proofing printer.

Sometimes the person who okays the proof is in a remote location. To avoid mail delays, some firms use remote proofers at their customers' sites. Files are transmitted over a digital telecommunications network. Once the client receives the file, they can output it on paper, using a digital printing device, or simply display it on a monitor (soft proof). The file that is sent can be an application file, a PostScript file, or a PDF file. This file can have either just the resolution necessary to output on the proofing device, or the full resolution of the final reproduction device. File size is an important issue for file transmission over digital networks; therefore, it makes more sense to have just the resolution needed to output on the proofing device. In any case, the most important consideration is to have the proofing devices accurately calibrated to the printing device.

Corrections

The aim of a proof is to detect any error or mistake in the file prior to printing the job. When corrections need to be done, decisions have to be made quickly. It is necessary to have excellent communication between customer and producer. Remote proofing, and digital proofing in general, is helping to speed up the process of correction and reproofing. Therefore, it is important to have corrections as a task in the workflow with a clearly defined methodology. If film is still used, it is output by an imagesetter, after the RIP stage. Film can be output either on single spreads or on a full-size imposed signature. The film is then used for plate exposure or for making analog proofs.

Plate output

Today there are two methods for producing a plate: the conventional way, using film, and the digital way, using a computer-to-plate device, also known as a platesetter. With a totally digital workflow, the second way is more suitable; however, many printers still use film due to the capital investment required. With computer-to-plate technology, film is eliminated from the production workflow, which represents many advantages for printers, and eliminates one level of variability in the system. Another issue with computer-to-plate is proofing. Proofing has to be done digitally; however, digital proofing, although it has improved in the past couple of years, is still not completely accepted as a contract proof by some critical customers. They demand a halftone-dot-based proof.

Blueline proof

The purpose of a blueline proof is to check final imposition and verify if there is any element missing or misplaced. The blueline can be printed in many paper formats; it can be a print of a single page or a big print of the entire press sheet imposition. These proofs are not intended to judge color or print quality in any aspect, they are just to verify the position of the elements in the page or the imposition.

Printing

Printing is the last task in a print production environment. Today we not only produce output using conventional printing methods, like offset lithography, flexography or gravure, but we also have a variety of optional digital printing devices available. Digital printers and presses use different technologies, and instead of ink, they use toner or inkjet ink.

Storage

Storage refers to the warehousing of electronic files from already completed jobs. Files can be stored on computer hard drives, CD-ROMs, tapes, or magnetic diskettes. Many storage technologies have been developed in recent years; however graphic arts files are known for huge sizes, and therefore storage can still be a problem more in the finding and retrieval than in the actual storage.

These are the most typical tasks in a print production workflow. Some others are omitted here but probably they are a subcategory of the ones we just mentioned. As you see, each one of the tasks has its own requirements. Workflows can be very different from one print shop to another. Each one may combine tasks that are highly automated with conventional or manual methods or they can have a fully digital workflow. The content creator must be aware of these issues before creating the file for printing.

One of the promises of PDF does lie with the originators. If they convert their layout program pages into PDF properly, and properly is the operative word, then workflow can be truly automatic. We must assume that some originators will not make good PDFs (and they probably did not make good application files either), so PDF may remain to be done when a job is accepted by the prepress or printing service. Many new utility programs will allow PDFs to be fully edited (except for certain layout features like justification and hyphenation) for changes and corrections at the last minute.

Variable data printing

Print no longer has to be simply a long-run, broadcast-oriented information distribution medium. Print is able to deliver a specific, targeted message to a specific, targeted audience.

At the front end, master pages must be formatted with provisions for entering information that will vary from printed unit to printed unit. Information must be imported from a database to fill the variable areas of the layout. Most of the programs for variable-data printing provide some way to define portions of QuarkXPress or PageMaker layouts as subject to variation.

Personalization is an outgrowth of the mail merge features dating back to word processors of the 1970s (and to "player-piano" typewriters of the 40s and 50s), which made it possible to merge a standard letter with a list of names, addresses, and personalized salutations. Personalization on today's digital color presses mostly takes the form of supplementing name and address data with other text in specific areas of a static page layout. The source of the variable information is a database or a delimited, sequential list of fields. A more advanced approach to personalization is adding not just text, but other content objects to the page, such as photos, graphics, scanned signatures, etc. They are retrieved from a database for placement in the layout.

A different aspect of variable printing is sometimes described as custom document assembly, or "versioning." This has been done in the office for years. Word processors in the 70s assembled individual paragraphs into reports, customized insurance policies, and other materials.

Short runs of specific layouts can incorporate variable data with some of the data varying from page to page, while other content is common to a series of pages. Many programs define the variable objects on the master page as a variable content box. Data areas on the page must be predefined (usually as rectangles of a fixed size). The database data is then linked by a variable data program and the master layout and the variable data are combined, either in the page (which then needs to be rasterized for each impression) or in the RIP.

Soon pages and layouts will be generated on the fly according to the defined content. The static master page must be rasterized and each of the variable-page components must also be rasterized fast enough to keep up with the print engine.

The RIP requirement becomes more complex as graphics and color-separated photos are included as components that vary from unit to unit. Print server configurations such as Barco's and new multi-processor RIP configurations such as Adobe's Extreme are working in this area. For now, most pages to be printed are prerasterized, assembled on the fly, and input to the print engine. The ability to pass these huge amounts of raster data through the pipeline to the print engine in such a way as to ensure that the device can run at its rated speed is the other major challenge. This task is complicated by the size of the pipeline to the print engine, that is, the maximum speed of data transfer to the engine, which at this stage of the technological evolution of engines is generally much slower than is required for true productivity. The suppliers of digital color printers and presses have each chosen a unique method for handling variable data and producing custom documents. They all face other technical considerations that contribute to the complexity of the overall variable-printing workflow, including the ability to handle input from a variety of database formats and mechanisms for ensuring and verifying job integrity.

Digital workflow is evolving rapidly to meet the demands of automated presses, printers, and systems. The printing industry must be competitive among the mass media. It must be able to handle long and short runs, static and variable data, now and not later.

The RIP

Almost every imaging device available today is a raster imager, using spots to build text, lines, pictures, etc. Thus, every imager, whether it is a lowly desktop printer or a giant computer-to-plate (CTP) system, must, out of necessity, have a RIP. And every RIP is just a little bit different. Many are based on Adobe's design, with some additional features, and some are legally derived from public information on the PostScript language. These have been called PostScript clones. Most of the small or home office market is dominated by Hewlett-Packard's PCL printer language, a PostScript wannabe, and many of the high-end CTP systems use non-Adobe PostScript interpreters.

When you send a document to a printer, the RIP does its job and out comes the page or pages. But today's digital workflow is much more complex and multiple RIPpings are often the norm. In a CTP workflow, the document might be RIPped to a color printer for color proofing, RIPped to an imposition proofer, RIPped to a remote proofer, and finally RIPped to the platesetter. In most cases this involves four different RIPs and four different imaging engines. And four chances for variation. Plus, there are "flavors" of PostScript based on versions from Adobe licensees and others who are not licensees.

RIP evolution

PostScript has become dominant in the computer printing world because of its device-independence and resolution-independence.

Device-independence means that the image (the page to print or display) is defined without any reference to specific device features (printer resolution, page size, etc.). A single page description can be used on any PostScript-compatible printer from a 300 dpi laser printer to a 3,000+ dpi imagesetter or platesetter. In our opinion, another reason for its success is that it supports high-end printing. Computer-to-plate and digital printing as we know them could not have developed without a standardized page description language.

Most applications that can print to a PostScript printer also let you "print" to a file. Printing to a file means that the application (or the computer running the application, with the help of a PostScript driver) converts the job data into PostScript commands and saves the data as a file instead of transmitting the code over a cable to a printer. You can then download the file to any PostScript printer to print it out. Downloading is different from printing in that no data conversion (from job data to PostScript) takes place, the file is merely sent to the printer. This allows you to directly send PostScript streams to printers, without opening any application program. The PostScript file contains all font and image data and can be stored on a disk and sent to a graphic arts service. Most computer platforms have a variety of PostScript downloaders available.

PostScript is device-independent … to a point. When you print, you print to a specific printer that has very specific features such as certain resolutions, page sizes, minimum margins, choice of paper trays, etc. Although the PostScript driver can send the PostScript job to any printer, it can't specify a tabloid page for a printer that does not have a tabloid tray, for example. To access features specific to the printer, PostScript uses PPDs (PostScript Printer Description files) which are stored in the System folder. However, color complicates things, as each device will render the color described in the PostScript code a different way. This is why color management is so important.

Hardware and software RIPs

There are so-called hardware RIPs and software RIPs. The distinction is not always clear. Initially all RIPs were proprietary, with a CPU, disk, RIP software, and related hardware enclosed in a cabinet and attached to an imaging recorder. There was no monitor and no keyboard, although a keypad and LCD panel on the recorder did allow some level of interface. You connected your network to the RIP and away you went. Then someone decided that they could sell you the RIP software and you could install it in your own computer. Usually they supplied a special computer board and cable to connect to the imager. The latter approach was called a software RIP.

PostScript 3

In September 1996, Adobe Systems Incorporated announced its newest printing systems solution, which includes the next generation of Adobe PostScript called PostScript 3 (the word "level" has been dropped). Adobe's integrated printing system solution focuses on changing the printing experience by allowing OEM customers to build best-in-class printing solutions and providing users the ability to print complex graphics and Web content, when and where they need it. Adobe has gone beyond offering a page description language to providing a total systems solution for delivering and printing digital documents.

Adobe has developed an advanced level of functionality in Adobe PostScript 3 to accommodate the new digital document creation process which includes varying sources, complex composition, and virtually unlimited destinations. Users are now accessing content for use in digital documents from varying sources, including electronic mail, web pages, intranets, on-line services, content providers, and digital cameras. Document composition now includes not only text but also complex graphics, clip art, corporate logos, Internet content, multiple fonts, scanned images, and color. Finally, the digital document's destination can be to printing systems anywhere in the world, such as personal printers, network printers, service bureaus, pay-for-print providers, or data warehouses for electronic archival. Images and documents now travel pretty well.

Enhanced Image Technology, a PostScript 3 feature, insures that documents print faster, easier, and with optimal quality. A key benefit to the user is that EHT recognizes image objects and automatically optimizes processing to deliver the highest possible quality, and at the same time speeds the return to the application. Adobe PostScript 3 will include new imaging features that support the increasingly complex documents available via the Internet, including support for three-dimensional images, photo-quality grayscaling, smooth gradients in graphic objects, image compositing, and full-color spectrums.

PostScript 3 will support direct processing of web content, including HTML and PDF. It will also extend the resident font set to provide compatibility with the resident fonts of all leading operating systems, enhancing performance by reducing font downloading. PostScript 3 provides users with a more robust ability to manage individual pages within a document, thereby improving control over the printing process.

Extreme

The high-speed data requirements of digital presses, large-format film "imposetters," and computer-to-plate systems demand radical changes in RIP and workflow architectures. Developers are also trying to eliminate PostScript processing bottlenecks and accelerate production times. RIP suppliers have been converting PostScript into contone (CT) and linework (LW) files via proprietary methods or converting PostScript into some editable internal format in an attempt to make the RIPping process more efficient.

Adobe's Extreme RIP architecture is a major step in RIP evolution. It is built around the 3.0/3.x version of Adobe's Portable Document Format. Acrobat 4 was released in early 1999. PostScript is an interpretive programming language; PDF is a compact, noninterpretive format designed for fast imaging to a screen. PDF has lacked the ability to handle high-resolution images easily and to handle screening for print—both of these are included within Extreme. Extreme also connects web and print publishing, as both will use the new version of PDF as the plug-in to web browsers.

Working with PostScript

Not all PostScript is equal; code generated by Photoshop conforms to PostScript's Document Structuring Conventions (DSC), some from QuarkXPress does not. Page structure can't be easily determined. Extreme converts such files automatically into PDF format, allowing separate processing. Extreme incorporates both Adobe PostScript language and Adobe Portable Document Format (PDF) for production printers, and Adobe PrintMill, an intranet-based printing and printer management solution. When you create a page in Quark-XPress or PageMaker, you are interfacing with the program as displayed on the screen.

The GUI describes the page on screen for the user. However, when you click Print, it is PostScript code that defines that page as it is sent to the printer or imagesetter. You can even save the PostScript file to disk and read it (if you can decipher it). But a page described in Post-Script is nearly uneditable without an understanding of the programming language itself. Admittedly there are unique people out there who can edit PostScript. PostScript is a voluminous file format. Placing a single "a" on a QuarkXPress page and "printing" the page to an ASCII file produces at least 16 pages of type.

Producing PostScript

There are four choices for producing a file from an application:

1. Click and print.
   Click Print and send the file to a printer on your in-house network. This is a great option if you're publishing a single copy for yourself. Or even a couple of dozen copies for the staff.

2. Let someone else worry.
   Send the application file to an outside service, but make sure you send the image files and all of the screen and printer fonts. This file can be changed by the service bureau, making its integrity questionable.This approach not only opens the door for further unpredictability, but it also raises some tricky legal issues. Due to font licensing, the service bureau must install the fonts you use and/or supply, print your job, and immediately

remove those fonts from their system. This must be done for each job and each time the file is printed. What if the service bureau has purchased a license to the same font? For instance, you supply a document that uses Garamond. Whose version of Garamond is it—Adobe's, ITC's, Monotype's, or some overnight type house's? If you don't specify and/or the service bureau doesn't have the correct version of your typeface, a font substitution will occur. Possible repercussions of an improper font substitution could be the reflowing of text, sometimes destroying the original design. Or maybe you like Courier, the ultimate font substitution.

But service bureaus deal with application files because they can open them, preflight check them, and make changes.

3. PostScript code.
Save the file to disk as PostScript code, which incorporates the images and fonts, and send it to an output service. This is a viable option if you have a very large external storage device to save all of that PostScript information. (Remember, a single "a" generates 16 plus pages of PostScript text. Well, that's not really fair, because the 16 pages of code could support many text pages. But PostScript code is voluminous, nevertheless.)

A drawback to this method is the lack of "correctability." If the correct page setup options were not chosen at the time of PostScript generation, the page may not reproduce as desired. Often, designers don't know the specifications of the imagesetter or output device of the service bureau. Without this information, specifications regarding page size, crop marks, line screen ruling, and many other variables can't be set. And once the PostScript file for that document is generated, it's too late. What if only a part of a page or a graphic created in a drawing program needs to be placed into a page layout application like QuarkXPress or PageMaker?

Thus was born the Encapsulated PostScript file—a file representing one page with, or in the early days without, a preview image.

This allows you to save a graphic in a standardized form and place it into a composite document where it can be scaled and manipulated to fit. However, the EPS file does not save font data and many artists have seen their beautiful graphics output with Courier because the original font was not available at the RIP. So, the EPS was portable only to a point. Adobe Illustrator now saves EPS with the font data as does Acrobat Exchange 3.x. And the new Placed PDF could replace EPS.

4. Create a PDF of your file.
- A PDF file can contain objects such as hypertext links that are useful only for interactive viewing.
- To simplify the processing of page descriptions, PDF provides no programming language constructs.
- PDF enforces a strictly defined file structure that allows an application to access parts of a document randomly.
- PDF files contain information such as font metrics to ensure viewing fidelity.
- PDF requires files to be represented in ASCII to enhance document portability.

PostScript conclusions

As a platform-independent page description language, PostScript has emerged as a de facto standard. Today, PostScript accounts for 95 percent or more of the final output of all commercial publications. On the downside, PostScript is extremely variable and page-dependent.

There's no doubt that PostScript has brought on revolutionary advances. But with every revolution comes the need for further refinement. Even Adobe admits that PostScript has many deficiencies for the role it is currently playing. The use of PostScript has far surpassed Adobe's original intention, and thus, they are in the midst of solving problems and advancing their core technology in order to fulfill the expectations of today's digital workflow demands. The wide variety of applications, platforms, and typefaces has caused many headaches for the publishing industry. There are just too many places for things to go wrong.

While you can easily move documents around by e-mail, network, or disk, you can't assume that everybody has the right fonts on their system, or that they have the right program to open your document, or even (in a cross-platform environment) the right setup to receive the document. You could spend a lot of time and money installing the same software and fonts, plus the requisite extra hard-disk space and RAM, on every system to allow document portability—and then train people on each program used to create the documents in the first place. But of course, this setup is inefficient and you don't have the capital to implement it, and neither does anyone else.

PostScript serves its purpose as a way to describe document pages in a design-rich fashion. But in today's world of ever-increasing efficiency, the need for speed, and the customer's insistence on jobs being printed "yesterday," research and development into document handling is a never-ending process. Files need to be transferred from place to place quickly, predictably, and efficiently. With the increasing use of digital presses, CTP technology, and completely digital workflows, the need for platform-independent digital file transfer standards is becoming more and more urgent. That brings us to the fourth alternative for communicating with graphic service providers and the outside world, the Portable Document Format.

PostScript and PDF are closely related as they have the same roots. PostScript is needed in order to produce PDF files for use in a prepress environment. The Acrobat Distiller strips out important imaging information concerning images contained in the resulting PDF file and plug-ins are needed to add functionality back into Acrobat so that the PDF file can be used in a prepress environment. One such plug-in commonly used in Acrobat is "addPS." This allows users to have more control over how files are imaged on a film imagesetter. Making a PDF file is a relatively simple process. The long way involves saving your document in PostScript form and then opening it in Distiller. However, programs will eventually save as PDF directly and this will be a major advantage. Do not use PDFWriter if your document contains images since it is really best for simple text pages.

To improve performance for interactive viewing, a PDF defines a more structured format than that used by most PostScript language programs. PDF also includes objects, such as annotations and hypertext links, that are not part of the page unit itself but are useful for interactive viewing.

Creating a PDF file

The two most common methods of creating a PDF are either through the application software in which the document was created or from PostScript files made from the document. Many applications can produce a PDF file directly. PDFWriter, available on both Apple Macintosh computers and computers running Microsoft Windows, acts as a printer driver. PDFWriter shows up as a printer in the Macintosh Chooser window. The user needs to choose that "printer" to create a PDF file. The user then "prints" their file to PDFWriter and an electronic file is produced. This is similar to "print to disk." The PDF file is platform-independent; it can be viewed or printed from Macintosh, Windows, PC, and UNIX platforms.

For more complex documents that involve high-resolution images and detailed illustrations, the PDF file must be created differently because of limitations of the system software. The application Acrobat Distiller was developed for this situation. Distiller was designed to produce PDF files from PostScript files that have been "printed to disk," that is, saved as a file in PostScript format. The Distiller application accepts any PostScript file, whether created by a program or hand-coded. The Distiller produces more efficient PDF files than PDF Writer for some application programs.

Prepress issues

PDF files can contain color separation information by saving specific color information as individual PDF pages. This is the manner in which the color separation process must be done since there is no color separation engine in Acrobat Exchange, Reader, or Distiller to perform the color separation at output or when files are being distilled. Page layout applications used in conjunction with a PostScript driver can create a distillable PostScript file that can contain multiple pages of color information. For four-color printing, the PDF file contains four pages that correspond to the four-color process inks. If the document has more than four colors, the PDF file would then contain more individual pages for the additional color information. Each color is given its own page in the PDF. The PDF file format has difficulties in translating trap information from some original applications. To apply traps in Adobe Illustrator, one must convert the text into outlines. The application then no longer considers this information as text and treats it as a graphic element. Some high-end imaging capabilities of PostScript have been left out of the PDF format.

Output

The Distiller strips out certain information in the process of making PDF files. A plug-in called "addPS" adds PostScript information to a PDF document that describes what the screen frequency and angle should be for the PDF file being imaged. This plug-in is used to send PostScript files to a RIP allowing the user to specify the default line screen and angle information of the imagesetter and RIP. The next file that is imaged at the imagesetter would be imaged according to those specifications. A separate PostScript routine needs to be sent each time a new color is imaged because the angles need to be offset for each separation. If an imagesetter cannot set the screen frequency and screen angles, "addPS" or some other utility must be used.

Workflow models

Workflows can take many configurations depending on factors like the software used and, more importantly, on the needs of the user. In this section we comment on various approaches that intend to solve workflow issues.

Traditional model

1. Workstations running OPI-capable application programs place images on the OPI or image server over the network.
2. Any workstation on the network sends the job to the appropriate print server queue.
3. The print server spools the job, releases the workstation, and transmits the job to the appropriate output device.

Transmission time is very fast because the job contains only a low-resolution image and a callout of the image. The RIP with the OPI integrating function reads the callout in the job and connects to the image server as directed. Because the same workstation may be used as both the image server and the RIP, the integrator needs only to retrieve the image from its disk and merge the high-resolution image into the job stream as the page is printed.

Once the publication is output, what happens to the images? In the old days, they were archived to tape. Today, publishers and service firms are interested in the future of their images. That means they want to store them in such a way that they can be found quickly, accessed rapidly, and converted (re-purposed) to various file formats for print or presentation. If your prepress group has only a couple of workstations, you keep the files you need on those workstations. If you have several workstations, you probably need to share files, create image databases, and improve network performance when sharing those files. You need servers.

- File servers
- Print servers
- OPI servers

File servers. When you need to find a file, it's nice to know where to look. A centralized file server that stores high-resolution images, fonts, layouts, and completed jobs can increase everyone's productivity. You can use any workstation that can share files as a file server. Both the Windows NT (server version) and the Power Macintosh platforms incorporate file sharing as a standard. If you use a

Windows NT platform as the server, Macs can also access those files. You can also equip the server and workstations with several utilities, such as RunShare and Extensis Portfolio (formerly Fetch), to make file sharing easier and quicker.

The most important feature for a file server isn't a high megahertz rating (although it helps), but a fast input/output speed. You can increase a workstation's input/output performance by using fast hard drives or disk arrays and SCSI accelerators. For critical applications where you can't ever let the server go down, you can configure it with an uninterruptible power supply (UPS) and hot swappable disk drives—disk drives you can replace without shutting down the computer.

Print servers. Everybody knows what it used to be like to send a long document to the printer: you used to sit there and wait while the computer flashed printer status messages in your face. You were basically out of commission until the printer released the computer. Print servers solved this problem by spooling print jobs from around the network and sending them to the appropriate output device. When you print your document, you actually send it to the print server; the print server accepts the job and releases your workstation right away. You get back to work; the print server continues to accept and print jobs from all users on the network.

The term "spooling" has nothing to do with winding something threadlike around a cylinder. "Spool" is actually an acronym for Simultaneous Print Operations On-Line. Every print server has a spooler. Print servers are necessary for maintaining a productive prepress department. A print server receives jobs from a user on a network, stores that job in a queue, and then forwards the job to a printer on the network. The device could be a low-resolution printer or a high-resolution imagesetter. A useful print server also includes such features as queue management, job logs, printer setup, and often can also store files for later printing.

OPI servers *(Auto-Swap)*

OPI addresses the problem inherent with any electronic graphics production environment—the large amount of data in image files. This data burden impedes productivity in some systems:

- It ties up the workstation while the image file is being printed.
- It creates a network bottleneck any time the image file is transmitted, whether to another workstation for page layout or to the output device for proofing or final imaging.

The OPI industry-standard convention defines how to embed instructions in a PostScript output file to tell the output device where and how to merge the various text and graphics components of a page. OPI enables users to work with low-resolution preview images in their page makeup programs, and keep the high-res graphic images close to the imagesetter.

To work within the OPI model, you create jobs like this:

1. Make up pages using any of a variety of desktop publishing programs. On these pages, compose and fit all the editorial content, line work, charts, ads, and other page elements.
2. Place photos or other high-resolution graphics on the page using a screen-resolution preview FPO (For Position Only) image, which is a low-resolution TIFF image created by a color-separation program such as Photoshop.
3. Send the job to the imagesetter.
4. The imagesetter, using OPI interpreter software, reads the pathname, fetches the high-res image from the server, and merges the image in position with the text and line work.

The preview is sometimes called a callout file, proxy image, FPO (for position only), or a view file. This preview image resides on the workstation and its storage path and filename must match the storage path and filename on the server.

In general, OPI works with TIFF files. OPI supports all the cropping and sizing commands issued in the page makeup program. When the page makeup program creates a PostScript output file of the job for the printer, it appends these commands, along with the pathname and filename, as PostScript comments in the job stream. When the OPI-compliant output device reads these comments, it acts upon them by retrieving and merging the high-resolution image. Many OPI solutions also support DCS (Desktop Color Separation), an industry-standard convention for handling color separations created with desktop publishing programs. DCS originated with Quark as a way to manage color separation files.

DCS works with EPS (Encapsulated PostScript) files. In producing color separations, DCS-compliant programs—such as Photoshop—generate a set of five EPSF files. These five files include a main, or "composite" file, as well as a file for each color separation—cyan, magenta, yellow, and black. The composite file contains the names of the cyan, magenta, yellow, and black EPS files and the pathname to their storage location, PostScript commands to print a non-separated version of the image, and a 72-dpi PICT version of the image for viewing on the screen.

APPENDIX

Agfa
100 Challenger Road
Ridgefield Park, NJ 07660-2199
(800) 685-4271
(508) 583-4168 FAX

Canon USA, Inc.
One Canon Plaza
Lake Success, NY 11042
(800) 848-4123, (516) 328-5960

Casio
Casio, Inc.
570 Mt. Pleasant Ave.
Dover, NJ 07801
(800) 962-2746

Chinon America
(800) 441-0222
(310) 533-0274

Dicomed, Inc.
12270 Nicollet Avenue
Burnsville, MN 55377
(612) 895-3000

Dycam, Inc.
9414 Eton Avenue
Chatsworth, CA 91311
(800) 883-9226
(818) 407-3966 FAX

Eastman Kodak Company
343 State Street
Rochester, NY 14650
(800) 242-2424
(800) 235-6325

EPix Imaging Systems, Inc.
2953 Bunker Hill Lane, Suite 202
Santa Clara, CA 95054
(408) 562-0901
(408) 562-0919 FAX

Epson America, Inc.
(800) 289-3776
(310) 782-4212 FaxBack

Fuji Photo Film, U.S.A., Inc.
555 Taxter Road
Elmsford, NY 10523
(800) 378-3854

Hitachi Home Elelectronics America
3890 Steve Reynolds Blvd.
Norcross, GA 30093
(770) 279-5600
(770) 279-5699 FAX

Jenoptik Laser
(800) EYELIKE

Konica U.S.A.
440 Sylvan Ave.
Englewood Cliffs, NJ 07632
(800) 285-6422, (201) 568-3100
(201) 569-2167 fAX

Leaf Systems, Inc./Sinar Bron Imaging
17 Progress Street
Edison, NJ 08820
(908) 754-5800
(908) 754-5807 FAX

Leica Camera
(201) 767-7500

MegaVision, Inc.
5765 Thornwood Drive
Goleta, GA 93117
(805) 964-1400
(805) 683-6690 FAX

Minolta Corporation
101 Williams Drive
Ramsey, NJ 07466
(201) 825-4000
(201) 818-3590 FAX

Nikon, Inc.
1300 Walt Whitman Road
Melville, NY 11747-3068
(516) 547-4355

Olympus America Inc.
Melville, NY
(800) 347-4027

Panasonic
(201) 348-7000

Pentax Corp.
35 Inverness Drive East
Englewood, CO 80112
(303) 799-8000
(303) 790-1131 FAX

Phase One United States, Inc.
24 Woodbine Ave, Suite 1
Northport, NY 11768
(516) 757-0400
(516) 757-2217 FAX

Polaroid Corporation
565 Technology Square
Cambridge, MA 02139
800-816-2611

Ricoh Consumer Products Group
Sparks, NV
(702) 352-1600
(702) 352-1615 FAX

Rollei
16 Chapin Road
Pine Brook, NJ 07058
(201) 808-9004

Samsung Opto-Electronics America
40 Seaview Drive
Secaucus, NJ 07094
(201) 902-0347
(201) 902-9342 FAX

Scanview, Inc.
330A Hatch Drive
Foster City, CA 94404
(415) 378-6360
(415) 378-6368 FAX

Sharp Electronics
(800) 237-4277

Sony Electronics Inc.
Sony Drive
Park Ridge, NJ 07656
(201) 930-7796
(201) 358-4942 FAX

Toshiba
(800) 288-1354

Umax
(800) 562-0311

Yashica
2301-200 Cottontail Lane
Somerset, NJ 08873
(908) 560-0060
(908) 560-9221 FAX

INDEX